Certificate in Combating Financial Crime

Combating Financial Crime

Edition 7, June 2020

This learning manual relates to syllabus version 7.0 and will cover exams from **11 August 2020 to 10 January 2022**

APPROVED WORKBOOK

Welcome to the Chartered Institute for Securities & Investment's Combating Financial Crime study material.

This manual has been written to prepare you for the Chartered Institute for Securities & Investment's Combating Financial Crime examination.

Published by:
Chartered Institute for Securities & Investment
© Chartered Institute for Securities & Investment 2020
20 Fenchurch Street
London EC3M 3BY
Tel: +44 20 7645 0600
Fax: +44 20 7645 0601

Email: customersupport@cisi.org
www.cisi.org/qualifications

Author:
Dr. Natalie Schoon

Reviewers:
Katerina Williams, Chartered MCSI
Karl Micallef

This is an educational manual only and the Chartered Institute for Securities & Investment accepts no responsibility for persons undertaking trading or investments in whatever form.

While every effort has been made to ensure its accuracy, no responsibility for loss occasioned to any person acting or refraining from action as a result of any material in this publication can be accepted by the publisher or authors.

All rights reserved. No part of this publication may be reproduced, stored in a retrieval system, or transmitted, in any form or by any means, electronic, mechanical, photocopying, recording or otherwise without the prior permission of the copyright owner.

Warning: any unauthorised act in relation to all or any part of the material in this publication may result in both a civil claim for damages and criminal prosecution.

Candidates should be aware that the laws mentioned in this workbook may not always apply to Scotland.

A learning map, which contains the full syllabus, appears at the end of this manual. The syllabus can also be viewed on cisi.org and is also available by contacting the Customer Support Centre on +44 20 7645 0777. Please note that the examination is based upon the syllabus. Candidates are reminded to check the Candidate Update area details (cisi.org/candidateupdate) on a regular basis for updates as a result of industry change(s) that could affect their examination.

The questions contained in this manual are designed as an aid to revision of different areas of the syllabus and to help you consolidate your learning chapter by chapter.

Workbook version: 7.1 (June 2020)

Important – Keep Informed on Changes to this Workbook and Examination Dates

Changes in industry practice, economic conditions, legislation/regulations, technology and various other factors mean that practitioners must ensure that their knowledge is up to date.

At the time of publication, the content of this workbook is approved as suitable for examinations taken during the period specified. However, changes affecting the industry may either prompt or postpone the publication of an updated version.

It should be noted that the current version of a workbook will always supersede the content of those issued previously.

Keep informed on the publication of new workbooks and any changes to examination dates by regularly checking the CISI's website: cisi.org/candidateupdate

Learning and Professional Development with the CISI

The Chartered Institute for Securities & Investment is the leading professional body for those who work in, or aspire to work in, the investment sector, and we are passionately committed to enhancing knowledge, skills and integrity – the three pillars of professionalism at the heart of our Chartered body.

CISI examinations are used extensively by firms to meet the requirements of government regulators. Besides the regulators in the UK, where the CISI head office is based, CISI examinations are recognised by a wide range of governments and their regulators, from Singapore to Dubai and the US. Around 50,000 examinations are taken each year, and it is compulsory for candidates to use CISI workbooks to prepare for CISI examinations so that they have the best chance of success. Our workbooks are normally revised every year by experts who themselves work in the industry and also by our Accredited Training Partners, who offer training and elearning to help prepare candidates for the examinations. Information for candidates is also posted on a special area of our website: cisi.org/candidateupdate.

This workbook not only provides a thorough preparation for the examination it refers to, it is also a valuable desktop reference for practitioners, and studying from it counts towards your Continuing Professional Development (CPD). Mock examination papers, for most of our titles, will be made available on our website, as an additional revision tool.

CISI examination candidates are automatically registered, without additional charge, as student members for one year (should they not be members of the CISI already), and this enables you to use a vast range of online resources, including CISI TV, free of any additional charge. The CISI has more than 40,000 members, and nearly half of them have already completed relevant qualifications and transferred to a core membership grade. You will find more information about the next steps for this at the end of this workbook.

The Background and Nature of Financial Crime	1
Money Laundering	27
Terrorist Financing	59
Bribery and Corruption	71
Fraud and Market Abuse	95
Tax Evasion	113
Financial Sanctions	125
Financial Crime Risk Management	135
The Role of the Financial Services Sector	179
Glossary	217
Multiple Choice Questions	223
Syllabus Learning Map	245

It is estimated that this manual will require approximately 80 hours of study time.

What next?
See the back of this book for details of CISI membership.

Need more support to pass your exam?
See our section on Accredited Training Providers.

Want to leave feedback?
Please email your comments to learningresources@cisi.org

Chapter One
The Background and Nature of Financial Crime

1. Definitions	3
2. Governmental and Quasi-Governmental Approaches to Combating Financial Crime (CFC)	8
3. Best Practice	16
4. Asset Recovery	18

This syllabus area will provide approximately 5 of the 50 examination questions

1. Definitions

Learning Objective

1.1.1 Know the following terms: financial crime; money laundering; predicate offences; terrorist financing; proliferation financing; fraud; market abuse; bribery; corruption; international financial sanctions; trade and investment sanctions; tax evasion; data protection

1.1 Financial Crime

Although frequently used, the term 'financial crime' has no internationally accepted definition. Until the late 20th century, financial crime had a limited scope and generally included corruption, bribery, fraud and money laundering (ML) of the proceeds of drug trafficking and other serious crimes. More recently, the term has expanded to include money laundering of the proceeds of any crime and also terrorist financing (TF), the financing of proliferation of weapons of mass destruction (WMDs), breaches of financial and trade sanctions, market abuse and tax evasion.

The UK's Financial Services and Markets Act 2000 (FSMA) now broadly defines the term to include:

'...any offence involving fraud or dishonesty; misconduct in, or misuse of information relating to, a financial market; or handling the proceeds of crime'.

Financial crime, therefore, covers a wide range of offences including insider trading, money laundering and also terrorist financing. The FSMA states that the term 'offence' is behaviour that:

'...includes an act or omission which would be an offence if it had taken place in the United Kingdom.'

Therefore, the remit of the legislation also includes conduct occurring outside the UK.

In 2012, the UK's then regulator of the financial services sector, the Financial Services Authority (FSA) (subsequently replaced by the Financial Conduct Authority (FCA) and the Prudential Regulation Authority (PRA)), introduced the following, similar, definition of financial crime:

'Any offence involving money laundering, fraud or dishonesty, or market abuse'.

1.2 Money Laundering

Money laundering is the process utilised by criminals to disguise the origin of the proceeds of crime (such as money made from trafficking drugs) by converting them into 'clean' money, ie, funds which no longer appear to have an illegal origin.

In effect, any handling of, or involvement with any proceeds of any crime (or monies or assets representing the proceeds of crime), can be regarded as money laundering. Criminals involved in money laundering include drug dealers, burglars, fraudsters, people traffickers, smugglers, **terrorists**, tax evaders and illegal arms dealers. Involvement in money laundering is not restricted to criminals, but may include professionals such as bankers, lawyers, accountants and financial advisers if they are performing an activity involving the proceeds of crime, or enabling others to commit financial crimes.

All crimes committed for financial gain are underpinned by the common need to launder the proceeds of these crimes. Robust mechanisms for combating money laundering are a major disincentive to undertaking financial crime.

In short, money laundering is a derivative crime in that the monies being laundered are derived from another criminal activity. The initial criminal activity is known as the 'predicate offence'.

1.3   Predicate Offences

The United Nations (UN) defines a predicate offence as one whose proceeds may become the subject of a money laundering offence. In other words, it is the underlying criminal conduct (eg, fraud or drug trafficking) that generates proceeds of crime to be laundered. International conventions and standards, such as those set by the Financial Action Task Force (FATF) require countries to apply the crime of money laundering to all serious offences with a view to including the widest possible range of predicate offences. In this context, a predicate offence may be described by reference to:

- all criminal offences, or
- a threshold linked to a category of serious offences, or
- the penalty of imprisonment applicable to the predicate offence (threshold approach), or
- a defined list of predicate offences, or
- a combination of these approaches.

1.4   Terrorist Financing

Terrorist financing is fundamentally a straightforward concept. It is the provision of funds or other assets, in any form, to support terrorism or of those who encourage, plan, or engage in it. Terrorist financing can include the raising, moving, storing and utilisation of financial resources for the purposes of terrorism. It includes the financing of terrorist acts, of terrorists and of **terrorist organisations**. Terrorist financing need not be linked directly to a terrorist attack.

Unlike money laundering, the funds may be small in value and are, therefore, difficult to detect. In addition, the origin of funds is often difficult to establish. Furthermore, it is not always possible to establish when funds become terrorist funds. For example, materials to manufacture explosives could be purchased with funds held in a bank account, an overdraft, or a small part of a personal loan.

1.5   Proliferation Financing

Proliferation financing (PF) has been described by the FATF as:

> 'the act of providing funds or financial services which are used, in whole or in part, for the manufacture, acquisition, possession, development, export, trans-shipment, brokering, transport, transfer, stockpiling or use of nuclear, chemical or biological weapons and their means of delivery and related materials (including both technologies and dual use goods used for non-legitimate purposes), in contravention of national laws or, where applicable, international obligations'.

The United Nations Security Council (UNSC) Resolution 1540 (2004) adopted under Chapter VII of the UN Charter is binding on all UN member countries. It sets out the basic obligations of UN member states for countering proliferation financing. FATF Recommendation 7 targets proliferation financing and requires countries to implement **targeted financial sanctions** to comply with UNSC resolutions and also to criminalise the act.

1.6 Fraud

Although the word fraud is used frequently, there is no exact legal definition of the term. Fraud includes acts such as conspiracy, embezzlement, misappropriation, false representation, concealment of material facts and collusion. In practice, the term has generally been used to refer to deception with the intention of obtaining a financial advantage or personal gain, avoiding an obligation or causing loss to another party.

In the financial sector, fraud occurs mostly in the context of a **firm's** relationship with a customer, client, or colleague on an individual or organisational basis.

The UK Fraud Act 2006 has created a single primary offence of fraud that is defined in Section 1. The Act has created a single primary offence stating a person is guilty if they are in breach of fraud by:

- false representation (Fraud Act 2006 Section 2)
- failing to disclose information (Fraud Act 2006 Section 3), or
- abuse of position (Fraud Act 2006 Section 4).

Other offences are created by more sector-specific laws such as those that prohibit bribery and corruption and deal with offences related to companies or financial services.

The Fraud Act 2006 largely replaced laws related to obtaining property by deception, obtaining a pecuniary advantage and other offences that were created under the Theft Act 1978. In the UK, the common law offence of conspiracy still exists and is applicable to all aspects of 'financial crime'.

1.7 Market Abuse

The term 'market abuse' covers a wide range of harmful behaviours, such as insider dealing and market manipulation, which may unreasonably disadvantage investors or other participants in financial markets, such as stock exchanges.

Insider dealing relates to buying or selling securities, for example shares or bonds, on the basis of non-public information that may affect the price if it was made public.

Market manipulation covers deliberate attempts to move the market price, such as lying about a company to drive its share price up or down in order to profit from the price movement.

1.8 Bribery

One definition of bribery is:

'...the offering, promising, giving, accepting or soliciting of money, gifts or other advantage as an inducement to do something that is illegal or a breach of trust in the course of carrying out an organisation's activities'.

The definition under the UK Bribery Act 2010 is slightly different and notes the purpose of a bribe as:

'...to induce a person to perform improperly a relevant function or activity'

or

'...to reward a person for the improper performance of such a function or activity'.

Whether the offer or receipt is intended for an employee's family or friends, or whether bribery takes place through third parties, it is still considered to be a bribe. Bribery can take many forms and can be of any size.

1.9 Corruption

There is no universally accepted definition of corruption. The *UN Guide for Anti-Corruption Policies* (2003) notes that:

'...definitions applied to corruption vary from country to country in accordance with cultural, legal or other factors and the nature of the problem as it appears in each country'.

A number of organisations, including Transparency International define it as:

'...the abuse of entrusted power for private gain'.

The World Bank defines a corrupt practice as the:

'...offering, giving, receiving or soliciting, directly or indirectly, of anything of value to influence improperly the actions of another party'.

Corrupt behaviour is very broad in its practical manifestations and is not always related specifically to bribery, but bribery can be regarded as a subset of the overall crime of corruption.

1.10 International Financial Sanctions

Financial sanctions are imposed by governments and may apply to individuals, entities and governments resident in the same country or abroad. Financial sanctions prohibit a firm from carrying out any transaction with a person, organisation or government who is the target of the sanction.

Recommendation 6 of the FATF requires countries to implement targeted financial sanctions to comply with the UN Security Council Resolutions (UNSCRs) relating to the prevention and suppression of terrorism and terrorist financing.

In the UK, financial sanctions are usually passed as secondary legislation based on an earlier act of parliament. The US sanctions countries that sponsor terrorism or violate human rights. In addition to countries, specific people and organisations are also subject to sanctions. These are typically political groups or organisations promoting violence or social unrest.

1.11 Trade and Investment Sanctions

Similar to financial sanctions, trade and investment sanctions are economic sanctions. They are an instrument of foreign policy and economic pressure. Trade and investment sanctions are generally aimed at governments and the main forms of trade and investment sanctions are:

- tariffs on goods imported
- quotas on the amount of goods that can be imported from or exported to the country
- embargoes preventing countries from trading with each other
- non-tariff barriers on imported goods including licensing and packaging requirements and product standards, and
- freezing or seizing assets so that they cannot be sold or moved.

Trade sanctions can be categorised as import- and export-based sanctions. Export sanctions block goods from entering a country and have generally less impact than import sanctions which block goods leaving a country. Their economic impact varies. When faced with an export sanction, a country may find alternatives for the goods and services they no longer receive. However, when faced with an import sanction, countries cannot sell their goods or services, which typically results in a large economic burden.

1.12 Tax Evasion

Tax evasion is defined as the illegal practice where a person, organisation or corporation intentionally avoids paying their true tax liability. Anyone caught evading tax is typically subject to criminal charges and substantial penalties. Money laundering is a form of tax evasion since criminals wilfully evade paying taxes on illegal income. Tax evasion typically entails deliberate misrepresentation of the true state of wealth and income and is illegal. Under Part 3 of the UK Criminal Finance Act, it is a criminal offence to facilitate tax evasion or fail to prevent the facilitation of tax evasion in the UK, or any foreign jurisdiction. The UK offence applies to any firm involved in the criminal facilitation of UK tax evasion, irrespective of where they are based in the world. The foreign offence applies to the criminal facilitation of foreign tax evasion by a firm that is incorporated in the UK, carries out (part of) their business in the UK, or if the foreign tax evasion facilitation took place in the UK. The offence of foreign tax evasion requires dual criminality which means the evasion and facilitation must be a criminal offence in both the foreign jurisdiction and in the UK.

Tax avoidance, on the other hand, is the legitimate reduction of taxes using methods included in tax law and by exploiting legal loopholes. A tax loophole can be defined as a technicality allowing someone to avoid the scope of a law or restriction without directly violating the law.

1.13 Data Protection

In the European Union (EU), data protection regulation has been unified in the General Data Protection Regulation (GDPR) which was approved and adopted by the EU parliament in April 2016 and implemented on 25 May 2018. The GDPR applies to organisations in the EU, as well as organisations located outside the EU who offer goods or services to, or monitor the behaviour of, EU data subjects. The GDPR applies to all companies processing and holding the personal data of 'data subjects' residing in the EU, regardless of the location of the company.

Within the context of the GDPR, personal data is defined as any information related to a natural person or data subject, that can be used to directly or indirectly identify the person or subject. Personal data includes names, photos, email addresses, bank details, social networking posts, medical information or computer IP addresses.

Fines for breaching the GDPR are tiered, with maximum fines of either 4% of annual global turnover or €20 million, whichever is higher. Lower fines could be imposed for minor breaches.

2. Governmental and Quasi-Governmental Approaches to Combating Financial Crime (CFC)

2.1 The Role of the Financial Action Task Force (FATF)

Learning Objective

1.2.1 Know the role and objectives of the FATF, its limitations and the legal context of its recommendations

The Financial Action Task Force (FATF) is an intergovernmental body established in 1989, headquartered in Paris. The organisation has 38 members – 36 member jurisdictions and two regional organisations (the European Commission (EC) and the Gulf Cooperation Council (GCC)). The objectives of the FATF as detailed in its document *Financial Action Task Force Mandate (2012–20) 20 April 2012 Washington, DC* are:

> '...to set standards and to promote effective implementation of legal, regulatory and operational measures for combating money laundering, terrorist financing and other related threats to the integrity of the international financial system'.

Initially, starting with the single mandate to combat money laundering (1989), the mandate of the organisation has expanded over the years to cover combating terrorist financing (2001), preventing of proliferation financing (2008) and sanctions breaches, tax evasion and related issues (2012). Although initially incorporated for a limited period of time, as of 2020, the FATF's mandate has been changed to be open ended. Starting in 2022, the ministers of the FATF will meet every two years to discuss strategic issues and progress.

The FATF is a 'policy-making body' that reviews money laundering/terrorist financing, develops countermeasures and promotes the adoption and implementation of the appropriate measures globally. In addition, it monitors the progress of members in implementing the measures to combat financial crime. The FATF, in collaboration with other international stakeholders (eg, the International Monetary Fund (IMF) and the World Bank), also works to identify national level vulnerabilities with the aim of protecting the international financial system from misuse by criminals, corrupt officials and politicians.

The FATF 40 Recommendations, which were last revised in 2012, are the accepted international standards to combat money laundering, terrorist financing and the financing of the proliferation of WMDs. The legal, administrative and operational frameworks and financial systems vary from country to country, therefore, the FATF Recommendations need to be implemented to reflect the circumstances of the individual country.

The FATF Recommendations set out the essential measures that countries should have in place to:

- identify the risks, and develop policies and domestic coordination
- pursue money laundering, terrorist financing and the financing of proliferation
- apply preventative measures for the financial sector and other designated sectors
- establish powers and responsibilities for the competent authorities (eg, investigative, law enforcement and supervisory authorities) and other institutional measures
- enhance the transparency and availability of beneficial ownership information of legal persons and arrangements, and
- facilitate international cooperation.

Countries are measured against these standards by a peer review process known as 'mutual evaluation'. Since 2013, the methodology for the evaluation consists of two parts – a technical evaluation, measuring the extent to which the standards have been adopted in the system of the country; and an **effectiveness evaluation**, measuring the success of the system in mitigating the risks and threats of money laundering, terrorist financing and proliferation financing. More than 190 jurisdictions around the world have committed to the FATF Recommendations through a global network of nine regional organisations, known as FATF Style Regional Bodies (FSRBs).

Although the FATF Recommendations are derived from international treaties and conventions, they are 'soft law' and not in themselves treaty obligations. Countries voluntarily sign up to implement the FATF standards and submit to mutual evaluation. The findings of these evaluations are published, but the FATF cannot itself impose any sanctions for failing to comply. However, the findings can be used both by **financial institutions** and other governments to inform themselves about the risks posed by jurisdictions. The FATF itself also maintains an International Cooperation Review Group (ICRG) and publishes updates three times a year on those countries and jurisdictions that have strategic deficiencies and that pose a risk to the international financial system.

2.2 The Role of Financial Regulators, Commissions and Institutions

Learning Objectives

1.2.2 Know the role of financial regulators, commissions and institutions in combating financial crime: Money Laundering Directives; European Supervisory Authorities; Office of Foreign Assets Control (OFAC); US Securities and Exchange Commission (SEC); Financial Conduct Authority (FCA); other domestic regulators

2.2.1 Money Laundering Directives

A directive issued by the EU is a legal act which requires member states to achieve a particular result, but does not dictate how the result has to be achieved. Each member state implements its own measures which may vary from one member state to the next. EU regulations, on the other hand, are automatically enforceable in all member states at the same time.

Most of the instructions to the EU member states concerning combating financial crime (CFC) have been disseminated through EU directives, providing flexibility to member states to legislate and implement the changes within the framework of local regulations and enforcement mechanisms.

To date, the EU has issued four successive directives on the prevention of the use of the financial system for the purpose of money laundering and terrorist financing. The directives implement the FATF Recommendations into European law. The First Money Laundering Directive (91/308/EEC) was issued in 1991 and amended in 2001 by the Second Money Laundering Directive (2001/97/EC).

The Third Money Laundering Directive (2005/60/EC) came into force on 15 December 2005. The Directive was implemented in the UK through the Money Laundering Regulations (MLR) 2007, which came into force on 15 December 2007.

The most recent, known as the Fifth Money Laundering Directive (2018/843) or 5MLD, was published in the Official Journal in May 2018 and amends 4MLD (2015/849). Amongst others, it includes changes specifically related to dealing with the ways in which terrorist groups are financed and conduct their operations.

2.2.2 The European Supervisory Authorities (ESAs)

In the aftermath of, and as a response to, the financial crisis of 2007, the EU proposed the creation of the **European Supervisory Authorities (ESAs)** and the European Systemic Risk Board (ESRB) in 2009. The European System of Financial Supervision (ESFS), as it came to be called, is the framework for financial supervision in the EU and has been operational since 2011.

There are three ESAs:

1. The European Banking Authority (EBA) located in London
2. The European Securities and Markets Authority (ESMA) located in Paris, and
3. The European Insurance and Occupational Pensions Authority (EIOPA) in Frankfurt.

Here are brief descriptions taken from the three authorities' websites:

- The **European Banking Authority (EBA)** is an independent EU authority which works to ensure effective and consistent prudential regulation and supervision across the European banking sector. Its overall objectives are to maintain financial stability in the EU and to safeguard the integrity, efficiency and orderly functioning of the banking sector.
- The **European Securities and Markets Authority (ESMA)** is an independent EU authority which aims to safeguard the stability of the EU financial system by ensuring the integrity, transparency, efficiency and orderly functioning of securities markets, as well as enhancing investor protection. It fosters supervisory convergence among national securities regulators (such as the FCA) and across financial sectors, working closely with the other ESAs.
- The **European Insurance and Occupational Pensions Authority's (EIOPA's)** core responsibilities are to support the stability of the financial system, transparency of markets and financial products as the protection of policyholders, pension scheme members and beneficiaries. EIOPA is commissioned to monitor and identify trends, potential risks and vulnerabilities stemming from the micro-prudential level, across borders and across sectors.

The three authorities work to ensure that competent authorities and institutions within their scope apply the provisions of European AML/CFT legislation effectively and consistently. They also work together through the Joint Committee Anti-Money Laundering to:

- develop a common understanding of the risk-based approach (RBA) to AML/CFT and how it should be applied
- produce guidelines on:
    - AML/CFT risk-based supervision, and
    - risk factors and simplified and enhanced customer due diligence (CDD).

2.2.3 The Office of Foreign Assets Control (OFAC)

The US government, like most others, imposes economic and trade sanctions in pursuit of its foreign policy and national security goals against targeted foreign countries, regimes, terrorists, international narcotics traffickers, those engaged in activities relating to the proliferation of weapons of mass destruction and those who pose other threats to US national security or the economy.

The OFAC of the US Department of the Treasury acts under presidential national emergency powers, as well as the authority granted to it by specific legislation, basically to impose controls on transactions and freeze assets under US jurisdiction.

OFAC administers and enforces these sanctions. Many of these sanctions are based on UNSC resolutions (binding on all countries) and other international mandates. Implementation of these sanctions also involves close cooperation of the US with other allied governments.

The organisation is also responsible for administering the specially designated nationals (SDNs) list. The SDN list is a publication of OFAC which lists individuals and organisations with whom US citizens and permanent residents are prohibited from transacting and doing business. This SDN list differs from the list maintained pursuant to Section 314(a) of the USA PATRIOT Act, which contains information regarding individuals and organisations engaged in terrorist or money laundering activities.

2.2.4 The US Securities and Exchange Commission (SEC)

The Securities and Exchange Commission (SEC) is an agency of the US federal government. It holds primary responsibility for enforcing US federal securities laws, proposing securities rules, and regulating the securities industry, the stock and options exchanges and the electronic securities markets in the US.

The SEC has a three-part mission to protect investors, maintain fair, orderly and efficient markets, and facilitate capital formation. It brings civil enforcement actions against individuals and companies alleged to have committed accounting fraud, provided false information, or engaged in insider trading or other violations of securities law. The SEC also works with criminal law enforcement agencies to prosecute both individuals and companies for offences that include a criminal violation.

The SEC is also part of, and an important member of, the three-member steering committee of the interagency Financial Fraud Enforcement Task Force (FFETF) established by the US President in 2009. The task force works with state and local partners to investigate and prosecute significant financial crimes, ensure just and effective punishment for perpetrators of financial crimes, address discrimination in the lending and financial markets and recover proceeds for victims. It is the broadest coalition of law enforcement, investigatory, and regulatory agencies ever assembled in the US to combat financial crime.

It is an important member of the International Organization of Securities Commissions (IOSCO) and works in collaboration with securities market regulators around the world, both in the context of multilateral memoranda of understanding (MMOUs) and bilateral arrangements to combat financial crime.

2.2.5 The Financial Conduct Authority (FCA)

The FCA was established on 1 April 2013 and its statutory aim is to ensure that relevant markets work well. It is responsible for the conduct supervision of financial services firms and prudential supervision of firms not supervised by its counterpart, the Prudential Regulatory Authority (PRA). The FCA is accountable to HM Treasury and Parliament.

The objectives of the FCA are to protect consumers, ensure the industry remains stable and promote healthy competition between financial services providers.

The FCA has a wide financial crime remit. It is the AML/CFT supervisor for financial services firms and investigates and prosecutes market abuse. As part of its responsibility to ensure the integrity of the UK's financial markets, the FCA requires regulated firms to have systems and controls in place to mitigate the risk that they might be used for financial crime. The FCA, as part of its Handbook, produces a *Financial Crime Guide* for firms which sets out its expectations and examples of good and poor practice that it has identified through its supervision work.

The FCA has regulatory requirements that apply to all authorised firms subject to the Money Laundering Regulations (MLRs), which must apply policies and procedures to minimise their money laundering risk. **Internal controls** effectively monitor and manage firms' compliance with anti-money laundering policies and procedures. The controls are expected to be appropriate to the size of the firm, the products it offers, the parts of the world where it does business and the types of customers who use its services.

2.2.6 Domestic Regulators

Many other sectors are subject to the MLRs in the UK, in accordance with the FATF standards. They all have an AML/CFT supervisor, appointed by HM Treasury under the MLRs. These include HM Revenue & Customs (HMRC), the Gambling Commission and professional bodies from the legal and accountancy professions. There are 27 supervisors in total, a mixture of self-regulatory bodies (SRBs) and regulators. According to HM Treasury:

'The supervisors in the UK are a highly diverse group including large global professional bodies, smaller professional and representative bodies, as well as public sector organisations. In each area of supervision, the supervisor's approach needs to be proportionate to the nature and associated risks of the members being supervised'.

2.3 Governmental Approaches to Combating Financial Crime

Learning Objectives

1.2.3 Know how regulators implement international standards and facilitate cross-border cooperation

1.2.4 Understand the role and scope of: intelligence gathering and analysis; investigating financial crime; asset recovery and repatriation

Financial markets have become increasingly globalised. Technological advances have facilitated the movement of capital across borders and increased investment opportunities for investors. The 2007 financial crises also demonstrated undeniable, strong interconnectedness of markets with their resulting contagion effects around the world.

In a global marketplace, the development of global solutions and the enforcement of international regulatory and supervisory standards are only possible through international cooperation and coordination. The problems faced by globalised markets require globally coordinated solutions.

2.3.1 Coordination and Cooperation

In recent years, there have been substantial efforts to expand and deepen the coordination between the financial market regulators to minimise cross-border frictions and to identify more harmonised standards or common approaches to regulation. National regulators, such as the US's SEC and the UK's FCA have realised that to be effective they need cooperative relationships and coordination with other jurisdictions.

The most obvious manifestation of international cooperation is the growing information sharing and cooperation across borders to combat financial crime under frameworks such as the Basel Committee on Banking Supervision (BCBS), the IOSCO and the International Association of Insurance Supervisors (IAIS).

2.3.2 Regulations – Best Practices

Significant work on the analysis of regulations and adoption of high-quality regulations has been undertaken by multilateral institutions, such as the BCBS, IOSCO and IAIS, along with the Financial Stability Board (FSB), G20, FATF and the EU. The work primarily focuses on considering appropriate regulations, standards and guidelines for international financial markets and the global economy. Historically, these multilateral institutions have tended to outline principles and recommendations that individual national regulators may choose to adopt as they deem fit and in the way they consider appropriate to achieve the results desired in the respective principle or the recommendation.

The development of regulations on common 'principles' and 'recommendations' helps squeeze out any differences that may have existed amongst the laws and regulations of different individual countries. Another benefit of these cooperative efforts is that they significantly enhance the credibility of the laws or regulations of the country implementing the principles. Developing countries are beneficiaries of the cooperative efforts as they gain from the experiences and capacities of other advanced national regulators by adopting high-quality regulations consistent with the internationally accepted regulatory best practices and principles.

2.4 Regulatory Consistency

Additionally, when national regulators cooperate to develop regulatory principles upon which they agree, they also adopt broadly consistent regulations, even if the manner of implementing these regulatory principles may differ from one country to another.

A tremendous benefit of this process to market participants is regulatory certainty in cross-border transactions, as regulations based upon broadly agreed principles result in almost consistent treatment of participants' actions. Regulatory certainty, in turn, reduces compliance costs and other frictions associated with cross-border transactions, resulting in greater efficiency in global markets.

In addition, continued and expanded international cooperation in information sharing and enforcement also serves to enhance market transparency and, therefore, investor confidence.

2.4.1 Intelligence Gathering and Analysis

Financial intelligence in general terms is understood to mean the gathering and analysis of information about the financial affairs of entities of interest, with the aim of understanding their nature and capabilities and predicting their intentions.

The process of collecting financial intelligence involves analysing and scrutinising a large volume of different transactional data which is generated at different stages of financial transactions. This data is usually provided by banks and other financial institutions in fulfilment of their regulatory requirements or in response to court orders or other legal requirements.

Financial institutions are required to submit various financial transaction reports to the regulators or the law enforcement agencies under different laws which all form part of financial intelligence gathering and analysis. In particular, FATF Recommendation 29 mandates that each country has a **financial intelligence unit (FIU)**, which is responsible for receiving, analysing and disseminating suspicious activity reports (SARs).

2.4.2 Investigating Financial Crime

A great variety of criminal activities can be classified as financial crime. As long as there are weaknesses that can be exploited for gain, criminals will try to take advantage of companies, other organisations and also private individuals. Financial crimes, by their very nature, involve complex money laundering schemes and sophisticated criminals. Investigations using proper financial investigative techniques are required to uncover the proceeds of crime, as well as to create the trail of evidence that leads investigators to the top of criminal enterprises.

In June 2012, the FATF issued the paper *Operational Issues Financial Investigations Guidance*, which provides useful guidance. A financial investigation involves the collection, collation and analysis of all available information with a view to assisting in the prosecution of crime and in the deprivation of the proceeds and instrumentalities of crime. Criminals usually like to maintain some degree of control over their assets and, as a result, there is usually a 'paper trail' that will lead back to the offender. This paper trail can also be followed to identify additional offenders and potentially the location of evidence and instrumentalities used to commit the crimes. In financial investigations, it is important to answer all questions relating to the proceeds of crime. A careful financial investigation that properly follows the trail of the money and other assets can reveal the complex structure of major criminal organisations and can lead to seizures and forfeitures of the proceeds of crime.

Different financial investigation IT systems have been developed and are available in the market. Some law enforcement agencies have also published toolkits in the form of guides or financial investigation checklists which provide valuable assistance in undertaking information gathering and analysis.

2.4.3 Asset Recovery and Repatriation

The FATF defines the term 'asset recovery' as '*the return or repatriation of the illicit proceeds, where those proceeds are located in foreign countries*'. However, the United Nations Convention against Corruption (UNCAC) defines the term as 'the recovery of the proceeds of corruption'. Such assets may include monies in bank accounts, real estate, vehicles, works of art and precious metals. In short, asset recovery and repatriation is any effort by governments to repatriate the proceeds of corruption hidden in foreign jurisdictions.

The FATF has also issued a paper entitled *Best Practices on Confiscation (Recommendations 4 and 38) and a Framework for Ongoing Work on Asset Recovery*, in October 2012. The paper sets out international best practices to assist countries in their implementation of its Recommendations 4 and 38, which address impediments to effective confiscation and asset recovery in the international context. FATF Recommendation 4 requires the countries to put in place measures to identify, trace and evaluate property which is subject to confiscation. Likewise, FATF Recommendation 38 requires that countries must establish an authority to take expeditious action in response to requests by foreign countries to identify property which may be subject to confiscation.

The World Bank and the United Nations Office on Drugs and Crime (UNODC) have also developed a partnership and started an initiative entitled 'The Stolen Asset Recovery (StAR) Initiative' aimed at helping developing countries recover the assets stolen by their corrupt rulers and officials.

3. Best Practice

Learning Objective

1.3.1 Know the role, evolution and practical application of best practice in CFC and establishing international standards

1.3.2 Understand the role of the FCA's financial crime guidance

1.3.3 Understand the importance of the JMLSG to UK financial services firms

3.1 Best Practice

The term 'best practice' can be defined as a method or technique that has consistently shown results superior to those achieved by other means, and which is used as a benchmark. It can evolve to become better as improvements are discovered. The term is also used by some to describe the process of developing and following a standard way of doing things that multiple organisations can use.

Regulation has evolved from a very prescriptive regime, based on extremely detailed rules, that was regarded as costly, confusing and resource intensive, particularly for smaller firms, to a more principles- and outcomes-based regime. A large volume of detailed, prescriptive and highly complex rules also diverted attention towards adhering to the letter, rather than the purpose of regulatory standards. Regulation tends to be more outcome-focused, allowing firms to decide how best to align their business with regulatory outcomes, while holding the senior management to account for delivering. However, to assist firms in their compliance efforts, regulators produce guidance, which often includes both good and poor practice.

The FATF, although not a regulator, adopts this approach and produces both guidance and best practice documents. Recent examples include *Guidance on Correspondent Banking* (October 2016), which explains the FATF's requirements in the context of correspondent banking services; and *Best Practices on Combating the Abuse of Non-Profit Organisations* (June 2015), aimed at preventing the misuse of non-profit organisations (NPOs) for the financing of terrorism while, at the same time, respecting their legitimate actions. The FATF documents can be used by jurisdictions in establishing their systems, regulators in producing their own guidance and by individual firms setting up their systems and controls.

3.2 The Role of the FCA's Financial Crime Guidance

The FCA's *Financial Crime Guide: A firm's guide to countering financial crime risk* (FCG) is intended to provide practical assistance and information for firms of all sizes and across all FCA-supervised sectors on actions firms can take to counter the risk that they might be used to further financial crime. The contents, instead of being prescriptive, have been drawn primarily from FCA-thematic reviews, with some additional material included to reflect other aspects of the FCA's financial crime remit.

The examples in the thematic reviews included in the Guide are regarded as the best practices for the industry. However, firms have the flexibility to comply with their financial crime obligations in ways other than following the good practice set out in the Guide, providing the desired results are achieved.

The Guide gives examples of good and poor practice of:

- governance
- structure
- risk assessment
- policies and procedures
- recruitment, vetting, training, awareness and remuneration
- quality of oversight.

The FCA also makes it clear that the:

'Guide is not a standalone document; it does not attempt to set out all applicable requirements and should be read in conjunction with existing laws, rules and guidance on financial crime. If there is a discrepancy between the Guide and any applicable legal requirements, the provisions of the relevant legal requirement prevail. If firms have any doubt about a legal or other provision or their responsibilities under FSMA or other relevant legislation or requirements, they should seek appropriate professional advice'.

The FCA's focus, when supervising firms, is on whether they are complying with FCA rules and their other legal obligations. The FCA expects the firms to be aware of what the regulations provide, where it applies to them and to consider applicable guidance when establishing, implementing and maintaining their anti-financial crime systems and controls. Best practices are not a substitute for law.

3.3 The Importance of the Joint Money Laundering Steering Group (JMLSG) to UK Financial Services Firms

The JMLSG consists of the leading UK trade associations in the financial services sector. The JMLSG published industry guidance papers defining best practice and practical advice related to the interpretation of the UK MLRs. The guidance which has been provided to the UK financial sector since 1990, is periodically reviewed and, if necessary, changes and additions are made. The JMLSG guidance provides UK financial services firms with a degree of discretion as to how to implement AML/CFT legislation and regulation, including any procedures that need to be put in place. The JMLSG guidance is used by the FCA to assess whether or not the conduct of a firm constitutes a breach of AML/CFT requirements. It is recognised and approved by HM Treasury, and needs to be taken into consideration by UK courts in legal proceedings.

4. Asset Recovery

Learning Objective

1.4.1 Know the importance of recovery for prevention, deterrence and justice

1.4.2 Know how the United Nations Office on Drugs and Crime (UNODC) and the World Bank Group (WBG) aim to assist developing countries and financial centres with their Stolen Asset Recovery initiative (StAR)

1.4.3 Know civil and criminal remedies to recovering assets and the implications of freezing orders: criminal confiscation; civil recovery; freezing orders; search orders; disclosure of information orders; tracing; monitoring; unexplained wealth orders

4.1 The Importance of Recovery for Prevention, Deterrence and Justice

In terms of impact, financial crimes such as corruption, bribery and money laundering are not simply economic crimes that affect only those who are directly involved in these criminal acts. The prevalence of corruption or money laundering in a society destabilises its basic economic structures and markets, destroys possibilities of good governance and undermines the supremacy of an impartial and predictable legal system. Corruption is the major, if not the only, reason for lack of economic, political and social development in most developing countries. Corruption not only increases poverty but also impedes the access of the poor to public services such as education, health and justice.

It is difficult to estimate the amount of money being laundered, but a report from the United Nations Office on Drugs and Crime (UNODC) estimated that, in 2009, criminal proceeds accounted for 3.6% of global gross domestic product (GDP), with 2.7% ($1.6 trillion) being laundered. This remains in line with the 2% to 5% of global GDP (Camdessus 1998), which amounts to between $800 billion and $2 trillion estimated by the International Monetary Fund (IMF) in 1998. In addition, the Anti-Corruption Resource Centre estimated that 25% of the GDP of African states is lost to corruption every year ($148 billion, 2007). However, it needs to be considered that due to the illegal nature of money laundering and the underlying offences, it is difficult to provide any exact estimates.

Organised crime and corruption are primarily profit-driven activities. Recovery of stolen or laundered assets deprives the criminal of their ill-gotten gains and acts as a deterrent to such activity by reducing its effectiveness. Returning stolen assets to their rightful owners as part of a restorative justice programme acts to mitigate the effects of the crime, both at an individual level, and most importantly at a national level.

4.2 How the United Nations Office on Drugs and Crime (UNODC) and Stolen Asset Recovery (StAR) Assist Developing Countries and Financial Centres

International institutions, such as the UN, World Bank and the IMF, view corruption as one of the main obstacles to the progress of developing countries.

StAR is a partnership between the World Bank Group and the UNDOC which supports international efforts to end safe havens for corrupt funds. The initiative is financed by the World Bank and UNODC. However, contributors to StAR's Multi-Donor Trust Fund (MDTF) also include France, Norway, Sweden, Switzerland, the Netherlands and the UK.

StAR works with client developing countries (countries who have requested StAR for assistance by sending a written request to the StAR Secretariat) as well as with donors (developed countries who provide resources) to improve the legal framework for asset retrieval, and it provides guidance, skill development and practical assistance to developing countries.

Stolen asset recovery is complex and challenging for developing countries as they lack capacity and experience in this area of work. StAR offers practical guidance on the strategy and management of asset recovery efforts and helps countries launch asset recovery cases. It supports the countries to overcome legal and operational issues hampering progress and promptly engages with financial centres where assets may be hidden. The initiative also helps by acting as a facilitator along with providing expertise focused on assisting in international cooperation on specific cases.

Asset recovery matters because depriving corrupt officials of their ill-gotten gains will always be a significant deterrent. Recovering even a reasonable portion of the annual estimated stock of stolen assets acquired illegally by corrupt leaders of poor countries would make a substantive difference for the ordinary hard-working people living in these developing countries.

StAR is currently the main international initiative that focuses solely on the recovery of assets stolen by corrupt officials and political leaders from the developing countries. This initiative is important to ensure that asset recovery remains high on the international agenda and that the tools needed are provided to countries willing to pursue asset recovery. On the policy front, StAR works with regulatory agencies, governments, global forums and other partners towards building stronger international standards against corruption and collective responsibility and action to detect, prevent and recover stolen assets.

In short, StAR works both with developing countries and financial centres to prevent the laundering of the proceeds of corruption and to facilitate a more systematic and timely return of stolen assets.

The World Bank's initiative to help developing countries in the recovery of their stolen assets has been unsuccessful primarily because of two linked factors. Developing countries that have been victims of government corruption are still ruled by the groups or individuals who are the perpetrators or beneficiaries of this corruption. Simultaneously, recipient countries or territories of these stolen funds are often reluctant to act against the powerful interest groups who benefit from these stolen funds, such as banks.

4.3 Civil and Criminal Remedies to Recovering Assets

4.3.1 Criminal Confiscation

The UN Convention against Illicit Traffic in Narcotic Drugs and Psychotropic Substances defines [Article 1(f)] that confiscation *'which includes forfeiture where applicable, means permanent deprivation of property by order of a court or other competent authority'*.

The ability of the law enforcement agencies to deprive criminals of their proceeds of crime is an essential part of the contemporary global strategy to combat financial crime. There are different mechanisms to deal with the proceeds of crime and include both criminal and civil confiscation regimes. This approach is also mandated by the FATF and some other international instruments including the Council of Europe Convention on Laundering, Search and Seizure of Proceeds from Crime 1990.

FATF Recommendation 4 on *'Confiscation and Provisional Measures'* reads as:

'Countries should adopt measures similar to those set forth in the Vienna Convention, the Palermo Convention, and the Terrorist Financing Convention, including legislative measures, to enable their competent authorities to freeze or seize and confiscate the following, without prejudicing the rights of bona fide third parties: (a) property laundered, (b) proceeds from, or instrumentalities used in or intended for use in money laundering or predicate offences, (c) property that is the proceeds of, or used in, or intended or allocated for use in, the financing of terrorism, terrorist acts or terrorist organisations, or (d) property of corresponding value'.

The objective of confiscation proceeding is simple and straightforward. It is to deprive the defendant of the financial benefit that have obtained from criminal conduct.

Confiscation is an essential tool in the prosecutors' toolkit to deprive offenders of the proceeds of their criminal conduct to deter the commission of further offences and to reduce the profits available to fund further criminal enterprises. Prosecutors almost invariably consider this asset confiscation in every case in which a defendant has benefited from criminal conduct.

Generally, it is appropriate for the prosecutors to apply for a confiscation order whenever a defendant has obtained a benefit from or in connection with their criminal conduct and has the means to pay a confiscation order. To do this, the courts in the UK normally decide whether the defendant has a criminal lifestyle. If it decides that they do, then the court calculates the benefit from general criminal conduct using the assumptions set out in the Proceeds of Crime Act (POCA) 2002. Offences are included within Schedule 2 of POCA on the basis that they are offences that are typically committed by criminals to acquire wealth.

Similar provisions exist in the laws of almost all countries. In the US, the Racketeer Influence and Corrupt Organization (RICO) Act 1970 and parallel provisions in the Comprehensive Drug Abuse Prevention and Control Act of 1970 can be regarded as the first modern federal statute to impose forfeiture as a criminal sanction directly on an individual defendant.

4.3.2 Civil Recovery

The FATF defines **non-conviction-based confiscation** as *'confiscation through judicial procedures related to a criminal offence for which a criminal conviction is not required'*. Recommendation 38 obliges countries that civil (non-conviction based) liability should be sought where criminal liability is unavailable. Recommendation 4 of the FATF requires countries to consider adopting measures that should allow proceeds of crimes to be confiscated without requiring a criminal conviction. The expectations and obligations emerging out of the FATF are explained in its best practices paper *On Confiscation (Recommendations 4 and 38) and a Framework for Ongoing Work on Asset Recovery* (October 2012).

In the UK, the principle of civil recovery is established in law under POCA Section 2A that grants non-conviction asset-seizing powers to relevant agencies. Part 5 deals specifically with the recovery of the proceeds of crime from unconvicted defendants through proceedings in the civil courts. Guidance notes published (November 2012) by the UK Attorney General's Office on Asset Recovery Powers for Prosecutors explain that:

> *'Civil recovery is a form of non-conviction-based asset forfeiture which allows for the recovery in civil proceedings before the High Court of property which is, or represents, property obtained through unlawful conduct. Importantly, the proceedings are against the property itself rather than against an individual.*
>
> *These proceedings are civil litigation and the civil standard of proof (the balance of probabilities) applies. As the action is against the property and not the person, the person who holds the assets which are the subject of the order might not be the person who carried out the unlawful conduct, and a civil recovery order is not a conviction or a sentence'.*

The courts do require some convincing evidence to be satisfied that property is, on the balance of probabilities, more likely to be the proceeds of unlawful conduct. However, for the prosecutors to prove that property was obtained through unlawful conduct, it is normally considered sufficient to prove that the property was obtained through offending of a particular type (eg, fraud).

Civil recoveries are also possible in other countries including the US under different laws including the Civil Asset Forfeiture Reform Act 2000 and the USA Patriot Act 2001.

4.3.3 Freezing Orders

A freezing order is an injunction which restricts a respondent from disposing of, or dealing with, their own assets. The purpose of a freezing order is to prevent a defendant from moving, hiding, or otherwise concealing any of their assets from beyond the jurisdiction of a court which might frustrate any potential judgment. In this context, an asset is anything owned that has value. Although a freezing order is typically nationwide, there is also the possibility of worldwide freezing injunctions which apply to assets located outside the jurisdiction where the order is obtained in addition to any assets within the jurisdiction.

A freezing injunction can apply to a wide range of assets such as land, vehicles, shares, bonds and other financial instruments as well as money held in bank accounts. Assets can also include those that are held beneficially for another party, eg, assets held by a bank or on trust by a third party.

The courts normally require certain conditions to be fulfilled before a freezing order is issued, such as:

1. The plaintiff has a strong case.
2. The plaintiff can present enough evidence regarding the existence and location of assets that will be affected by the injunction, if made.
3. There is a risk of dissipation of the assets before a judgment can be enforced.
4. The freezing order is 'just and convenient'.

The granting of a freezing order does not give the plaintiff the right to the property that is subject of the order, nor does it give the plaintiff any lien on the defendant's property. It also gives no priority to the potential creditor over other claimants before or after judgment, nor does it affect the laws relating to insolvency.

The defendant is only restrained from disposing of their assets in the sense that to do so will constitute contempt of court. Freezing orders are considered by some as harsh on defendants because the order is often granted at the pre-trial stage in *ex parte* hearings. However, on balance the concept is designed to prevent injustice being done to a successful claimant by preserving assets and funds from being disposed of or dissipated before a judgment is satisfied.

Any breach of the terms of the order can result in proceedings for contempt of court. This is punishable by a fine, imprisonment or the seizure of the assets subject to the injunction.

4.3.4 Search Orders

A search order is a court order that provides the right to search premises and seize evidence without prior warning. This is primarily intended to prevent destruction of relevant evidence, particularly in cases of financial crimes.

The purpose of a search order is usually to preserve evidence or property which is, or possibly can be, the subject of an action, or as to which a question arises in an action. In the UK, the High Court's power to grant search orders is derived from Section 7(1) of the Civil Procedure Act 1997.

It is essentially an *ex parte* court injunction that requires a defendant to allow the plaintiff to:

- enter the defendant's premises
- search for and take away any material evidence, and
- force the defendant to answer some questions.

This order is not a 'search warrant', but the defendant is in contempt of court if he refuses to comply.

Because such an order does not give the accused party the ability to defend themselves, orders are only issued exceptionally and according to a three-step test.

Such legal provisions are commonly found in English and common law systems and are now known as 'search orders' in England and Wales, as well as in New Zealand, Australia and India. In other jurisdictions, there can be a similar type of order or there may not be any statutory provision at all.

4.3.5 Disclosure of Information Orders

Disclosure in general terms is the act or process of making known something that was previously unknown; it is thus simply a revelation of facts. In a legal context, it is defined as the mandatory divulging of information to a litigation opponent according to procedural rules (Black's Law Dictionary).

Also known as the 'initial disclosure' in the US, it is a civil procedure in the federal practice that requires that parties make available to each other, without first receiving a discovery request the relevant information like: contact details of the persons having the discoverable information; a copy or description of all relevant **documents**, data compilation, and tangible items under a party's possession or control.

Disclosure of documents reflects the initial stage of the civil litigation process when each party is required to disclose the documents that are relevant to the issues in dispute to the other party. It normally takes place after each party has set out its position in their statement of case.

The disclosure exercise is important as it impacts upon the eventual outcome of the proceedings. Credibility at trial can be affected if a party fails to give proper disclosure and the court can also impose sanctions on a party that does not comply with its disclosure obligations.

The question of whether a document should be disclosed is determined by reference to the issues raised in the parties' statements of case. The term 'document' has a wide meaning, incorporating all media on which information is recorded. It includes, for example not only paper, but also all data including retrievable deleted electronic documents and other media including tapes, videos and photographs.

4.3.6 Tracing

Tracing in general terms is defined as:

> '...the process of tracking property's ownership or characteristics from the time of its origin to the present' (Black's Law Dictionary).

In a general and private legal context, tracing is only a process, not a remedy, by which a claimant can demonstrate as to what has happened to their property. Through the process, they can identify its proceeds and those persons who have handled or received it and ask the court to award a proprietary claim against the property, or an asset substituted for the original property or its proceeds. Tracing allows transmission of legal claims from the original assets to either the proceeds of sale of the assets or new substituted assets.

The process of tracing is easy to understand through an example.

Example

If Karl has money in a solicitor's account and the solicitor takes out that money to buy a painting, Karl may be able to make a claim against the painting. This claim will take priority even if the solicitor is bankrupt and has other unsecured claims against him.

In the context of CFC, the process of identifying and tracing the proceeds of crime is a tool of 'financial investigations' (Interpretive Note to FATF Recommendation 30) and is a means of enquiry into financial affairs related to a criminal activity, with a view to identifying the extent of criminal networks and/or the scale of criminality; terrorist funds or any other assets that are, or may become, subject to confiscation.

FATF Recommendation 16 (Wire Transfers) obliges countries to ensure that basic information on the originator and beneficiary of wire transfers is immediately available to assist law enforcement and/or prosecutorial authorities in detecting, investigating and prosecuting terrorists or other criminals, and tracing their assets.

4.3.7 Monitoring

An account **monitoring** order in the UK allows for real-time financial surveillance. The order is available for money laundering, criminal forfeiture, and cash seizure investigations and enables the investigator to observe the transactions in an account. Analysis of the product can establish typologies being used and provides opportunities for cash seizure, for example, targeting the locations of frequent large cash withdrawals.

Section 370 POCA provides for account monitoring orders. Section 371 spells out the requirements for *'making of these account monitoring orders',* subject to fulfilment of which an *'account monitoring order'* may be issued by the court. However, for the order to be issued there must be reasonable grounds for suspecting that the person specified in the application for the order has benefited from their criminal conduct. The orders are normally issued in the cases of confiscation investigation, a civil recovery investigation or a money laundering investigation.

Freezing Order: Scope

A freezing order can be used to freeze assets and monies suspected of being the proceeds of corruption, pending the outcome of the claim. It is an interim injunction and may be made by the court wherever it is *'just and convenient'* to do so (Section 37(1) of the Senior Courts Act 1981). There is also a possibility of worldwide freezing injunctions which apply to assets located outside the jurisdiction, as well as assets within the jurisdiction.

Freezing Injunction: Breach

Freezing injunctions are granted by the court and any breach of the terms of the 'order' can result in proceedings for contempt of court. This is punishable by a fine, imprisonment or the seizure of the assets subject to the injunction.

4.3.8 Unexplained Wealth Orders

Unexplained wealth orders are a part of the UK's Criminal Finance's Act 2017. They are an investigative tool in that can be used to strip individuals of the proceeds of their alleged crimes. The orders can only be issued by the court and only when concerning a politically exposed person (PEP) or if it is someone involved in, or connected to a person involved in, serious crime. Although the terms of each order can vary depending on the circumstances, the purpose is always for the recipient to explain how they were able to obtain the property or wealth subject to the order. Contrary to many other parts of the law, it is not up to the applicant to prove guilt, rather it is up to the recipient to prove their innocence.

End of Chapter Questions

Think of an answer for each question and refer to the appropriate section for confirmation.

1. What is the offence of money laundering?
   Answer reference: Section 1.2

2. What is a predicate offence?
   Answer reference: Section 1.3

3. What is bribery?
   Answer reference: Section 1.8

4. What are the objectives of the Financial Action Task Force (FATF)?
   Answer reference: Section 2.1

5. Which areas of focus are added in the 5th Money Laundering Directive (5MLD) of the EU?
   Answer reference: Section 2.2.1

6. What is the European Securities and Markets Authority (ESMA)?
   Answer reference: Section 2.2.2

7. What are the functions of Office of Foreign Assets Control (OFAC)?
   Answer reference: Section 2.2.3

8. What is the intention of the Financial Conduct Authority's (FCA's) *Financial Crime Guide*?
   Answer reference: Section 3.2

9. How is Joint Money Laundering Steering Group (JMLSG) guidance used by the FCA?
   Answer reference: Section 3.3

10. What is the StAR programme?
    Answer reference: Section 4.2

11. What is 'civil recovery'?
    Answer reference: Section 4.3.2

12. What is the purpose of freezing orders?
    Answer reference: Section 4.3.3

13. What is an unexplained wealth order?
    Answer reference: Section 4.3.8

Chapter Two
Money Laundering

1. Background	29
2. International Anti-Money Laundering (AML) Standards	38
3. The Financial Action Task Force (FATF)	42
4. The Role of Other International Bodies	48

This syllabus area will provide approximately 8 of the 50 examination questions

1. Background

Learning Objectives

2.1.1 Understand the models of the money laundering process: placement, layering, integration (PLI) model; the 'enable, distance, and disguise' model

2.1.2 Know these associated activities as defined by the Proceeds of Crime Act (POCA) 2002: concealment; arrangements; acquisition, use and possession; failure to disclose; tipping off, consent regime, criminal property, criminal conduct

2.1.3 Know the role, purpose and scope of The Money Laundering, Terrorist Financing and Transfer of Funds (information on the payer) Regulations (MLR 2017)

2.1.4 Understand how the stages of the money laundering process are detected by financial services firms in the regulated sectors

1.1 Introduction

Money laundering (ML) is traditionally defined as a process to conceal the true origin of the proceeds of crime in such a way that the unlawfully gained money or assets appear to have been derived from legitimate origins or to constitute legitimate assets.

In its 2015 report, *'Why is Cash Still King? A Strategic Report on the Use of Cash by Criminal Groups as a Facilitator for Money Laundering'*, Europol explains that:

> *'There are many different ways in which the laundered money can be integrated back with the criminal; however, the major objective at this stage is to reunite the money with the criminal in a manner that does not draw attention and appears to result from a legitimate source'.*

Once a criminal is reunited with their funds or assets, they can freely spend them without necessarily drawing attention to it.

Money laundering takes many forms, including:

- trying to turn money raised through criminal activity into 'clean' money
- handling the benefit of acquisitive crimes such as theft, fraud and tax evasion
- handling stolen goods
- being directly involved with any criminal or terrorist property, or entering into arrangements to facilitate the laundering of criminal or terrorist property, and
- criminals investing the proceeds of their crimes in a whole range of financial products.

The techniques used by money launderers, like those of other criminals, constantly evolve.

1.2 The Money Laundering Process

1.2.1 The Placement, Layering, and Integration (PLI) Model

The traditional money laundering process normally takes place over three distinct stages:

- **Placement** – this is the initial entry of the 'dirty' cash or proceeds of crime into the formal financial system. Generally, this stage serves two purposes:
    a. it relieves the criminal of holding and guarding large amounts of cash, and
    b. it places the money into the legitimate financial system.

    Cash generated from criminal activities is converted into some form of monetary instrument, such as money orders or travellers' cheques, or deposited into accounts at financial institutions or placed in some assets that store value like jewellery, real estate or different capital market equity and debt instruments. It is during the placement stage that money launderers are most vulnerable and risk being caught. This is because placement of large amounts of money into the legitimate and formal financial system may raise suspicions of financial services firms and law enforcement.
- **Layering** – this is the most complex stage and often entails international movement of the funds and use of formal remittance services. The primary purpose of this stage of the process is to separate the illegal money from its source. This is done through the sophisticated layering of financial transactions that are intended to obscure the audit trail and thus cut the link of the money with the original crime. The money launderers may, during this stage, begin by moving funds from one country to another, then divide them into investments placed in advanced financial options or overseas markets; constantly moving them to elude detection. These funds may be left invested for some time in countries with weak anti-money laundering enforcement systems before moving to the third stage of the process.
- **Integration** – it is at this stage where the money is eventually returned or reunited back to the criminal from what seems to be a legitimate source. Having been placed initially as cash or other similar assets and layered through a number of transactions, the criminal proceeds by this time are now fully integrated into the financial system and can be used and enjoyed by the criminals, for any purpose.

There are many ways in which the laundered money can be integrated back with the criminal; however, the major objective at this stage is to reunite the money with the criminal in a manner that does not draw attention and appears to result from a legitimate source. For example, the criminals with this reunited money can now freely spend it and enjoy their illegal profits without necessarily drawing attention to them.

1.2.2 Enable, Distance and Disguise (EDD) Model

The enable, distance and disguise (EDD) model of money laundering recognises a wider range of conduct related to the facilitation of money laundering than the PLI model.

- **Enable** – financial products or services have many legitimate uses, but may also be used to enable financial crime. The main question to be asked in order to establish whether or not firms run facilitation risk in relation to money laundering is 'why'? Why does the client request this specific product or service, and what is the advantage for the client?

- **Distance** – criminals distance themselves from the asset using a company, trust or a foundation, for example when an asset is owned by a company in which the criminal is the majority shareholder.
- **Disguise** – using a multi-layered, opaque ownership structure effectively disguises the ownership of the company, trust or foundation. Shares of a company can be issued in bearer form, further disguising ownership.

In this context, the use of a company is attractive for the following reasons:

1. The company is a legal person with the ability to open bank accounts, enter into contracts, and apply for credit cards.
2. It can (in)directly be owned by the criminal either in their own name, via bearer shares or via nominees.
3. Formal structure provides a sense of trust and reliability.

Trusts are not legal persons and in the context of financial crime, are attractive due to the fact that they are generally not registered, enable the criminal to pass the legal ownership of a property to a trustee while retaining control over the property, and are portable.

Although often associated with benevolent purposes, foundations can also exist for commercial purposes. Foundations have specific objectives to be achieved by means of an endowment. They are typically controlled by a foundation council, who manages the foundation for the benefit of the beneficiaries. Similar to trusts and companies, foundations have a variety of legitimate uses. They are, however, vulnerable to criminal exploitation due to the inherent possibility to disguise ownership while retaining control of the asset.

Corporate service providers can be engaged to provide company directors, registered offices, company secretaries, nominee shareholders or trustees. The use of such services creates a further disconnect between the company, trust, or foundation and the ultimate owner. When transacting with a corporate service provider, an assessment of the vulnerability of their services to be used for financial crime, and licensing obligations and corporate law in the jurisdiction they operate in, are important to assess.

1.3   Proceeds of Crime Act (POCA) 2002

Part 7 of the Proceeds of Crime Act (POCA) 2002 (Sections 327–340) contains the primary UK anti-money laundering (AML) legislation, including provisions requiring businesses within the regulated sector (financial institutions: such as banks, investment companies, **money service businesses**, and some other professions, for example, auditors, insolvency practitioners, tax advisers, independent legal professionals, estate agents and high value dealers) to report to the authorities the knowledge or suspicions of money laundering by their clients. Under the Act of 2002, money laundering offences are committed when a person undertakes any of the following acts:

- concealment
- arrangements
- acquisition, use and possession
- failure to disclose
- tipping-off, or
- consent.

Offence	Description
Concealment	A person commits an offence of concealment under Section 327 of POCA 2002 if criminal property is: • concealed, disguised, converted, transferred or removed from the jurisdiction or area of authority under which the law applies (for example, it is moved overseas) • concealing or disguising criminal property includes concealing or disguising its nature, source, location, disposition movement or ownership of any rights with respect to it. This offence is committed by the person being investigated in relation to the proceeds of either their own criminal activity or that of someone else.
Arrangements	Assisting someone to keep the proceeds of crime. Thus, a person commits an offence when they know or suspect they are helping someone to acquire, retain, use or control criminal property. Examples of arrangements under Section 328 of POCA include a: • lawyer who knowingly helps a person buy a house with criminal money • person who arranges for their partner or parent to put a vehicle which is criminal property in their name.
Acquisition, use and possession	The acquisition, possession or use of criminal property. Examples of acquisition, use and possession under Section 329 of POCA include when a person: • carries, holds, or looks after criminal property (for example, cash) • acquires criminal property for 'inadequate consideration' (this means an item is bought for significantly less than the market value, for example a car worth £50,000 is bought for £5,000).
Failure to disclose	Failure to report knowledge or suspicion of money laundering, or failure to report where there are reasonable grounds to know or suspect that another person is engaged in money laundering (see section 1.3.1 below).
Tipping-off	In the context of money laundering, tipping-off is related to the disclosure of the fact that a suspicious transaction report (STR) or related information is being filed with the FIU (see section 1.3.2 below).
Consent	Appropriate consent is the consent provided by a nominated officer, police officer, or customs officer to undertake a prohibited act provided an authorised disclosure is made. As long as the person is not informed within seven working days that they may not undertake the act, they will have received consent.

In the context of POCA, criminal conduct is any conduct that constitutes an offence under UK law, even when it is undertaken in a geographical area that is not part of the UK. A person benefits from criminal conduct if they directly or indirectly obtain a property or a financial gain in relation to the criminal activity. Criminal property is defined as the proceeds of any crime.

1.3.1 Failure to Disclose

FATF Recommendation 21 obliges countries that their financial institutions, their directors, officers and employees should be:

> *'protected by law from criminal and civil liability for breach of any restriction on disclosure of information imposed by contract or by any legislative, regulatory or administrative provision, if they report their suspicions in good faith to the FIU, even if they did not know precisely what the underlying criminal activity was, and regardless of whether illegal activity actually occurred'.*

POCA allows reporters (financial institutions) a defence against the money laundering offence by making an authorised disclosure, known as a suspicious activity report (SAR), to seek the consent of the National Crime Agency (NCA) prior to undertaking an activity which the reporter suspects may constitute one of the three (Sections 327–329 of POCA) money laundering offences or 'prohibited acts'. The 'consent regime' is described in more detail in section 6 of chapter 9.

Failure to disclose knowledge or suspicion of money laundering falls under Sections 330–332 of POCA and amendments to the disclosure regime by the Serious Organised Crime and Police Act (SOCPA) 2005 (Section 104).

Section 338 of POCA

Section 338 of POCA provides the basic clarifications as to what constitutes the authorised disclosures with references to the prohibited acts mentioned in Sections 327, 328 and 329. The form and manner in which a disclosure under Sections 330, 331, 332 or 338 must be made are detailed in Section 339.

The UK National Crime Agency (NCA) explains that no offence is committed if a person (normally the firm's money laundering reporting officer (MLRO)) or nominated officer (NO) makes an 'authorised disclosure' under Section 338 of POCA to a constable or more usually the NCA. The defence also applies to those who intended to make such a disclosure but had a reasonable excuse for not doing so.

In general terms, a disclosure is regarded as an 'authorised disclosure' if it is undertaken:

- before a person carries out the act prohibited by Sections 327–329
- while a person is carrying out the act prohibited by Sections 327–329, the act having begun at a point when the discloser did not know or suspect that the property was the proceeds of crime and the disclosure is made on the discloser's own initiative as soon as is practicable after they first knew or suspected that the property is the proceeds of crime, or
- after the act prohibited by Sections 327–329 and is made on the discloser's own initiative as soon as practicable after the act, and there is good reason for failure to make the disclosure before the act.

Authorised disclosures protect the reporter from being involved in money laundering offences. POCA also created new offences of failing to disclose knowledge; or suspicion of money laundering activity. The sections are:

POCA Section	
Section 330	Failure to disclose: regulated sector
Section 331	Failure to disclose: nominated officers in the regulated sector
Section 332	Failure to disclose: other nominated officers

Each offence carries a maximum penalty on conviction of:

- five years imprisonment
- a fine, or
- both.

These offences create different requirements for the regulated and non-regulated sectors. To commit the offence, a person must know or suspect that someone is involved in money laundering and that they can identify the money launderer or whereabouts of the laundered property, but fail to disclose this. The knowledge or suspicion must be based on information that has come to them in the course of their business. The test of knowledge or suspicion for the regulated sector is expanded to include when they had 'reasonable grounds for suspecting', even if they did not actually form a suspicion.

Authorised disclosures (SARs) are also required to be made under the provisions of Sections 19(2) and 21 of the Terrorism Act 2000 in case of terrorist financing.

The NCA has issued detailed guidance for firms submitting SARs.

1.3.2 Tipping Off

In the context of money laundering, 'tipping off' is regarded as a situation where any individual discloses information that could affect an investigation, particularly following the submission of a SAR. A firm that reports a customer to the FIU is not allowed to tell the customer they have done so. Recommendation 21(b) states that:

> 'Financial institutions, their directors, officers and employees should be:
>
> (b) prohibited by law from disclosing ('tipping off') the fact that a suspicious transaction report (STR) or related information is being filed with the FIU'.

In the UK, Section 333 of POCA creates the offence of 'tipping off' when a person knows or suspects that a disclosure falling within Section 337 or 338 of the POCA has been made. The person commits an offence under Section 333 of POCA if a disclosure is made that is likely to prejudice a money laundering investigation, eg, informing an individual of the disclosure to the NCA. The offence carries a maximum penalty on indictment of five years' imprisonment, or a fine, or both.

Section 342 of POCA contains a separate offence of prejudicing an investigation by:

- alerting individuals to an investigation being, or about to be undertaken
- destroying, concealing or falsifying relevant documents.

The MLRs 2017 provide that the firm cannot, at the time, tell a customer that a transaction is being delayed because the law enforcement authority is conducting an investigation and a report is awaiting consent from NCA. This cannot be disclosed even later, unless law enforcement agrees, or a court order is obtained permitting disclosure. Only then the firm can inform a customer that a transaction or activity was delayed because a report had been made under POCA or the Terrorism Act.

1.3.3 Penalties

POCA imposes legal obligations on every individual within all regulated sector firms to ensure that AML provisions are strictly adhered to. Any breach of the obligations provided under the Act carry tough penalties some of which are:

Offence	Penalty
Concealment Arrangements Acquisition, use and possession	Up to 14 years in prison and/or an unlimited fine
Failure to disclose Tipping off	Up to 5 years in prison and/or an unlimited fine

1.4 Detecting the Stages of the Money Laundering Process

Financial services firms carry out transaction monitoring to try to detect money laundering. Monitoring systems, manual or automated, can vary considerably in their approach to detecting and reporting unusual or uncharacteristic behaviour and possible acts of financial crime.

There are many automated transaction monitoring systems that are available in the market. These systems use a variety of techniques to detect and report unusual/uncharacteristic transactions/activities. The techniques used range from artificial intelligence to simple rules. These systems generally 'flag' certain transactions for review, which allows analysts to scrutinise some or all transfers, often using link analysis.

Link analyses are important to help identify relationships among individual accounts, people, and organisations. However, an effective use of link analysis requires a variety of readily available data, which provides analysts with indicators of possible money laundering activity.

Staff in financial institutions are also trained to spot suspicious activity when dealing with customers face-to-face, such as at a counter.

Example

In November 2019, Australia's financial intelligence agency, AUSTRAC, started legal action against WestPac in relation to 23 million breaches of AML and counter-terrorism finance laws amounting to $11 billion in transactions. Although made aware of child exploitation risks in one of their payment systems in 2013, WestPac did not resolve this issue until June 2018. Therefore, they failed to detect inappropriate behaviour on client accounts in a timely manner.

Regulators, supervisory and even law enforcement agencies of different countries such as the UK, Canada, Belgium and Ireland have developed non-exhaustive lists highlighting risk indicators to help the financial firms detect acts of possible financial crime. Some international bodies, like the International Association of Insurance Supervisors (IAIS), have also developed such risk indicators for their sectors of financial services. The role of the financial services sector in combating financial crime (CFC), and their relations with regulators, will be examined in more detail in chapter 7 (particularly section 1).

1.5   MLR 2017

The Money Laundering, Terrorist Financing and Transfer of Funds (information on the payer) Regulations 2017 (MLR 2017) came into force in the UK on 26 June 2017. MLR 2017 transposes the Fourth Money Laundering Directive (4MLD) into UK law and replaces the Money Laundering Regulations and the Transfer of Funds (information on the payer) Regulations, both of 2007.

MLR 2017 enhances existing rules, expands their scope and brings them up to date. The new Regulations do not make any radical changes to the UK's financial crime prevention regime, but they do tighten the existing rules in a number of important ways. The main changes are related to relevant persons, the risk-based approach, politically exposed persons (PEPs), third parties and reckless statements. Each of these is detailed below.

1.5.1   Relevant Persons

The Regulations now cover all gambling providers and no longer only the holders of casino operation licences. In addition, there is an extended obligation on trustees to reveal the beneficiaries of a trust.

The Regulations do not cover relevant persons engaging in financial activities on an occasional or very limited basis which is defined as:

- an annual turnover from financial activity below £100,000 (increased from £64,000)
- transactions not exceeding €1,000 per customer, or
- financial activity ancillary to a larger business, no more than 5% of the total turnover of the larger business and only offered to customers of the main business.

1.5.2 The Risk-Based Approach

All businesses subject to MLR 2017 are required to adopt a risk-based approach to financial crime, specifically in relation to customer and transaction screening. Specific procedures are outlined for the analysis of exposure to financial crime risk. The findings of the analysis have to address (among others) customers, jurisdiction, products and services, and types and volumes of transactions. Policies, procedures and controls need to be in writing and are subject to periodic review and, if necessary, amended. Policies must be proportionate to the risks of the business.

Where previously businesses could default to simplified due diligence for any transaction, under the new regulations, businesses need to actively assess whether enhanced due diligence (EDD) would be more appropriate. In addition, EDD is compulsory for any transactions associated with a risky jurisdiction. A list of high-risk jurisdictions is included in the Regulations.

1.5.3 Politically Exposed Persons (PEPs)

The Regulations are extended to include local and foreign politically exposed persons (PEPs). All PEPs are subject to EDD on transactions.

1.5.4 Third Parties

It remains permitted to rely on due diligence carried out by a third party, provided the third party is subject to the new Regulations or an equivalent level of regulations in another jurisdiction. The third party must be able to provide all relevant information within two working days.

1.5.5 Reckless Statements

The offence of knowingly providing false or misleading statements about financial crime has been extended to include statements that are not knowingly false but are made recklessly, with little regard as to whether or not they are false.

2. International Anti-Money Laundering (AML) Standards

2.1 The Role of International Agencies

Learning Objective

2.2.1 Know the role of international financial institutions in combating money laundering: the International Monetary Fund (IMF); the World Bank

2.1.1 The International Monetary Fund (IMF)

The role of the International Monetary Fund (IMF) and its programmes in the area of AML/**combating the financing of terrorism (CFT)** have evolved over the years in line with the growing recognition of the need to combat financial crime and the fast emerging importance of financial integrity issues. According to the IMF, money laundering and terrorist financing:

> '...can undermine the integrity and stability of financial institutions and systems, discourage foreign investment, and distort international capital flows. They may have negative consequences for a country's financial stability and macroeconomic performance, resulting in welfare losses, draining resources from more productive economic activities, and even have destabilising spillover effects on the economies of other countries'.

The IMF includes AML/CFT issues in its regular assessments of financial stability, and carries out AML/CFT assessments to the FATF standards and supports capacity development activities and research projects. The IMF has observer status at the FATF and endorses the FATF standards and assessment methodology. In 2009, the IMF launched a fund to finance AML/CFT capacity development. More than $25 million was pledged by a number of countries for the second five-year phase from 2014. The IMF assists over 30 countries each year with technical assistance and training relating to AML/CFT. It also produced a methodology for carrying out national risk assessments and assists countries through this process.

2.1.2 The World Bank

AML/CFT was introduced by the World Bank in its work programmes after the 9/11 terrorist attacks in 2001. AML/CFT issues are now a mandatory element of the Bank's Financial Sector Assessment Programme (FSAP) in individual developing countries. The approach undertaken by the World Bank reflects the belief that the integrity of a country's financial system is critical to maintaining its stability and advancing its development.

The World Bank assists countries with their AML/CFT efforts in several ways, for example via grants to help build capacity and knowledge aimed at enhancing compliance with the FATF Recommendations. Similar to the IMF, it provides technical assistance to develop laws, regulations and institutional frameworks. It also provides training to **supervisors**, investigators, prosecutors and judges, disseminating good practice on new financial products, regulations and financial investigation.

It has also developed a national risk assessment methodology and offers guidance and help in undertaking these assessments. In partnership with the United Nations Office on Drugs and Crime (UNODC), the World Bank runs the Stolen Asset Recovery Initiative (StAR) that supports international efforts to end safe havens for corrupt funds. StAR works with developing countries and financial centres to prevent the laundering of the proceeds of corruption and to facilitate more systematic and timely return of stolen assets.

2.2 International Instruments and Conventions

Learning Objective

2.2.2 Know the role, purpose and scope of international instruments and conventions: UN Conventions; Directives/Regulations of the European Union – 2015/849/EC (4th Money Laundering Directive) 2018/843/EC (5th Money Laundering Directive), 2018/1673/EC (6th Money Laundering Directive), 2015/847/EC (Fund Transfer Regulations)

2.2.1 UN Conventions

Over time, a number of UN conventions have been held on the subject of AML/CFT which are typically named after the city where they were held. The following conventions are relevant in this context:

a. The **Vienna Convention**, or the 1988 UN Convention against Illicit Traffic in Narcotic Drugs and Psychotropic Substances, provided a strategy to counter international drug trafficking, coupled with provisions to provide the law enforcement community with the necessary tools to undermine the financial power of the cartels and other groups. The primary concept was to take the profit out of crime. However, the predicate offences were limited to drug trafficking offences, and did not include unrelated crimes such as fraud, kidnapping and theft. Over time, it has been accepted that predicate offences for money laundering are more extensive than just drug trafficking.

b. The **Palermo Convention,** or the UN Convention against Transnational Organised Crime (2000), provided tools to address organised crime as a global problem with enhanced international cooperation. The convention was an important event in the reinforcement of the fight against organised crime. The definition of money laundering offences is extended to include the laundering of proceeds of transnational organised crime, widening the scope of AML/CFT considerably beyond drug trafficking offences. The convention required countries to:

> '...institute a comprehensive domestic regulatory and supervisory regime... in order to deter and detect all forms of money laundering'.

These include matters covered in the FATF Recommendations such as customer due diligence (CDD), record keeping, the reporting of suspicious transactions, and the need to ensure appropriate resources for law enforcement and regulatory efforts.

c. The **Merida Convention,** or the UN Convention against Corruption (UNCAC) of 2005, resulted in the first globally agreed international anti-corruption instrument. It is unique in its global coverage as well as the extent and detail of its provisions. UNCAC requires the countries that have ratified the Convention to implement several anti-corruption measures, some of which may affect existing laws, institutions and working practices. The Convention aims to promote the prevention, detection and sanctioning of corruption and certain criminal conduct. In addition, it aims to improve the cooperation between state parties, and to strengthen the enforcement of international law, thereby providing effective legal mechanisms for asset recovery and judicial cooperation. The Convention also provides for exchange of information, and mechanisms for implementation of the Convention and technical assistance to the developing countries. In terms of Article 63 of the Convention, the Conference of the state parties to the UNCAC was also established to improve the capacity of and cooperation between state parties to achieve the objectives set out in the Convention and to promote and review its implementation.

Article 23 of UNCAC requires countries to criminalise money laundering and to seek to apply the offences to *'the widest range of predicate offences'*. As a minimum, money laundering offences should be applied against a comprehensive range of criminal offences established in accordance with the Convention. Some jurisdictions, including the UK, now apply an 'all crimes' regime, applying money laundering to the proceeds of any crime, while the FATF has developed a list of crimes that must be included as predicate offences.

2.2.2 European Regulations and Directives

The most recent EU Directive on the prevention of the use of the financial system for the purposes of money laundering or terrorist financing is Directive 2015/849/EC of 20 May 2015. It is also referred to as the 'Fourth (4th) Money Laundering Directive' or simply '4MLD'. The Fourth Directive was needed to bring EU legislation in line with the international standards on combating money laundering and terrorist financing set out in the FATF 40 Recommendations, which were revised in 2012.

The Directive implements the risk-based approach, through requiring a European-wide **risk assessment**, as well as national and institutional assessments. It covers customer due diligence and other requirements on financial institutions and designated non-financial businesses and professions (DNFBPs), in accordance with the FATF Recommendations (see section 3 of this chapter). DNFBPs are non-financial sectors identified to be vulnerable to money laundering abuse, such as lawyers, accountants, real estate agents and some types of businesses that deal in high-value goods.

Significantly, the Directive extends the definition of PEPs, that is individuals who hold prominent public positions, to include domestic PEPs, ie, those in the home country of the institution holding a relationship with them. 4MLD also requires companies to hold information on their beneficial owners and includes tax crimes as a predicate offence for money laundering.

The **European Commission (EC)** produced proposals to amend some of the provisions of 4MLD in 2016. In response to terrorist attacks in Belgium and France, it proposed new requirements relating to virtual currencies and pre-paid cards being potentially misused by terrorists. In addition, and in response partly to the 'Panama Papers' affair, when leaked documents highlighted the use of anonymous companies, the EC proposed more measures relating to the transparency of companies and trusts, including pubic registries of beneficial ownership, and central registries of bank accounts. At the time of publishing, these amendments had not been finalised.

The 5th and 6th Money Laundering Directives (5MLD and 6MLD) build further on 4MLD as follows:

- **5MLD** – builds on 4MLD by adding a legal definition of virtual currencies, and making virtual currency exchanges obliged entities. The Directive also imposes reporting requirements on FIUs. In addition, 5MLD further reduces the limit on prepaid cards to €150 without identity checks, and to €50 for remote or online transactions. Prepaid cards issued outside the EU cannot be used in the EU unless they are issued in a jurisdiction with similar AML/CFT regulation. With the introduction of 5MLD, high value goods traders such as art, oil, arms and precious metal, traders must now undertake 'know your customer' (KYC) procedures for any transaction in excess of €10,000. Within 5MLD, ultimate beneficial ownership lists must be made public within a period of 18 months, trusts must observe the beneficial ownership rules in the same way and ultimate beneficial ownership lists must be inter-connected at an EU level. Any customers from high-risk third countries are subject to enhanced CDD. All member states as well as international organisations must compile and publish a functional list of politically exposed public functions. A combined list will be published at the EU level and updated periodically.
- **6MLD** – provides a more harmonised definition of money laundering offences with the 22 predicate offences now extended to include cybercrime and environmental crime, reflecting the changing nature of the threat. Aiding and abetting money laundering has been added as an offence, and criminal liability has been extended to legal persons. The maximum imprisonment in each EU member state has to be at least four years (was previously one year), and additional sanctions including a full shut-down of the business can be applied. 6MLD is scheduled to be implemented in December 2020, with regulated entities having until June 2021 to comply.

The Fund Transfer Regulation (2105/847/EC), known as FTR, accompanies 4MLD and includes rules on information relating to payers and payees that is required to accompany instructions to transfer funds. It applies to transfers in any currency where one of the payment service providers (the companies handling the transfer) is established in an EU member state.

These new pieces of European legislation have to be implemented in the UK by changes to domestic legislation. In March 2017, the government published draft regulations, *The Money Laundering, Terrorist Financing and Transfer of Funds (Information on the Payer) Regulations 2017*, for consultation. These new Money Laundering Regulations (MLR) came into force on 26 June 2017 covering the provisions of both 4MLD and FTR.

The AML/CFT regime in the UK imposes a number of obligations on firms and their senior management to:

- apply CDD measures (to identify/verify customers and to understand the nature and purpose of the proposed relationship)
- maintain appropriate systems and controls for AML/CTF purposes
- monitor customer transactions and activities
- report suspicious activity, both internally and, if appropriate, externally
- keep appropriate records and train staff
- comply with the UK financial sanctions regime.

3. The Financial Action Task Force (FATF)

3.1 International Instruments and Conventions

3.1.1 The Financial Action Task Force's (FATF's) Risk-Based Approach (RBA)

Learning Objective

2.3.1 Know the FATF's risk-based approach to AML and combating the financing of terrorism (CFT)

A risk-based approach (RBA) means that countries, competent authorities and financial institutions identify, assess, and understand the money laundering and terrorist financing risk to which they are exposed and in accordance with the level of risk take the appropriate mitigating measures. This flexibility allows for an efficient use of resources. Financial institutions, countries and competent authorities can decide on the most effective way to mitigate the money laundering/terrorist financing risks they have identified. It enables them to focus their resources and take enhanced measures in situations where the risks are higher and apply simplified measures where the risks are lower.

The FATF Recommendations create a regime for application of an RBA by governments and regulators and provide basic guidelines to the industry for adopting it. The approach is central to the effective implementation of the Recommendations and the global fight against financial crime.

Recommendation 1 of the FATF creates the basic obligation that:

> 'Countries should identify, assess, and understand the money laundering and terrorist financing risks for the country, and should take action, including designating an authority or mechanism to coordinate actions to assess risks, and apply resources, aimed at ensuring the risks are mitigated effectively. Based on that assessment, countries should apply a risk-based approach (RBA) to ensure that measures to prevent or mitigate money laundering and terrorist financing are commensurate with the risks identified. This approach should be an essential foundation to efficient allocation of resources across the anti-money laundering and countering the financing of terrorism (AML/CFT) regime and the implementation of risk based measures throughout the FATF Recommendations. Where countries identify higher risks, they should ensure that their AML/CFT regime adequately addresses such risks. Where countries identify lower risks, they may decide to allow simplified measures for some of the FATF Recommendations under certain conditions'.

Countries are also mandated to require their financial institutions and DNFBPs to identify, assess and take effective action to mitigate their money laundering and terrorist financing risks.

The general principle of an RBA is that, where there are higher risks, countries should require financial institutions and DNFBPs to take enhanced measures to manage and mitigate those risks and correspondingly, where the risks are lower, simplified measures may be permitted. Simplified measures should not be permitted whenever there is a suspicion of money laundering or terrorist financing.

Specific recommendations set out more precisely how this general principle applies to particular requirements.

Countries may also, in strictly limited circumstances and where there is a proven low risk of money laundering and terrorist financing, decide not to apply certain recommendations to particular types of financial institution or activity, or DNFBP.

By adopting an RBA, competent authorities, financial institutions and DNFBPs should be able to ensure that measures to prevent or mitigate money laundering and terrorist financing are commensurate with the risks identified, and enable them to make decisions on how to allocate their own resources in the most effective way.

The interpretive notes (INR 1) to the FATF Recommendation 1 (*Assessing Risks and Applying a Risk-Based Approach*) explain the obligations arising out of the Recommendation. In determining how the risk-based approach should be implemented in a sector, the FATF recommends that countries should consider the capacity and AML/CFT experience of the relevant sector. Countries should understand that the discretion afforded, and responsibility imposed on, financial institutions and DNFBPs by the RBA is more appropriate in sectors with greater AML/CFT capacity and experience.

3.1.2 Obligations for Financial Institutions (FIs) and Designated Non-Financial Bodies and Professions (DNFBPs)

Assessing Risk

Financial institutions (FIs) and DNFBPs are required to take appropriate steps to identify and assess their money laundering and terrorist financing risks (for customers, countries or geographic areas, products, services, transactions and delivery channels). They should document those assessments to be able to demonstrate their basis, keep them up to date and have appropriate mechanisms to provide risk assessment information to competent authorities or an appropriate **self-regulatory body (SRB)**. The nature and extent of any assessment of money laundering and terrorist financing risks should be appropriate to the nature and size of the business. FIs and DNFBPs should always understand their money laundering and terrorist financing risks, but competent authorities or SRBs may determine that individual documented risk assessments are not required, if the specific risks inherent to the sector are clearly identified and understood.

Risk Management and Mitigation

FIs and DNFBPs are required to have policies, controls and procedures that enable them to effectively manage and mitigate the risks that have been identified (either by the country, or by the FI or DNFBP). They must also monitor the implementation of those controls and to enhance them, if necessary.

The policies, controls and procedures should be approved by, and have the full commitment of, senior management. Measures taken to manage and mitigate the risks (whether higher or lower) should be consistent with national requirements and in conformity with the guidance from competent authorities and SRBs.

Where higher risks are identified, FIs and DNFBPs are required to take enhanced measures to manage and mitigate them.

Where lower risks are identified, countries may allow FIs and DNFBPs to take simplified measures to manage and mitigate them.

When assessing risk, FIs and DNFBPs must consider all the relevant risk factors before determining what is the level of overall risk and the appropriate level of mitigation to be applied. FIs and DNFBPs may differentiate the extent of measures, depending on the type and level of risk for the various risk factors (eg, in a particular situation, they could apply normal CDD for customer acceptance measures, but enhanced CDD for ongoing monitoring, or vice versa).

The mutual evaluations of countries by the FATF identify shortcomings or gaps existing in their AML/CFT regimes. These national-level vulnerabilities identified in the mutual evaluation reports may be used by an FI to develop a country- or sector-specific risk profiling of a jurisdiction when dealing with the entities working in the financial system of that country.

3.2 The Categories of FATF Recommendations

Learning Objective

2.3.2 Know the broad categories of what the Recommendations cover

The 40 Recommendations are broken down into categories, as follows:

a. **AML/CFT Policies and Coordination (1–2)**
    These two Recommendations set out the obligation to apply the RBA, as described above, and to have in place coordination mechanisms at the national level on AML/CFT.

b. **Money Laundering and Confiscation (3–4)**
    These Recommendations oblige countries to criminalise money laundering in accordance with the Vienna and Palermo Conventions and to have mechanisms in place to allow the confiscation of criminal proceeds, including what are called provisional measures to assist in this, such as investigative tools, and freezing/seizure powers.

c. **Terrorist Financing and Financing of Proliferation (5–8)**
    Terrorist financing must be criminalised and mechanisms established to put in place targeted sanctions regimes against terrorist financing and proliferation financing (PF) in accordance with United Nations Security Council Resolutions (UNSCR). Recommendation 8 deals specifically with non-profit organisations (NPOs), such as charities, to ensure that they cannot be abused for terrorist financing purposes.

d. **Preventive Measures (9–23)**
    This large group of Recommendations deals with the obligations to be placed on FIs, such as customer due diligence and record-keeping; additional measures to be taken in respect of specific high-risk customers and activities, such as PEPs or correspondent banking; how firms can operate with others within their own group and the responsibilities of foreign branches and subsidiaries; measures in respect of high-risk countries; reporting suspicious transactions to the authorities, namely the FIU; and requirements relating to tipping off and confidentiality.

    Recommendations 22 and 23 extend CDD obligations and other measures to DNFBPs.

e. **Transparency and Beneficial Ownership of Legal Persons and Arrangements (24–25)**
   These measures are designed to increase the transparency of those who own companies (legal persons) or trusts (legal arrangements), either directly or indirectly ('beneficial ownership'). FIs must understand the true ownership of their customers.

f. **Powers and Responsibilities of Competent Authorities and Other Institutional Measures (26–35)**
   Having placed extensive obligations on the private sector, this set of Recommendations outlines the requirements for the public authorities, including the AML/CFT supervisors of both FIs and DNFBPs; the FIU, law enforcement and other investigative authorities. It also requires them to be given the powers they need to carry out their functions and outlines the types of punishments that can be imposed on firms in breach of their obligations.

   Recommendations 33 and 34 deal with the need to collect statistics on money laundering/terrorist financing and to provide feedback to FIs and DNFBPs, so that they can improve their prevention and detection.

g. **International Cooperation (36–40)**
   Money laundering is a global phenomenon and often involves money moving across borders. These final five Recommendations outline how jurisdictions should cooperate with other countries including sharing information, freezing and confiscation, and extradition powers.

3.3 Categorisation of Jurisdictions by the FATF

Learning Objective

2.3.3   Know the categorisation of jurisdictions which the FATF considers to have strategic deficiencies

2.3.4   Understand the role, activities and coverage of the FATF style regional bodies (FSRB)

Through its mutual evaluation process, the FATF assesses how well the countries have achieved the objective of fighting money laundering and terrorist financing.

Since 2013, the country evaluation methodology comprises two interlinked components:

- technical compliance assessment, and
- effectiveness assessment.

The technical compliance assessment addresses the specific requirements of each of the FATF Recommendations, principally as they relate to the relevant legal and institutional framework of the country, and the powers and procedures of competent authorities.

These represent the fundamental building blocks of an AML/CFT system. They are rated as follows:

Technical Compliance Ratings		
Rating	Symbol used in assessment	Understanding/meaning
Compliant	C	There are no shortcomings.
Largely compliant	LC	There are only minor shortcomings.
Partially compliant	PC	There are moderate shortcomings.
Non-compliant	NC	There are major shortcomings.
Not applicable	NA	A requirement does not apply, due to the structural, legal or institutional features of a country.

The effectiveness assessment evaluates the extent to which the country achieves a defined set of outcomes that are central to a robust AML/CFT system and analyses the extent to which a country's legal and institutional framework is producing the expected results. How effectively each of the outcomes in the assessment methodology is achieved by a country is set out in the evaluation report and the country is assigned the following ratings against each FATF Recommendation:

Effectiveness Ratings	
Rating	Understanding/meaning
High level of effectiveness	The immediate outcome is achieved to a very large extent. Minor improvements needed.
Substantial level of effectiveness	The immediate outcome is achieved to a large extent. Moderate improvements needed.
Moderate level of effectiveness	The immediate outcome is achieved to some extent. Major improvements needed.
Low level of effectiveness	The immediate outcome is not achieved or achieved to a negligible extent. Fundamental improvements needed.

Based on the results of these evaluations, countries may be urged to adopt action plans and report their progress to the FATF on a regular basis. However, some countries are deemed to be too deficient or may not be prepared to engage with the FATF. These countries are referred to the FATF's International

Cooperation Review Group (ICRG), a process which involves further dialogue with the jurisdiction and review of progress against an agreed plan.

Because these countries pose a high risk, they are publicly identified at each FATF plenary, which are held three times each year. At these meetings, the FATF agrees and publishes two documents.

The first document, the FATF's *Public Statement*, identifies jurisdictions that have strategic AML/CFT deficiencies and:

1. to which countermeasures apply
2. that have not made sufficient progress in addressing the deficiencies or have not committed to an action plan developed with the FATF to address the deficiencies.

In addition, the FATF identifies jurisdictions with strategic AML/CFT deficiencies that have provided a high-level political commitment to address the deficiencies through implementation of an action plan developed with the FATF. The situation differs in each jurisdiction and therefore each of these jurisdictions presents different degrees of money laundering/terrorist financing risks. Updates on jurisdictions under increased monitoring are published three times a year.

The FATF expects its members to consider the strategic deficiencies identified in the second public document and these countries are often included in financial institutions' assessments of high-risk jurisdictions.

3.3.1 FATF-Style Regional Bodies (FSRBs)

The FATF recognised that to combat global issues such as money laundering and terrorist financing, it needed to expand its reach beyond its members. It has achieved this through the establishment of a network of FATF-Style Regional Bodies (FSRBs), with which it works to achieve global implementation of sound AML/CFT measures based on the 40 Recommendations. These FSRBs are voluntary and cooperative organisations of countries. Membership of these bodies is open to any country or jurisdiction within the given geographic region that is willing to abide by the rules and objectives of the organisation. Some members of FATF are also members of the FSRBs. Combined, the FATF and the FSRBs cover almost 200 jurisdictions.

As part of the process, the FSRBs undertake mutual evaluation of the AML/CFT regimes of other member countries. These bodies also develop regional and individual country technical assistance programmes in coordination with international donors and executing agencies to facilitate implementation of the FATF Recommendations. Like the FATF, the FSRBs meet several times each year and publish reports and guidance on their websites.

There are currently nine regional bodies. The geographic focus of each one can be gleaned from their titles. MONEYVAL includes members of the EU and Council of Europe that are not main FATF members.

- Asia/Pacific Group on Money Laundering (APGML)
- Caribbean Financial Action Task Force (CFATF)
- Eastern and Southern Africa Anti-Money Laundering Group (ESAAMLG)
- Eurasian Group on Combating Money Laundering and Financing of Terrorism (EAG)
- Financial Action Task Force of Latin America (GAFILAT)

- Inter-Governmental Action Group against Money Laundering in West Africa (GIABA)
- Middle East & North Africa Financial Action Task Force (MENAFATF)
- Committee of Experts on the Evaluation of Anti-money Laundering Measures and the Financing of Terrorism of the Council of Europe (MONEYVAL)
- Task Force on Money Laundering in Central Africa (GABAC).

The nine FSRBs have an essential role in promoting the effective implementation of the FATF Recommendations by their membership and in providing expertise and input in FATF policymaking. Over 180 jurisdictions around the world have declared their commitment to the FATF Recommendations through the global network of FSRBs including FATF memberships.

4. The Role of Other International Bodies

Learning Objective

2.4.1 Know the role other bodies play in combating money laundering and establishing best practice: the Basel Committee on Banking Supervision (BCBS); the International Organization of Securities Commissions (IOSCO); the International Association of Insurance Supervisors (IAIS); the Egmont Group of Financial Intelligence Units; the Wolfsberg Group; regulatory and supervisory bodies; professional bodies

2.4.2 Understand the importance of guidance issued by European Supervisory Authorities (ESAs)

2.4.3 Know the categorisations of jurisdictions which the EU considers to have strategic deficiencies

4.1 The Basel Committee on Banking Supervision (BCBS)

The Basel Committee was established in 1974 as the Committee on Banking Regulations and Supervisory Practices by the governors of the central banks of the G10 countries in the aftermath of serious disturbances in international currency and banking markets. It provides a forum for regular cooperation between its member countries on banking supervisory matters.

It seeks to improve supervisory understanding and the quality of banking supervision worldwide to do this in three principal ways by:

- exchanging information on national supervisory arrangements
- improving the effectiveness of techniques for supervising international banking business, and
- setting minimum supervisory standards in areas where they are considered desirable.

The BCBS formulates broad supervisory standards and guidelines and recommends 'statements of best practices' on a wide range of bank supervisory issues. These standards and guidelines are adopted by the BCBS with the expectation that the appropriate authorities within each country will take all necessary steps to implement them through detailed measures, statutory, regulatory or otherwise, that best suit that country's national system.

Three of the BCBS's supervisory standards and guidelines concern money laundering issues and are:

1. **Statement of Principles on Money Laundering**
   In 1998, the Basel Committee issued its *Statement on Prevention of Criminal Use of the Banking System for the Purpose of Money Laundering* (commonly known as the 'Statement on Prevention'). This outlines basic policies and procedures that bank management should ensure are in place to assist in suppressing money laundering through the banking system, both domestically and internationally. The BCBS notes that the most important safeguard against money laundering is:

   'the integrity of bank's managements and their vigilant determination to prevent their institutions from becoming associated with criminals or being used as a channel for money laundering'.

   There are essentially four principles contained in the Statement on Prevention:

   - **proper customer identification** – banks are advised to make reasonable efforts to determine and verify the true identity of all customers and as part of a bank's policies specific procedures for customer identification should be adopted
   - **high ethical standards and compliance with laws** – banks should ensure that business is conducted in conformity with high ethical standards and that banks should adhere to laws and regulations pertaining to financial transactions
   - **cooperation with law enforcement authorities** – banks should cooperate fully with national law enforcement authorities to the extent permitted by local laws or regulations relating to customer confidentiality
   - **policies and procedures to adhere to the statement** – banks should adopt formal policies consistent with the Statement on Prevention.

   Furthermore, banks should ensure that all staff members are aware of its policies and given proper training in matters covered by the bank's policies. Finally, the internal audit function within the institution should establish an effective means of testing for compliance and providing assurance to the board or governing body.

2. **Core Principles for Banking**
   In 1997, the Basel Committee issued its *Core Principles for Effective Banking Supervision* (Core Principles), which provides a comprehensive blueprint for an effective bank supervisory system and covers a wide range of topics. Of the total 25 Core Principles, one, number 15, deals specifically with money laundering and provides:

   'Banking supervisors must determine that banks have adequate policies, practices and procedures in place, including strict 'know your customer' rules, that promote high ethical and professional standards in the financial sector and prevent the bank from being used; intentionally or unintentionally, by criminal elements'.

   These **know your customer (KYC)** policies and procedures are a crucial component of an effective AML/CFT institutional framework for any institution.

   In addition to the 'Core Principles', the BCBS issued a *Core Principles Methodology* in 1999, which contains 11 specific criteria and five additional criteria to help assess the adequacy of KYC policies and procedures. These additional criteria include specific reference to compliance with the FATF's 'The Forty Recommendations' which in practical terms means that FATF recommendations are part of the principles.

3. **Management of Risks related to Money Laundering and Financing of Terrorism**

   The BCBS has consolidated several previous pieces of guidance into one document, *Sound management of risks related to money laundering and terrorist financing*. These guidelines describe how banks should include risks related to money laundering and financing of terrorism within their overall risk management framework and are consistent with the revised FATF standards. They include guidance on customer due diligence, account monitoring and reporting of suspicions.

4.2 International Organization of Securities Commissions (IOSCO)

The International Organization of Securities Commissions (IOSCO) is the international body that brings together the world's securities regulators and is recognised as the global standard setter for the securities sector. IOSCO develops, implements and promotes adherence to internationally recognised standards of best practices for securities markets regulation. These standards have been agreed by the body as best practices for the industry and regulators and have been issued as *Objectives and Principles of Securities Regulation*. These comprise 38 securities regulation principles, that in turn are based upon three common objectives of these securities regulators.

The three objectives are:

1. protecting investors (the term includes customers or other consumers of financial services)
2. ensuring that markets are fair, efficient and transparent, and
3. reducing systemic risk.

The member countries are expected to implement the 38 Principles under their relevant legal frameworks to achieve the three objectives of regulation. The capital market structures and working practices of individual countries are evaluated against these principles. The principles are geared to combat financial crime basically by trying to create transparency, save the market from systemic risks and protect the investors from fraudulent behaviour.

In 1992, IOSCO passed the *Resolution on Money Laundering*. Similar to comparable international organisations, IOSCO does not have law-making authority. Like the BCBS and IAIS, it relies on its members to implement its recommendations within their respective countries. The resolutions that each IOSCO member should consider are:

- The extent to which customer identifying information is gathered and recorded by financial institutions under its supervision, with a view to enhancing the ability of relevant authorities to identify and prosecute money launderers.
- The extent and adequacy of record-keeping requirements, from the perspective of providing tools to reconstruct financial transactions in the securities and future markets.
- Together with their national regulators charged with prosecuting money laundering offences, the appropriate manner in which to address the identification and reporting of suspicious transactions.
- The procedures in place to prevent criminals from obtaining control of securities and futures businesses, with a view to working together with foreign counterparts to share such information as needed.
- The appropriate means to ensure that securities and futures firms maintain monitoring and compliance procedures designed to deter and detect money laundering.

- The use of cash and cash equivalents in securities and futures transactions including the adequacy of documentation and the ability to reconstruct any such transactions.
- The most appropriate means, given their particular national authorities and powers, to share information in order to combat money laundering.

4.3 International Association of Insurance Supervisors (IAIS)

The International Association of Insurance Supervisors (IAIS), established in 1994, is an organisation of insurance supervisors from more than 100 different countries and has more than 60 observer members. The primary objectives of IAIS are to:

- promote cooperation among insurance regulators
- set international standards for insurance supervision
- provide training to members
- coordinate work with regulators in the other financial sectors and international financial institutions.

The IAIS covers virtually all areas of insurance supervision and it specifically deals with money laundering in one of its papers. In October 2004, it issued its guidance paper on AML/CFT.

The guidance paper is a comprehensive discussion of money laundering and combating of financing of terrorism in the context of the insurance industry. Like similar documents issued by other international bodies and industry associations, the *AML/CFT Guidance Notes* issued by the IAIS are also intended to be implemented by individual countries considering the products offered within the country, and the country's own financial system, economy, constitution and legal system and the particular insurance companies involved.

This guidance paper is structured around the core themes of the FATF Recommendations as follows:

- **Sections 2 and 3** constitute a risk-based approach regarding the combating of money laundering and terrorist financing in the insurance sector and mitigations such as:
  - elements of CDD
  - reporting of suspicion
  - measures affecting the organisation and staff of the insurer.
- **Section 4** is addressed to supervisors and deals with their application of the insurance core principles, including the monitoring of compliance by insurers with AML/CFT standards and cooperation by supervisors with other organisations involved in AML/CFT.

The guidance paper also provides a comprehensive non-exhaustive list of behaviour in the sector that can suggest risk of money laundering/terrorist financing.

4.4 The Egmont Group of Financial Intelligence Units (FIUs)

FATF Recommendation 29 requires that countries should establish an FIU that plays a central role in the country's AML/CFT operational network, and provides support to the work of other competent authorities. There are different models of FIU. Some FIUs are located in central banks while some are independent. FATF Recommendation 29 does not prejudge a country's choice for a particular model, and applies equally to all of them.

In 1995, a group of FIUs meeting at the Egmont Arenberg Palace in Brussels recognised the benefits that would accrue with the development of a network of FIUs and decided to establish an informal group for the stimulation of international cooperation and information sharing in the global fight against money laundering and terrorist financing.

The interpretative notes to Recommendation 29 explain the core mandate that an FIU should have and the functions that should be entrusted to an FIU. The notes provide further clarity on the obligations contained in the standard. The recommendation obliges that the FIU should serve as a national centre for the receipt and analysis of:

a. suspicious transaction reports
b. other information relevant to money laundering, associated predicate offences and terrorist financing, and for the dissemination of the results of that analysis.

The Notes provide that the countries should ensure that the FIU has regard to the *Egmont Group Statement of Purpose and its Principles for Information Exchange between Financial Intelligence Units for Money Laundering and Terrorism Financing Cases* and that the FIU must also apply for membership in the Egmont Group.

The Egmont Group provides a forum for FIUs to exchange information, experience and enhance support to their respective governments. The contributions made by the Egmont Group process include:

1. Expansion and systematising international cooperation in the exchange of financial intelligence.
2. Increasing the effectiveness of FIUs by offering training to improve the expertise and capabilities of the FIU personnel.
3. Fostering better and more secure communication among FIUs through the application of technology, presently via the Egmont Secure Web (ESW).
4. Promoting the establishment of FIUs in jurisdictions that are without or have weak national AML/ financing of terrorism programmes. The Egmont Group meets regularly to find ways to cooperate, especially in the areas of information exchange, training and the sharing of expertise.

The UKFIU (the NCA) is an active member of the Egmont Group. The membership of the Egmont Group allows the UKFIU to share and obtain financial intelligence from other members of the Group to support the NCA's own operations and projects. This sharing and access to the information helps in the channelling of this important resource for use by other law enforcement agencies in the UK.

4.5 The Wolfsberg Group

The **Wolfsberg Group** is an association of 13 global banks which aims to develop frameworks and guidance for the management of financial crime risks, particularly with respect to KYC and AML/CTF policies. The group was named after Château Wolfsberg in north-eastern Switzerland where it was formed. The Group neither has a written constitution nor any formalised set of rules or statutes. It has established four sets of principles for private banking that were published in October 2000 and revised in June 2012.

These principles are in general based on the FATF recommendations and are:

1. **Anti-money Laundering Principles for Private Banking** – these represent the group's view of appropriate anti-money laundering guidelines when dealing with high net worth individuals (HNWIs) and the private banking departments of FIs. The principles deal with customer identification, including establishing beneficial ownership for all accounts, and situations involving extra due diligence, such as unusual or suspicious transactions.
2. **Statement on the Suppression of the Financing of Terrorism** – this describes the role that FIs should play in combating terrorist financing, with a view toward enhancing the contribution FIs can make toward this international problem.
3. **Anti-money Laundering Principles for Correspondent Banking** – the Wolfsberg Group has adopted a set of 14 principles to govern the establishment and maintenance of correspondent banking relationships on a global basis. The principles prohibit international banks from doing business with shell banks.
4. **Monitoring Screening and Searching** – this set of principles identifies issues that should be addressed in order for FIs to develop suitable monitoring, screening and searching processes, using a risk-based profile approach.

The Wolfsberg Group also issued a statement against corruption in 2007 that was replaced by the Wolfsberg Anti-Corruption Guidance in 2011. This guidance has been developed in close cooperation with Transparency International and the Basel Institute on Governance. It takes account, in particular, of legal and regulatory developments in recent years, such as the US Foreign Corrupt Practices Act (FCPA) and also the requirements set out in the UK Bribery Act.

Most recently, in January 2017, the Wolfsberg Group in conjunction with the International Chamber of Commerce and Bankers' Association for Finance and Trade (BAFT) (the leading global financial services association for international transaction banking) issued a revised set of principles in relation to money laundering and financial crime risks in the area of trade finance.

The Wolfsberg Group has also published reports on emerging payments methods, such as its Guidance on *Prepaid & Stored Value Cards*, which considers the money laundering risks and mitigants of physical *Prepaid and Stored Value Card Issuing* and *Merchant Acquiring Activities*.

In conjunction with Bankers Almanac, the Wolfsberg Group developed a due diligence repository, to assist FIs in carrying out due diligence on their counterparties, including a standard questionnaire, which provides an overview of an FI's anti-money laundering policies and practices.

4.6   Regulatory and Supervisory Bodies

The terms regulation and supervision are often used interchangeably but intrinsically have different meanings.

- **Regulation** is primarily to do with rule making by a country's authorities. For example, the EU has transposed the FATF Recommendations into EU law via their successive Money Laundering Directives. These are then transposed into the regulations of the individual member states. In other jurisdictions, the FATF recommendations are directly transposed into laws and regulations.

- **Supervision** is primarily a function of monitoring, and FIs follow the rules correctly and uniformly, so that they adequately manage their risks and adhere to certain minimum standards. Supervisory bodies also examine the systems of banks and FIs as a whole to detect prudential risks affecting the entire financial system. Supervisors, can also issue binding decisions and impose penalties on those institutions that do not adhere to the rules.

FATF Recommendation 26 requires FIs to be subject to adequate regulation and supervision in respect of AML/CFT matters. Supervisors must ensure that criminals and their associates are not involved in the ownership or management of such institutions. Recommendation 27 states:

'Supervisors should have adequate powers to supervise or monitor, and ensure compliance by, financial institutions with requirements to combat money laundering and terrorist financing, including the authority to conduct inspections. They should be authorised to compel production of any information from financial institutions that is relevant to monitoring such compliance, and to impose sanctions, in line with Recommendation 35, for failure to comply with such requirements. Supervisors should have powers to impose a range of disciplinary and financial sanctions, including the power to withdraw, restrict or suspend the financial institution's license, where applicable'.

Recommendation 28 deals with the regulation and supervision of DNFBPs. Casinos are expected to have a similar regime to FIs, but other sectors may be supervised in one of two ways, on a risk-sensitive basis by:

- a supervisor, or
- an appropriate self-regulatory body, providing it can ensure that its members comply with their obligations to combat money laundering and terrorist financing.

In the UK, the MLRs provide for several bodies to be supervisory authorities for different parts of the regulated sector and these are listed in Schedule 3 to the Regulations.

Presently the Treasury has 27 appointed AML/CTF supervisors which oversee eight broad sectors of the economy and a diverse range of firms comprising:

- credit institutions
- FIs
- auditors
- insolvency practitioners
- external accountants and tax advisers
- independent legal professionals
- trust or company service providers
- estate agents
- high value goods and services dealers
- casinos.

The appointed supervisors include, as well as the FCA:

- Gambling Commission (GC)
- HM Revenue & Customs (HMRC).

Professional bodies such as:

- Association of Chartered Certified Accountants (ACCA)
- Chartered Institute of Management Accountants (CIMA)
- Chartered Institute of Taxation (CIOT)
- Institute of Chartered Accountants in England and Wales (ICAEW)
- Law Society/Solicitors Regulatory Authority (SRA).

In March 2017, the government announced its intention to create a new Office for Professional Body Anti-Money Laundering Supervision (OPBAS), hosted within the FCA. The Office will help ensure the professional body supervisors fulfil their obligations under the MLRs and have overarching responsibility to strengthen the UK's supervisory regime by improving coordination between AML supervisors and with law enforcement.

Firms must register with the supervisor that regulates their industry sector. It is illegal if the firm carries on a business activity covered by the Regulations, but does not register with the supervisory authority.

4.7 Professional Bodies

The AML/CFT supervisors mentioned above include several professional SRBs such as the Law Society and the accountancy bodies. Such organisations fall within the FATF definition of SRBs, and have the advantage of understanding the work of their professional members. However, the independence of supervision by professional bodies, even if they have the appropriate powers, has been called into question. See for example the comment made in Sir David Clementi's 2004 report on the supervision of legal services:

> *'It is difficult to understand how one body can effectively both regulate a profession and also represent and lobby for its interests without prejudice to either its regulatory or representative functions'.*

This has led to the separation of representative and supervisory functions for lawyers in England and Wales, but there remains a perception of possible conflicts of interest in other bodies. Using professional bodies also results in a larger number of AML/CFT supervisors, which poses challenges of consistency and information sharing. The UK Treasury is examining possible changes to the UK's AML/CFT supervisory structure.

4.8 European Supervisory Authorities (ESAs)

The joint committee of the three European Supervisory Authorities (ESAs) has published guidelines on money laundering/financing terrorism (ML/FT). The guidelines promote a common understanding of the risk-based approach to AML/CFT, promoting a consistent and effective approach. The guidelines focus on factors to consider when assessing the ML/FT risks associated with a transaction and set out customer due diligence measures. The guidance is used by competent authorities, such as the FCA and PRA, when assessing ML/FT-related risk assessment and management systems and controls.

The guidelines set clear, regulatory expectations of the way credit and financial institutions should discharge important AML/CFT obligations in line with international best practice.

4.9 Jurisdictions with Strategic Deficiencies – EU Categorisations

The EU has a methodology in place to identify high-risk third countries. The methodology takes into account the following components:

- Criminalisation of money laundering and terrorist financing.
- CDD measures, record-keeping and reporting requirements for FIs and designated non-financial businesses and professions.
- Powers and procedures of the competent authority in relation to AML and terrorist financing.
- Existence of dissuasive, proportionate and effective sanctions.
- Practise in cooperation and exchange of information.
- Accuracy and timeliness of provision of beneficial ownership information.
- Implementation of targeted financial sanctions.

The methodology ensures a robust, objective and transparent process is applied in the identification of jurisdictions that have strategic deficiencies in their national AML/CFT regimes and that pose significant threats to the financial system of the EU.

End of Chapter Questions

Think of an answer for each question and refer to the appropriate section for confirmation.

1. What is the purpose of money laundering?
   Answer reference: Section 1.1

2. What are the three stages of the traditional money laundering process?
   Answer reference: Section 1.2.1

3. What is POCA 2002?
   Answer reference: Section 1.3

4. What is an authorised disclosure?
   Answer reference: Section 1.3.1

5. What is tipping off in the context of money laundering?
   Answer reference: Section 1.3.2

6. What activities do both the IMF and World Bank carry out in relation to money laundering?
   Answer reference: Sections 2.1.1 and 2.1.2

7. Within the EU's 6MLD, predicate offences are now included to which crimes?
   Answer reference: Section 2.2.2

8. What is the risk-based approach to AML/CFT?
   Answer reference: Section 3.1.1

9. What are the seven categories of FATF Recommendations?
   Answer reference: Section 3.2

10. What is the Egmont Group?
    Answer reference: Section 4.4

11. What do the ESA AML/CFT guidelines promote?
    Answer reference: Section 4.8

Chapter Three
Terrorist Financing

1. Background	61
2. Measures to Combat the Financing of Terrorism (CFT)	62
3. Standards for Combating the Financing of Terrorism (CFT)	64

This syllabus area will provide approximately 4 of the 50 examination questions

1. Background

Learning Objective

3.1.1 Understand the similarities and differences between: money laundering and financing terrorism; proliferation finance and terrorist financing

1.1 The Similarities and Differences between Money Laundering and Terrorist Financing

Terrorist financing involves the solicitation, collection or provision of funds with the intention that they may be used to support terrorist acts of individuals, groups or organisations. Funds may stem from both legal (eg, donations from legitimately earned income) and illicit sources (such as the proceeds of crimes). The primary goal of individuals or entities involved in terrorist financing is, therefore, not necessarily to conceal the sources of the money but to conceal both the financing and the nature of the financed activity.

More precisely, according to the International Convention for the Suppression of the Financing of Terrorism, a person commits the crime of financing terrorism:

> 'if that person by any means, directly or indirectly, unlawfully and wilfully, provides or collects funds with the intention that they should be used or in the knowledge that they are to be used, in full or in part, in order to carry out'

an offence within the scope of the Convention.

Money laundering and terrorist financing often display similar features, mostly having to do with concealment. Those who finance terrorism transfer legal or illicit funds in ways that conceal their source and more importantly their ultimate use, which is the support of terrorism.

Many of the controls firms have in place in relation to combating the financing of terrorism will overlap with their anti-money laundering measures; for example, risk assessment, customer due diligence checks, transaction monitoring, reporting of suspicions and liaison with the authorities. A firm needs to develop risk-based systems that include identification of sources of information on terrorist financing risks, such as media reports, alerts from the relevant authorities in their jurisdiction, Financial Action Task Force (FATF) typologies, court judgements and similar other sources.

However, there are two major differences between terrorist and criminal property:

- often only small amounts are required to commit individual terrorist acts, thus increasing the difficulty of tracking terrorist property
- terrorists can be funded from legitimately obtained income, including charitable donations, and it is extremely difficult to identify the stage at which legitimate funds become terrorist property.

Terrorist organisations can also require quite significant funding to resource their infrastructure. They may control property and funds from a variety of sources and employ modern techniques to manage these funds and to move them between jurisdictions, like other criminals.

1.2 Proliferation Financing (PF) and Terrorist Financing (TF)

The proliferation of weapons of mass destruction (WMDs) is a significant security concern, and in 2008, this topic was included in the FATF's mandate. To combat this threat, the FATF has adopted a new recommendation (Recommendation 7) that is aimed at ensuring consistent and effective implementation of targeted financial sanctions when these are called for by the UN Security Council (UNSC).

Proliferation is the manufacture, acquisition, possession, development, export, transshipment, brokering, transport, transfer, stockpiling or use of nuclear, chemical or biological weapons and their means of delivery and related materials (including both technologies and dual-use goods used for non-legitimate purposes), in contravention of national laws or, where applicable, international obligations.

Proliferation financing (PF) is the act of providing funds or financial services which are used, in whole or in part, to support proliferation. UNSC Resolution 1803 adopted in March 2008 in light of international concerns surrounding the nuclear development programme in Iran placed obligations on financial institutions to exercise vigilance on transactions with Iranian entities. The implementing European Regulation (423/2007, amended by 1110/2008) requires financial institutions to report suspicions of proliferation financing to their FIU or other designated competent authority, in much the same way as money laundering or terrorist financing suspicions are reported.

UK guidance for firms on how to proceed with reporting in a situation of proliferation financing is available in the UK Financial Intelligence Unit (UKFIU) publication *National Crime Agency (NCA) Guidelines for Counter Proliferation Financing Reporting*.

2. Measures to Combat the Financing of Terrorism (CFT)

Learning Objective

3.2.1 Know the main provisions of the United Nations International Convention for the Suppression of the Financing of Terrorism

3.2.2 Know the work of the United Nations Security Council in relation to the financing of terrorism

2.1 United Nations International Convention for the Suppression of the Financing of Terrorism

The Terrorist Financing Convention (formally, the International Convention for the Suppression of the Financing of Terrorism) is a 1999 United Nations (UN) treaty designed to criminalise terrorist financing acts. The Convention covers the prosecution of persons accused of involvement in the financing of terrorist activities. Countries who are party to the convention must undertake to prosecute terrorist financiers or extradite them to a country that can prosecute them.

The Convention prohibits any person(s) from directly or indirectly, unlawfully, and wilfully providing or collecting funds with the intention that they should be used, or in the knowledge that they are to be used, to carry out an act of terrorism (defined as an offence under one of the nine treaties listed in Annex 1 to the Convention).

The Convention obligates each state party to establish these offences as criminal offences under its domestic law, thus making them punishable by appropriate penalties.

The Convention also requires each party to take appropriate measures, for the detection and **freezing**, seizure or forfeiture of any funds used or allocated for the purposes of committing the offences. Countries must also cooperate in preventative measures and countermeasures, and exchange information and evidence needed in related criminal proceedings.

2.2 The Work of the United Nations Security Council (UNSC)

The UNSC has primary responsibility for the maintenance of international peace and security. It has 15 members and all UN member countries are obliged to comply with Council decisions. The Council has a variety of options open to it to respond to threats to peace and security, one of them being enforcement measures, including economic sanctions, arms embargoes, financial penalties and restrictions, and travel bans. It has applied these measures to countering terrorism, including terrorist financing.

The internationally-binding combating the financing of terrorism (CFT) sanctions regime was first established by United Nations Security Council Resolution (UNSCR) 1267 (1999) of 15 October 1999. The regime has been modified and strengthened by subsequent resolutions. Sanctions now apply to designated individuals and entities associated with Al-Qaida and other terrorist organisations, wherever located.

The names of the targeted individuals and entities are placed on the sanctions list. The consolidated list of sanctions also contains the narrative summaries of reasons for listing of the individuals, groups, undertakings and entities.

The resolutions have all been adopted under Chapter VII of the UN Convention and are binding on all states, obliging them to take the measures stipulated in the resolutions with respect to any named individual or entity associated with terrorist activities.

Resolution 1267 (1999) and Successor Resolutions, including 2253 (2015)

UNSCR 1267 was adopted on 15 October 1999. The Council designated Osama bin Laden and associates as terrorists and established a sanctions regime to cover individuals and entities associated with Al-Qaida, Osama bin Laden and the Taliban wherever these might be located.

The sanctions regime in terms of the resolution has since been reaffirmed and modified by several further UNSCRs. UNSCR 1988 (2011) split the regime into two groups – the Al-Qaida regime and the Taliban (Afghanistan regime). The sanctions have been applied to individuals and organisations in all parts of the world and now include the Islamic State of Iraq and the Levant (ISIL) (Da'esh) since Resolution 2253 (2015) was adopted in December 2015.

According to the UN:

'The criteria for adding a name to the ISIL (Da'esh) & Al-Qaida Sanctions List is set out in paragraphs 3 to 5 of resolution 2253 (2015). States are required to impose the measures upon Al-Qaida or ISIL (Da'esh) and other individuals, groups, undertakings and entities associated with them.

Acts or activities indicating that an individual, group, undertaking or entity is associated with ISIL (Da'esh) and Al-Qaida include:

- *participating in the financing, planning, facilitating, preparing, or perpetrating of acts or activities by, in conjunction with, under the name of, on behalf of, or in support of*
- *supplying, selling or transferring arms and related material to*
- *recruiting for; or otherwise supporting acts or activities of, ISIL (Da'esh), Al-Qaida or any cell, affiliate, splinter group or derivative thereof'.*

The regime developed under the resolution comprises a UNSC Committee, which has developed a consolidated list of people and entities that it has determined as being associated with the organisations listed on the *ISIL (Da'esh) and Al-Qaida Sanctions List*. The committee also monitors and oversees the laws which must be passed within each member nation to implement the sanctions, namely to:

- freeze assets
- prevent entry into/transit through their territories
- prevent the direct or indirect supply, sale and transfer of arms and military equipment.

The Committee is supported by a Monitoring Team, consisting of eight experts based in New York. As well as assisting the Committee to monitor implementation, the Monitoring Team is responsible for studying the changing nature of the threat from Al-Qaida, ISIL (Da'esh) and the Taliban, and for assisting the Committee in considering listing proposals and reviewing names on the sanctions lists.

3. Standards for Combating the Financing of Terrorism (CFT)

3.1 Financial Action Task Force (FATF) Recommendations

Learning Objective

3.3.1 Know the FATF Recommendations relative to terrorist financing

In the aftermath of the September 2001 terrorist attacks in the US, the FATF expanded its mandate beyond anti-money laundering (AML) to include CFT. In October 2001, a set of eight Special Recommendations (SRs) on terrorist financing was adopted to complement the existing 40 Recommendations aimed at countering the laundering of the proceeds of crime. A ninth SR was added in October 2004.

Since 2001, significant work has been undertaken by the FATF to examine how financial measures applied by states, the private sector and the non-profit/charitable sectors, play a role to:

- deter crime and terrorism in the first place – by increasing the risk and lowering the reward faced by perpetrators
- detect the criminal or terrorist abuse of the financial system, and
- disrupt criminal and terrorist activity – to save lives and hold the guilty to account.

Firms are now required to look at money laundering and terrorist financing as part of an overall strategy to tackle financial crime. In the 2012 revision of the FATF standards, it was decided to absorb the SRs into the main body of the 40 Recommendations.

Most of the FATF's 40 Recommendations (2012) are equally applicable to CFT – for example, the preventative measures (customer due diligence (CDD), record-keeping, monitoring and reporting) imposed on financial institutions and designated non-financial businesses and profession bodies (DFNBPs). However, some of the revised Recommendations are specific to combating terrorist financing, which are set out in Section C of the FATF Recommendations. These are:

- Recommendation 5 (the criminalisation of terrorist financing)
- Recommendation 6 (targeted financial sanctions related to terrorism and terrorist financing), and
- Recommendation 8 (measures to prevent the misuse of non-profit organisations).

Detecting terrorist involvement in otherwise legitimate financial activity requires financial institutions to implement the FATF standards through strong application of the know your customer (KYC) and CDD policies and procedures. These are also fundamental to the reporting of suspicious transactions which may indicate criminal activity supporting terrorism.

To assist financial institutions in combating terrorist financing countries are expected to adopt measures which include implementing targeted financial sanctions programmes, protecting vulnerable sectors including the charitable sector and money-service businesses, and encouraging effective reporting of suspicious activity.

3.2 EU Combating the Financing of Terrorism Initiatives

Learning Objective

3.3.2 Know EU CFT initiatives: money laundering directives; regulations of fund transfers; the Payment Services Regulation

3.2.1 Money Laundering Directives

The 4th Money Laundering Directive (4MLD) implemented the FATF Recommendations in European Union (EU) law and, therefore, reflected the issues mentioned above. Many of the measures in the Directive refer to the risks from money laundering and terrorist financing, following the approach of the FATF. There is no terrorist financing section of the Directive.

However, following terrorist outrages in Belgium and France in recent years, in February 2016, the EU adopted an Action Plan to strengthen the fight against terrorist financing. The Action Plan focuses on two main strands of action:

- tracing terrorists through financial movements and preventing them from moving funds or other assets
- disrupting the sources of revenue used by terrorist organisations, by targeting their capacity to raise funds.

The European Commission (EC) has amended 4MLD to reflect the changed environment, thus, including measures to:

- enhance the powers of EU financial intelligence units (FIUs) and facilitating their cooperation
- strengthen the rules surrounding cryptocurrencies, including a legal definition and reporting requirements
- address risks linked to anonymous prepaid instruments (eg, prepaid cards)
- expand the requirements for AML/CFT reporting to traders of high value goods
- strengthen the rules surrounding ultimate beneficial ownership
- harmonise stronger checks on a list of high-risk third countries.

These amendments came into force on 10 January 2020 as 5MLD.

In addition to 5MLD, EU directive 2017/541 on combating terrorism contains a requirement (Article 11) on member states to criminalise the provision of funds that are used to commit terrorist offences and offences related to terrorist groups or terrorist activities.

3.2.2 Regulations of Fund Transfers

In May 2015, Regulation (EU) 2015/847 on information accompanying transfers of funds replaced the previous Fund Transfer Regulation (1781/2006). The EU Regulation basically transposes FATF Recommendation 16 into EU law. This relates to wire transfers and obliges countries to ensure that financial institutions include accurate originator information and beneficiary information on wire transfers and related messages, and that the information remains with the wire transfer or related message throughout the payments chain.

The EU Payments Regulation sets out rules for the information about the payer (the person transferring the funds) that must be sent with a 'transfer of funds' by a payment services provider (PSP). The payer can transfer funds from one bank account to another, or they can give the funds they want to transfer to the payment services provider in cash, by cheque or by credit card. The funds can then be transferred electronically using SWIFT or transmitted in some other manner.

When a PSP transfers funds they must normally send the complete information on the payer with the transfer. This allows the authorities to trace payments if necessary. If the PSP used by the payer and the person receiving the funds are both within the EU then, unless full details are requested, the sender need only give the account number of the payer or another unique identifier selected by the PSP. Firms must comply with the EU Payments Regulation rules when transferring funds if they are a money services business (MSB) operating as a PSP in the EU. The rules apply to all transfers of funds in any currency.

Information on the Payer

Firms must have complete information on the payer, ie, the person transferring the funds when they make or receive any transfer of funds.

This means that firms need:

- the name of the payer
- the payer's address and/or their date and place of birth
- either their customer identification number, which is provided by the PSP, or a national identity number (which is usually their passport number)
- the payer's account number or a unique identifier which allows the transaction to be traced back to them.

Firms also need to verify this information by using documents, electronic ID data or information from a reliable and independent source such as a passport, a photocard driving licence, or photo identification documents issued by a government department.

However, for one-off transfers of under €1,000, and when this transaction is unlikely to become a regular business, firms do not need to verify the information the payer gives them.

In the case of linked transactions, information on the payer must be verified if the amount of the funds to be transferred is less than €1,000 and:

- there are several transactions which appear to be linked
- the linked transactions, when added together, exceed €1,000 or the equivalent in another currency.

The firm must verify the complete information on the payer for one-off transfers of €1,000 or more before making the transfer.

Regular Transfers

Firms need to verify the complete information on the payer if they are handling transfers for a 'payer' on a regular basis and have developed a 'business relationship'.

If the information has been verified once the firms do not have to do so for every transaction. Instead they should verify it at regular intervals and keep the information updated depending on their assessment of the risk.

Information on the Payer

In the case of transferring funds outside the EU, firms must send the complete information on the payer to the PSP acting for the person receiving the funds (the payee). However, if the payee's PSP is within the EU, then the payer's PSP will only need to send either the account number or a unique identifier, which allows the transfer to be traced back to the payer.

Firms must make sure that they receive the complete information on the payer from the payer's PSP if they are acting as PSP for the payee. If complete information on the payer is missing they should ask for it or consider rejecting the transfer. Missing or incomplete payer information may indicate that the transfer of funds is suspicious and should be reported to the NCA through the firm's internal SAR processes.

Record-Keeping

There are regulatory obligations to keep all complete information on the payer records (ID and transactions) for five years, even if the firm is an 'intermediary payment services provider' and neither the payer's nor the payee's PSP.

Records of transactions (whether undertaken as occasional transactions or under a business relationship) are to be kept for five years beginning on the date on which the transaction is completed. All other records must be kept for five years beginning on the date on which the business relationship ends.

There are financial penalties and/or potentially prosecution including imprisonment for up to two years for improper record-keeping.

Third-Party Payments

Third-party payments are money transmissions where the receivers of the money remittance order(s) are based in one country, but where settlement for the order(s) is made by the payment of an invoice to a beneficiary (often in another country). This is sometimes described as 'third-party pooling' or 'cover payments'. This type of remittance and settlement involves two separate transactions, each of which requires the appropriate customer due diligence or **enhanced due diligence (EDD)**.

These transactions are inherently high-risk. Firms should ensure that their risk assessment includes indicators of risk and consider applying EDD to the overseas recipient and keep records of settlement accounts.

Inward Remittances

An inward remittance occurs when a customer in one country wishes to carry out a transfer of funds to a beneficiary in another country. MSBs must apply CDD and where appropriate, ongoing monitoring if an overseas customer deals directly with the firm in the recipient country. If the transfer of funds is sent from an overseas MSB, the receiving firm must treat them as their customer. If bulk transfers are received (representing a collection of underlying transactions) the situation is high-risk and firms should consider carrying out EDD.

3.2.3 Payment Services Directive (PSD)

The Directive of the European Parliament and of the Council of 13 November 2007 on payment services in the internal market, also known as the Payment Services Directive (PSD), is aimed at ensuring that payments within the EU, in particular credit transfers, direct debits and card payments, become as easy, efficient, and secure as domestic payments within the member states.

The Directive provides the legal foundation for the creation of an EU-wide single market for payments and the necessary legal platform to make the single euro payments area (SEPA) possible. The PSD was implemented in the UK through the Payment Services Regulations (PSRs).

In the last few years, it was felt that the EU rules on payment services still needed to be updated to improve security, widen consumer choice and keep pace with innovations. The EC felt that although significant progress had been made in integrating retail payments in the EU into the current legislative framework on payments, several important areas of the payments market, such as card, internet and mobile payments, were still fragmented along national borders.

A new directive (PSD2) was adopted in 2015 and is fully in force as of 2018. It should be noted that PSD1 remains in force, with PSD2 designed to:

- make it easier and safer to use internet payment services
- better protect consumers against fraud, abuse, and payment problems
- promote innovative mobile and internet payment services
- strengthen consumer rights, and
- strengthen the role of the European Banking Authority (EBA) to coordinate supervisory authorities and draft technical standards.

In the UK, PSD2 was implemented in the Payment Services Regulations of 2017.

End of Chapter Questions

Think of an answer for each question and refer to the appropriate section for confirmation

1. What is the generally accepted definition of terrorist financing?
   Answer reference: Section 1.1

2. What is proliferation financing?
   Answer reference: Section 1.2

3. What does the UN Convention require states to do in relation to terrorist financing?
   Answer reference: Section 2.1

4. Do the FATF Recommendations oblige countries to criminalise terrorist financing?
   Answer reference: Section 3.1

5. What are the main strands of the EU Action Plan on terrorist financing?
   Answer reference: Section 3.2.1

6. What are the aims of the new Payment Services Directive?
   Answer reference: Section 3.2.3

Chapter Four
Bribery and Corruption

1. Bribery and Corruption — 73
2. UK Bribery Act 2010 — 73
3. The Foreign Corrupt Practices Act (FCPA) 1977 — 82
4. Corrupt Practice — 84
5. Combating Corruption — 87
6. Mutual Legal Assistance (MLA) — 92

This syllabus area will provide approximately 6 of the 50 examination questions

1. Bribery and Corruption

1.1 The Difference Between Bribery and Corruption

Learning Objective

4.1.1 Know the difference between bribery and corruption

Black's Law Dictionary defines bribery as *'the corrupt payment, receipt, or solicitation of private favour for official action'*. Bribery is thus a specific offence which concerns the practice of *'offering something or acceptance of some sort, usually money, to gain any advantage illegitimate or otherwise'*.

Corruption can be regarded to be any abuse of a position of trust in order to gain an undue advantage and includes any illegitimate use of office and it includes a range of different types of criminal behaviour. Corruption, in short, is most commonly defined *'as the misuse or the abuse of public office for private gain'* (World Bank, 1997, United Nations Development Programme (UNDP), 1999).

Corruption is, therefore, a much broader criminal behaviour and not always related specifically to bribery but bribery can be regarded as a subset of the overall crime of corruption.

2. The UK Bribery Act 2010

2.1 The Extra-Territorial Reach

Learning Objective

4.2.1 Know the extra-territorial reach of the UK Bribery Act (2010)

The Bribery Act 2010 has extra-territorial reach both for UK companies operating abroad and for overseas companies with a presence in the UK. In the case of companies registered in the UK, a company can commit an offence under Section 7 of the Act *'failure of commercial organisation to prevent bribery'* if an employee, subsidiary, agent or service provider (associated persons) bribes another person anywhere in the world to obtain or retain business or a business advantage. The UK Bribery Act because of its extra-territorial reach has a significant impact on many foreign companies.

A foreign subsidiary of a UK company can cause the parent company to become liable under Section 7 of the Act when the subsidiary commits an act of bribery in the context of performing services for the UK parent. If the foreign subsidiary is acting entirely on its own account it will not cause the UK parent to be liable for failure to prevent bribery under Section 7 as it is not then performing services for the UK parent. However, the UK parent company may still be liable for the actions of its subsidiary in other ways such as false accounting offences or under the Proceeds of Crime Act (POCA) 2002.

For example, a French oil and gas exploration company, which happens to have a UK subsidiary, appoints an intermediary to facilitate business in Africa, and the intermediary pays a bribe to a local official. Whether or not the French parent or the UK subsidiary is aware of the actions of the intermediary, or whether any benefit accrues to the UK subsidiary, in some circumstances, the French parent could be liable under the UK Bribery Act for failing to prevent bribery. The Act is engaged simply by virtue of the existence of a UK operation.

Also, using the same example, the UK subsidiary is itself at risk of prosecution if a person or company associated with it is involved in bribery, as are any French nationals working for the UK subsidiary and, therefore, ordinarily resident in the UK, if they are found to have paid or received a bribe.

2.2 The Offences

Learning Objective

4.2.2 Know the global reach of the UK Bribery Act (2010) and the offences: bribing another person; receiving bribes; bribery of a foreign public official (FPO); failure of commercial organisations to prevent bribery

The UK Bribery Act 2010 came into force on 1 July 2011, replacing some previous legislation notably the Public Bodies Corrupt Practices Act 1889 and the Prevention of Corruption Acts 1906 and 1916. The 2010 Act reformed the criminal law to provide a modern and comprehensive scheme of bribery offences that was aimed at enabling the courts and prosecutors in the UK to respond more effectively to offences of bribery at home as well as overseas.

The Bribery Act establishes four key criminal offences. The first two offences relate to offering and receiving a bribe. The third, a new offence introduced by the Act relates to the bribing of a foreign public official. All the three offences can be committed by an individual or a corporate body. The fourth is also a new offence and relates to the failure of commercial organisations to prevent bribery.

1. **Bribing another person (Bribery Act, Section 1)** – it is an offence to offer, promise or give a financial or some other advantage to induce another person where the briber intends the advantage to bring about an improper performance by another person of a relevant function or activity, or to reward improper performance of such a function or; the briber knows or believes that the acceptance of the advantage offered, promised or given in itself constitutes the improper performance of a relevant function or activity. The advantage can be offered, promised or given by the briber directly or through someone else, eg, if a bribe is paid by a third party (such as a partner organisation) for their benefit, in this case they can be found guilty of offence.
2. **Being bribed (Bribery Act, Section 2)** – it is an offence to request, agree to receive or accept a financial or other advantage with the intention that, as a consequence, a relevant function or activity should be performed improperly. It does not matter if the bribe is received directly or through someone else. It is immaterial whether or not the recipient or the person acting as a conduit to receive the bribe, knows or believes the performance of the function or activity is improper.

3. **Bribing a foreign public official (Bribery Act, Section 3)** – it is an offence if a person offers, promises or gives any advantage to a foreign public official with the requisite intention to influence the foreign public official in the official capacity and to obtain or retain business or an advantage in the conduct of business. However, unlike the general bribery offences in Sections 1 and 2, there is no requirement to show that there has been improper performance. The offence of bribing a foreign public official only covers the offering, promising and giving of bribes and not the acceptance of them.
4. **Failure of a relevant commercial organisation to prevent bribery (Bribery Act, Section 7)** – it is a strict liability offence, which in practical terms means that, if a commercial organisation fails to prevent someone associated with it from bribing another person with the intention to obtain or retain business or an advantage in the conduct of business for the organisation, it will be guilty of an offence under the Act. The commercial organisation's only defence to this offence will be if it can prove that, despite a particular case of bribery, it nevertheless had adequate procedures in place designed to prevent persons 'associated' with it from undertaking such a conduct.

The FCA fined JLT Specialty ltd (JLTSL) over £1.8 million for failing to have in place appropriate checks and controls to guard against the risk of bribery or corruption when making payments to overseas third parties in 2013. An example taken from the FCA website and is available at: www.fca.org.uk/news/firm-fined-18million-for-unacceptable-approach-to-bribery-corruption-risks-from-overseas-payments

2.2.1 Facilitation Payments

The Bribery Act does not make an exemption for facilitation or 'grease payments' (the practice of paying a small sum of money to a public official or other person as a way of ensuring that they perform their duty, either more promptly or at all). The position is, however, different in the US and some other members of the Organisation for Economic Co-operation and Development (OECD) where anti-corruption legislation includes a specific exception or defence for small facilitation payments in certain circumstances.

In the UK, there have been successful prosecutions under the Bribery Act, which have either involved the offering of or the acceptance of a bribe. The cases have made it apparent that prosecutors will not be deterred from prosecuting small value bribes as the sums involved in some cases ranged from £300 to £5,000.

Those found guilty under the Bribery Act face fines and imprisonment:

- for summary offences, the maximum fine is £5,000 and a maximum term of imprisonment of 12 months
- for conviction on indictment, an imprisonment of up to ten years and/or an unlimited fine.

2.3 Foreign Public Officials (FPOs)

Learning Objective

4.2.3 Know the definition of an FPO

The term 'foreign public official' refers to a person who acts in an official capacity for a foreign government. The term is chiefly used in the context of provisions of international conventions and national laws against corruption related to international trade in goods and services.

Section 6 (Subsections 5 and 6) of the Bribery Act defines a foreign public official as an individual who:

a. holds a legislative, administrative or judicial position of any kind, whether appointed or elected, of a country or territory outside the United Kingdom (or any subdivision of such a country or territory)
b. exercises a public function:
i. for or on behalf of a country or territory outside the United Kingdom (or any subdivision of such a country or territory), or
ii. for any public agency or public enterprise of that country or territory (or subdivision), or
c. is an official or agent of a public international organisation.

'Public international organisation' means an organisation whose members are any of the following:

a. countries or territories
b. governments of countries or territories
c. other public international organisations
d. a mixture of any of the above

2.4 Associated Persons

Learning Objective

4.2.4 Understand the liabilities corporate entities face from 'associated persons'

An organisation is liable under Section 7 of the Bribery Act, if a person associated with it bribes another person with the intention of obtaining or retaining business or a business advantage for the organisation.

A person associated with a commercial organisation is defined under Section 8 of the Act as someone who 'performs services' for or on behalf of the organisation. This person can be an individual or an incorporated or unincorporated body. Section 8 of the Act provides that the capacity in which a person performs services for or on behalf of the organisation does not matter, so employees (who are presumed to be performing services for their employer), agents and subsidiaries can all possibly be included.

The concept of a person who performs services for or on behalf of the organisation gives Section 7 of the Bribery Act a broad scope. This concept covers the entire range of persons connected to the organisation who might be capable of committing bribery for or on the behalf of the organisation. It may also include joint venture partners, associated business and other connected individuals.

Section 8(4) elaborates and makes it clear that the question as to whether a person is performing services for an organisation is to be determined by reference to all the relevant circumstances and not merely by reference to the nature of the relationship between that person and the organisation.

2.5 Strict Liability and Adequate Procedures

Learning Objective

4.2.5 Understand strict liability and the meaning of 'adequate procedures'

In a legal context, strict liability refers to the liability that does not depend on actual negligence or intent to harm, but that is based on the breach of an absolute duty. It is an absolute duty of the directors and managers of any commercial organisation that undertakes a business or part of its business in the UK to be aware of Section 7 of the Bribery Act 2010 offence of failing to prevent bribery. It is a strict liability offence, which in practical terms means that if an associate, whether an employee or a third-party service provider, has paid a bribe to obtain or retain a business or business advantage, the organisation concerned will be guilty of an offence. It makes no difference or provides any defence if the organisation or its directors/managers were unaware that the act of bribery has taken place.

There is only one defence available: the organisation must be able to show that, despite the particular act of bribery having taken place, it nevertheless had put in place adequate procedures designed to prevent and deter bribery from taking place. The question that arises here is that what constitutes adequate procedures.

Section 9 (1) provides that:

> 'the Secretary of State must publish guidance about procedures that relevant commercial organisations can put in place to prevent persons associated with them from bribing as mentioned in Section 7(1)'.

2.6 Bribery Prevention

Learning Objective

4.2.6 Understand the six principles for bribery prevention and their legal context

The risks of bribery need to be clearly understood by the management in an organisation to put in place robust and proportionate measures. Bribery risk assessment and prevention should essentially form part of any institution's overall risk management process; irrespective of it being in the public or private sector.

In March 2011, the UK Ministry of Justice published guidance suggesting procedures which relevant commercial organisations should put into place to prevent persons associated with them from bribing. The legal context of this guidance should be seen in terms of the stipulations of Section 9 of the Bribery Act and thus these principles drive their statutory validity from the Act.

2.6.1 The Six Principles

The guidance paper helps commercial organisations understand what sort of procedures they need to put in place for prevention from bribing or being bribed. The guidance recommends adoption of a risk-based approach to the problem and identifies six key management principles for the prevention of bribery in an organisation.

The principles are flexible so that each organisation can tailor its policies and procedures in a manner that are proportionate to the nature, scale and complexity of the activities of the organisation.

The six principles are:

1. **Proportionate procedures** – actions taken within the firm should be proportionate to the risks faced and the size of the firm.
2. **Top level commitment** – those at the top are responsible for establishing a culture across the organisation in which bribery is unacceptable.
3. **Risk assessment** – knowing and keeping up to date with the bribery risks in the firm and market.
4. **Due diligence** – knowing who you are doing business with or who provides services to the firm; knowing why, when and to whom the firm is releasing funds and seeking reciprocal anti-bribery agreements.
5. **Communication (including training)** – ensuring staff and those who provide services to the firm are aware of policies and procedures and what to look out for.
6. **Monitoring and review** – risks and effectiveness of procedures may change over time, so a firm needs to review their policies and procedures.

The six principles are not listed in order of importance and all are equally important and jointly provide the foundations of a successful anti-bribery framework. Each of them needs to be considered independently by the organisation to determine and implement the most suitable anti-bribery governance and culture framework.

2.7 Applicable Penalties Under the Act

Learning Objective

4.2.7 Know the maximum penalties applicable to individuals found guilty under the Act

Section 11 of the Act explains the penalties for individuals and companies found guilty of committing a crime under the Act. If an individual is found guilty of a bribery offence, and it is tried as a summary offence, they may be imprisoned for up to 12 months and fined up to £5,000.

Someone found guilty on indictment, however, faces up to ten years' of imprisonment and an unlimited fine. The crime of a commercial organisation failing to prevent bribery is punishable by an unlimited fine.

In addition, a convicted individual or organisation may be subject to a confiscation order under the POCA, while a company director who is convicted may be disqualified under the Company Directors Disqualification Act (CDDA) 1986.

2.8 Corporate Liability

Learning Objective

4.2.8 Understand the circumstances under which directors and senior officers of a corporation may be found liable under the Act: consent or connivance; passive acquiescence; failure to implement adequate procedures and potential civil liability

Bribery, whether committed in the UK or abroad, is a criminal offence under the Bribery Act 2010. As discussed above, the Act introduces a new offence for commercial organisations of failing to prevent bribery. It is a defence for firms charged with this offence to show that they had adequate procedures in place to prevent bribery. The Ministry of Justice (MoJ) has published guidance on adequate anti-bribery procedures.

The FCA regards the financial crime risk to include the risk of corruption as well as bribery, and so its scope is wider than that of the Bribery Act. The FCA may take action against a firm with deficient anti-bribery and corruption systems and controls regardless of whether or not bribery or corruption has taken place.

Principles 1, 2 and 3 of the FCA's *Principles for Business* are of particular relevance to bribery and corruption. Principle 1 obliges the firms to conduct their business with integrity, which is especially relevant in cases where firms and their employees may be engaged in corrupt practices. Principle 2 states that a firm must *'conduct its business with due skill, care and diligence'* and Principle 3 sets out the obligation that a *'firm must take reasonable care to organise and control its affairs responsibly and effectively, with adequate risk management systems'*.

A firm's senior management is responsible for ensuring that the firm conducts its business with integrity and tackles the risk that the firm, or anyone acting on its behalf, engages in bribery and corruption. Firms' senior management should, therefore, keep themselves updated and stay fully abreast of bribery and corruption issues.

Board and senior management should have a good understanding of the bribery and corruption risks faced by the firm, the materiality to its business and how to apply a risk-based approach to anti-bribery and corruption. The senior management should directly contribute to the firm's anti-bribery and corruption efforts and should approve and periodically review the strategies and policies for managing, monitoring and mitigating bribery risk. Staff must be made aware of the interest of senior management in this area, eg, integrity and compliance with relevant anti-corruption legislation should be considered when discussing business opportunities.

The FCA regards it as examples of good practice if the:

- firm is committed to carrying out business fairly, honestly and openly
- senior management lead by example in complying with the firm's anti-corruption policies and procedures
- responsibility for anti-bribery and corruption systems and controls is clearly documented and apportioned to a single senior manager or a committee with appropriate terms of reference and senior management membership who reports ultimately to the board.

Similarly, measures such as anti-bribery systems and controls being subject to audit and management information submitted to the board ensuring that they are adequately informed of internal and external developments are also regarded as good practices. Examples of poor practice by the FCA include:

- a lack of awareness of, or engagement in, anti-bribery and corruption at senior management or board level
- an 'ask no questions' culture
- little or no management information being sent to the board.

Example

In 2017, Rolls Royce issued a public apology and paid £671 million in penalties in relation to large-scale bribery covering six countries over a period of 30 years. The bribery was described by one judge as '*truly vast corrupt payments*'. Bribes were made to individuals who could influence decisions to favour Rolls Royce. By settling out of court under a deferred prosecution arrangement (DPA), Rolls Royce avoided having to give evidence. Further investigation into the prosecution of senior executives was abandoned in 2019.

2.8.1 Consent or Connivance

Section 14 of the Bribery Act provides (in circumstances where there is **consent**, connivance or neglect) for the personal criminal liability of directors, managers, secretaries and management committee members of bodies corporate and unincorporated for offences committed by or on behalf of such a body. Directors, or so-called senior officers, who consent or connive to commit bribery, commit the same offence (ie, there is no separate 'consent' and 'connivance' offence).

It is straightforward under the Bribery Act to prosecute senior officers of an organisation if it can be shown that bribery was committed with their consent or connivance. The Bribery Act (Section 14) establishes serious consequences for conniving senior officers. If any organisation is guilty under Sections 1, 2 or 6 of the Act, a senior officer of that organisation can also be convicted if they have given their consent or had any connivance in the criminal conduct. In other words, if an offence has been committed, the Act provides that a senior officer (or a person purporting to act in that capacity) of the organisation is guilty of the same offence if they have:

1. consented to or connived in the commission of that offence, and
2. a close connection to the UK as defined in Section 12(4) of the Act.

The term 'senior officer' in this context is broad and means a director, manager, company secretary or other similar officer of a body corporate.

2.8.2 Passive Acquiescence

In general, the term 'acquiescence' is regarded as *'the act or condition of acquiescing or giving tacit assent'* (*Random House Dictionary of English*). Passive acquiescence implies agreement or consent by silence or without objection. However, in a legal context, acquiescence occurs when a person knowingly stands by without raising any objection to the infringement.

If a senior officer did not give obvious consent or connive directly in bribery or corruption, an offence could still be committed by the passive acquiescence of the director or the responsible senior manager as brought out by the failure to put in place adequate procedures in the organisation.

2.8.3 Failure to Implement Adequate Procedures and Potential Civil Liability

A commercial organisation commits the offence of failing to prevent bribery if a person associated with it bribes another person (anywhere in the world) intending to obtain or retain business (or an advantage in the conduct of business) for the organisation unless the organisation can prove that it had adequate procedures to prevent bribery in place.

The Act has very wide territorial application which is also reflected in this offence. The UK courts will have jurisdiction not only over commercial organisations who were established or incorporated in the UK, but also against all other commercial organisations that conduct part of their business in the UK. This means that foreign companies could find themselves liable under the Act (as well as potentially under their local laws) even if the corrupt activity takes place outside the UK.

In the case of an organisation failing to put in place adequate procedures designed to prevent persons associated with organisation from undertaking criminal conduct of bribery as defined in the Act, the organisation will be guilty under Section 7 of the Act and also under the FCA guidelines. The Bribery Act carries: *'a maximum penalty of ten years imprisonment for all the offences, except the offence relating to commercial organisations, which carry an unlimited fine'*. The potential civil liability for the organisation is, in simple words, unlimited.

Example

Scarlad ltd, a supplier of technical products to steel manufacturers, self reported bribery to the UK Serious Fraud Office (SFO), admitting corporate criminal liability, and consequently, entered into a DPA. They paid penalties of £6.5 million. The company admitted to failure to prevent corrupt payments over a period of eight years. Three individuals were charged but were subsequently acquitted.

3. The Foreign Corrupt Practices Act (FCPA) 1977

3.1 The Objectives and Scope of the FCPA (1977)

Learning Objective

4.3.1 Understand the objectives and scope of the FCPA (1977)

The Foreign Corrupt Practices Act (FCPA) 1977 is a US federal law known primarily for its two main provisions:

1. accounting transparency requirements under the Securities Exchange Act of 1934, and
2. the bribery of foreign officials.

The Act was passed to make it unlawful for certain classes of persons and entities to make payments to foreign government officials in order to assist in either obtaining or retaining business. The FCPA made it illegal for companies and their management to influence foreign government officials with any personal payments or rewards. The FCPA applies to any person who has a certain degree of connection to the US and engages in foreign corrupt practices.

The Act also applies to any act by US businesses, foreign corporations trading securities in the US, American nationals, citizens and residents acting in furtherance of a foreign corrupt practice whether or not they are physically present in the US. In the case of foreign natural and legal persons, the Act covers their deeds if they are in the US at the time of the corrupt conduct.

Further, the Act governs not only payments to foreign officials, candidates, and parties, but also to any other recipient if part of the bribe is ultimately attributable to a foreign official, candidate, or party. These payments are not restricted to monetary forms and include anything of value.

3.2 UK Bribery Act (2010) vs the FCPA (1977)

Learning Objective

4.3.2 Know the key differences between the UK Bribery Act (2010) and the FCPA (1977)

The UK Bribery Act 2010 came into force on 1 July 2011 whereas the FCPA is fairly old and dates back to 1977. The Bribery Act of 2011 reflects a broader international trend and has a wider application than the FCPA. Therefore, organisations may consider that their anti-corruption procedures are sufficiently robust for the purposes of the FCPA, but these may not be sufficient under the Bribery Act.

Under the Bribery Act, commercial organisations may be vulnerable to prosecution if they carry on a business, or part of their business, in the UK and irrespective of where the bribe takes place. It is, therefore, important for organisations to be aware of the differences between the FCPA and the Bribery Act.

The Bribery Act and the FCPA have many common aspects like their extensive extra-territorial jurisdiction but the main differences between the Bribery Act and the FCPA are:

- **Bribery of foreign (public) officials** – both the Bribery Act and the FCPA make it an offence to bribe foreign (public) officials. Under the Bribery Act a 'foreign public official' is defined more narrowly than under the FCPA but still include:
    - anyone who holds a foreign legislative or judicial position
    - individuals who exercise a public function for a foreign country, territory, public agency or public enterprise, or
    - any official or agent of a public organisation.
- **Private-to-private bribery** – the FCPA does not cover bribery on a private level, unlike the Bribery Act, although such conduct can be caught under other US legislation.
- **Active and passive bribery** – the FCPA only covers active bribery, that is to say the giving of a bribe. In contrast, the UK's Bribery Act prohibits both active and passive bribery, ie, giving and the taking of a bribe.
- **Failure to prevent bribery** – the Bribery Act creates a strict liability corporate offence for failure to prevent bribery (as opposed to vicarious liability) subject to being able to establish that a company has adequate procedures. Under the FCPA, however, a company subject to US jurisdiction can be held vicariously liable for acts of its employees and agents. The UK offence extends to acts of associated persons which means anyone who performs services for or on behalf of the commercial organisation.
- **Intent** – under the FCPA it must be proved that the person offering the bribe did so with a 'corrupt' intent. The Bribery Act does not require the intent to be 'corrupt' or 'improper' in relation to the bribery of a foreign public official, although the requirement remains for the general bribery offence.
- **Facilitation payments** – the FCPA creates an exemption for facilitation payments whereas the Bribery Act makes no such exception. The UK's MoJ has, however, issued guidance in this context that confirms that prosecutors will exercise discretion in determining whether to prosecute in such a situation.
- **Promotional expenses** – the FCPA provides a defence to promotional expenses in so far as it can be demonstrated that they were a reasonable and bona fide expenditure. There is no such defence concerning promotional expenses under the Bribery Act, in relation to foreign public officials, although the MoJ has provided some comfort on this aspect in its guidance.
- **Penalties** – an individual found to have committed an offence under the Bribery Act is liable to imprisonment of up to ten years and/or to an unlimited fine. A company found guilty is subject to an unlimited fine.

For offences committed under the FCPA, an individual can be fined up to US$250,000 per violation and may also be given up to five years' imprisonment. A company guilty under the FCPA is liable for a fine of up to US$2,000,000 per violation. For offences committed under the Bribery Act there is a maximum penalty of ten years imprisonment for all the offences, except the offence relating to commercial organisations who can be subject to an unlimited fine.

4. Corrupt Practice

4.1 The Main Components of, and Differences in, Corrupt Practice

Learning Objective

4.4.1 Understand the main components and differences between types of corrupt practice: active and passive bribery; embezzlement; trading in influence; abuse of office; illicit enrichment; concealment

The term 'active bribery' refers to the offence committed by the person who promises or gives the bribe, as opposed to 'passive bribery' which is the offence committed by the official who receives the bribe. Active bribery occurs on the supply side while passive bribery is on the demand side.

In legal terminology (according to the Council of Europe's Criminal Law Convention on Corruption), the active bribery of public officials is defined as:

'the promising, offering or giving by any person, directly or indirectly, of any undue advantage ... for himself or herself or for anyone else, for him or her to act or refrain from acting in the exercise of his or her functions'. 'Passive bribery' is defined as 'the request or receipt...directly or indirectly, of any undue advantage, for himself or herself or for anyone else, or the acceptance of an offer or a promise of such an advantage, to act or refrain from acting in the exercise of his or her functions'.

4.1.1 Embezzlement

Embezzlement is the misappropriation of property or funds which are legally entrusted to someone in their formal position as an agent or guardian. It is usually a premeditated crime performed methodically, with the embezzler taking precautions to conceal their activities of the criminal conversion of the property of another person as the embezzlement occurs without the knowledge or the consent of the affected person.

It is not always a form of theft or an act of stealing, but is more generically an act of deceitfully extracting assets by one or more persons that have been entrusted with such assets. The person(s) entrusted with these assets may or may not have an ownership stake in them.

It is a breach of trust and a type of financial fraud, eg, a lawyer might embezzle funds from the trust accounts of their clients, a financial adviser might embezzle the funds of investors, and a somebody might embezzle funds from a bank account jointly held with their spouse.

In some cases, embezzlement can be conducted and concealed through creative bookkeeping practices. An accountant can set up a programme to deposit money in an account while changing the numbers to make it seem as if the company never had the money in the first place. An individual can also write out cheques without permission or create ghost employees with pay cheques that are sent to the embezzler.

Another very common form of embezzling is to overstate the costs of a particular operation and then steal the excess funds.

To prove embezzlement, it must be shown that the employee had possession of the goods 'by virtue of employment', that is, that the employee was formally delegated the authority to exercise substantial control over the goods. Typically, in determining whether the employee had sufficient control, the courts look at factors such as job title, job description and the particular operational practices of the firm or organisation.

Proper internal controls, separation of duties and oversight mechanisms are commonly used defences against embezzlement. For instance, accountants may be regularly observed by a senior accountant. Another way is through a proper division and clear segregation of duties and job rotations. Tasks where the risk of embezzlement exists can be designed in a manner that they require two individuals to carry out one function. Both individuals would then have to collaborate in order for embezzlement to occur.

4.1.2 Trading in Influence

The term 'trading in influence' (or 'influence peddling') refers to a situation where a person misuses their influence over the decision-making process for a third party (a person, institution or government) in return for their loyalty, money or any other material or immaterial undue advantage.

Article 18 of UNCAC and Article 12 of the Council of Europe Criminal Law Convention on Corruption both oblige member states to criminalise the act of trading in influence if it is intentional, ie, when a decision maker accepts a gift or advantage from someone who could benefit from the decision-making process.

4.1.3 Abuse of Office

Abuse of office, in the form of 'malfeasance in office' or 'official misconduct', is the commission of an unlawful act, carried out in an official capacity, which affects the performance of official duties. Abuse of office can also mean a person using the power they have for their own personal gain. It is often grounds for a 'for cause' removal of an elected official by statute or recall election.

Public office is abused for private gain when an official accepts, solicits, or extorts a bribe. It is also abused when private agents actively offer bribes to circumvent public policies and processes for competitive advantage and profit. Even if no bribery occurs, public office can also be abused for personal benefit through patronage and nepotism, the theft of state assets, or the diversion of state revenues.

The World Bank has settled for a more straightforward definition: *'the abuse of public office for private gain'*, which sums up almost all the corruption of public office holders in practical terms.

4.1.4 Illicit Enrichment

UNCAC defines 'illicit enrichment' as the *'significant increase in the assets of a public official that he cannot reasonably explain in relation to his lawful income'*. Article 20 of the Convention criminalises the conduct. Illicit enrichment is also criminalised and prescribed as an offence under other national and international instruments, such as the Inter-American Convention against Corruption (IACAC) and the African Union Convention on Preventing and Combating Corruption under comparable definitions.

The rationale for criminalising illegal enrichment is simple and straightforward as sometimes this enrichment is the only tangible evidence that a crime has taken place and that money has changed hands between the corruptor and the corruptee. In response, some states have adopted the offence of illicit enrichment to strengthen their ability to fight corruption and recover assets.

UNCAC, in its Article 20 titled *Illicit Enrichment*, provides that:

> *'Subject to its constitution and the fundamental principles of its legal system, each state party shall consider adopting such legislative and other measures as may be necessary to establish as a criminal offence, when committed intentionally, illicit enrichment, that is, a significant increase in the assets of a public official that he or she cannot reasonably explain in relation to his or her lawful income'.*

Illicit enrichment is criminalised under the UNCAC. However, the criminalisation of illicit enrichment is still not universally accepted as an anticorruption measure.

> *'A study on the subject found that 44 jurisdictions have criminalised illicit enrichment. Several jurisdictions that prosecute illicit enrichment perceive it as a valuable complement to the traditional toolkit for combating corruption. However, the statistical information collected indicates that only a limited number of these jurisdictions regularly investigate or prosecute the offense'.*

Source: On the Take: Criminalizing Illicit Enrichment to Fight Corruption, Lindy Muzila, Michelle Morales, Marianne Mathias, Tammar Berger, World Bank-UNODC, 2012.

4.1.5 Concealment

Concealment is primarily the act of refraining from making a disclosure, therefore it is an act by which a person prevents or obstructs the discovery of something. In short, it is a cover-up.

Concealment is confirmatory conduct which is aimed at keeping another person from learning of a fact which that person would have otherwise come to know but for this confirmatory conduct. This behaviour or conduct is always a misrepresentation and in all its forms it would have the ultimate effect that any misrepresentation would have. Concealment can occur in many forms, and is classified accordingly, eg, active concealment, fraudulent and passive concealment.

Concealment by words or actions of something that a person has a duty to reveal is known as 'active concealment'; while 'fraudulent concealment' is the affirmative suppression or hiding, with the intent to deceive or defraud, of a material fact or circumstances that one is legally or morally bound to reveal. 'Passive concealment' is the act of maintaining silence when one has a duty to speak (Black's Law Dictionary).

Officials who have benefited from illicit enrichment may be under an obligation to declare their wealth. If they fail to declare the proceeds of their corruption, they are guilty of concealing it, which may amount to a money laundering offence.

5. Combating Corruption

5.1 Associated Bodies

Learning Objective

4.5.1 Know the role international bodies play in combating corruption

There are a large number of international bodies that are working on combating corruption and although their role varies, their aim is similar.

5.1.1 United Nations Convention Against Corruption (UNCAC)

UNCAC was the first internationally agreed instrument to combat the threat of corruption (UN General Assembly Resolution 58/4 of 2003) and entered into force in December 2005. The Convention presents a comprehensive set of standards, measures and rules that all state parties should apply to strengthen their legal and regulatory regimes to fight corruption. Aspects covered by the Convention include:

- **Prevention** – measures directed at both the public and private sectors. These include model preventive policies, such as the establishment of anti-corruption bodies and enhanced transparency in the financing of election campaigns and political parties.
- **Criminalisation** – introduction of criminal offences to cover a wide range of acts of corruption, such as bribery and the embezzlement of public funds, but also trading in influence and the concealment and laundering of the proceeds of corruption. Other offences likened to corruption, including money laundering and obstructing justice, are also dealt with.
- **International cooperation** – cooperation between countries regarding prevention, investigation and prosecution. Specific mutual legal assistance, including collection of evidence and extradition.
- **Asset recovery** – a major part of the Convention, including requirements to return assets from public sector embezzlement to the state requesting them. This is particularly important for developing countries which lose huge amounts of badly needed resources to corruption.

5.1.2 Organisation for Economic Co-operation and Development (OECD)

The OECD is an international economic organisation of 34 countries, primarily aimed at stimulating economic progress and world trade. It provides a platform to compare policy experiences, seek answers to common problems, identify good practices and coordinate the domestic and international policies of its members.

In 1994, the OECD Ministerial Council adopted the recommendation of the Council on Bribery in International Business Transactions which led to the *Convention on Combating Bribery of Foreign Public Officials in International Business Transactions* which came into force on 15 February 1999. The OECD anti-bribery convention aims at reducing corruption in developing countries by encouraging sanctions against bribery in international business transactions carried out by companies based in the Convention member countries.

The OECD anti-bribery convention establishes binding standards to criminalise the bribing of foreign public officials in international business transactions and provides for a host of related measures that make this effective. It is the first and only international anti-corruption instrument focused on the supply side of the bribery transaction. The OECD member countries including the UK and seven non-member countries – Argentina, Brazil, Bulgaria, Colombia, Latvia, Russia, and South Africa – have adopted this convention.

It establishes a peer-driven monitoring mechanism to ensure the thorough implementation of the international obligations that countries have taken on under it. This monitoring is carried out under the framework of the OECD Working Group on Bribery which is composed of members of all state parties (ratifying countries).

5.1.3 The Council of Europe's Group of States against Corruption

The Group of States against Corruption (GRECO) is the Council of Europe's anti-corruption monitoring body established in 1999 with its headquarters in Strasbourg. Membership of GRECO is open to non-European states; it currently it has 49 members, including two states that are not members of the Council of Europe (the United States and Belarus). All Council of Europe members are members of GRECO.

The objective of GRECO is to improve the capacity of its members to fight corruption by monitoring their compliance with Council of Europe anti-corruption standards through a process of mutual evaluation and peer review. It helps to identify deficiencies in national anti-corruption policies, with a view to prompting the necessary legislative, institutional and practical reforms. GRECO's monitoring process comprises an evaluation procedure based largely on information gathered via questionnaires and on-site visits. There is also a compliance follow-up procedure designed to assess the measures subsequently taken by its members to implement the recommendations emanating from GRECO's evaluations.

GRECO works in cycles, called evaluation rounds, with each round covering certain specific themes.

- GRECO's **first evaluation** round (2000–02) dealt with the independence, specialisation and means of national bodies engaged in the prevention and fight against corruption. It also dealt with the extent and scope of immunities of public officials such as arrest and prosecution.
- The **second evaluation** round (2003–06) focused on the identification, seizure and confiscation of corruption proceeds, the prevention and detection of corruption in public administration and the prevention of legal persons (ie, corporations) from being used as shields for corruption.
- The **third evaluation** round (launched in January 2007) addressed the penalties provided for in the Criminal Law Convention on Corruption and the transparency of party funding.
- The **fourth evaluation** round (which began in January 2012) dealt with corruption related to parliament, judges and prosecutors.
- The **fifth evaluation** round (2017) concerns the prevention of corruption and integrity matters regarding high-level executive functions within central governments and law enforcement agencies.

GRECO does not have a mandate to measure the occurrence of corrupt practices in its individual member states. The thematic evaluations carried out so far by GRECO showed that, in many European states, there are currently no regulations to deal with the conflicts of interest that parliamentarians, judges and prosecutors might face, hence the focus of the most recent round of evaluations and that, in some countries, legislative frameworks are so complex or are so frequently amended that the stability and the clarity of the legislation is undermined.

5.1.4 United Nations Global Compact (UNGC)

The Global Compact is a UN initiative to encourage businesses worldwide to adopt sustainable and socially responsible policies and to report on their implementation. UNGC is a principles-based call that corporate sustainability starts with a company's value system and a principled approach to doing business. This means operating in ways that, at a minimum, meet fundamental responsibilities in the areas of human rights, labour, environment and anti-corruption.

UNGC's ten principles are derived from the:

- Universal Declaration of Human Rights
- International Labour Organization's Declaration on Fundamental Principles and Rights at Work
- Rio Declaration on Environment and Development, and
- United Nations Convention against Corruption.

Individual cities can join UNGC through the Cities Programme.

UNGC was initially launched with nine principles. In 2004, during the first Global Compact Leaders' Summit, a tenth principle 'against corruption' was added in accordance with UNCAC, which had been adopted a year earlier in 2003.

UNGC is not a regulatory instrument or a certifying body, but rather a forum for discussion and a network for communication between governments, companies and labour organisations. UNGC makes it clear that once companies declare their support for the principles: *'this does not mean that the Global Compact recognises or certifies that these companies have fulfilled the Compact's Principles'*.

5.1.5 United Nations Development Programme (UNDP)

The UNDP is an organisation that tries to help developing countries in the eradication of poverty and the reduction of inequalities through development of policies, skills, institutional capabilities and in achieving resilience by way of sustainable development outcomes.

When public money is stolen for private gain, it means that fewer resources are left to build facilities like schools, hospitals, roads and water treatment services. When foreign aid is diverted into private bank accounts, important infrastructure or poverty reduction projects can come to a halt. Corruption hinders economic development, strikes at the heart of democracy, democratic institutions and public trust in leaders. For the vast majority of the poor, women and minorities in the developing countries, corruption means even less access to jobs, justice or any fair and equal opportunities.

The UNDP, through the global programme on Anti-Corruption for Development Effectiveness (PACDE), regional and country-level programmes (2008–13), was a major provider of anti-corruption technical support to developing countries. Presently, the vision of the UNDP's Global Anti-Corruption Initiative (GAIN) (2014–17) is to *'help countries achieve the simultaneous eradication of poverty and significant reduction of inequalities and exclusion'*.

UNDP work on anti-corruption cuts across all three development pathways of the new strategic plan: sustainable development, democratic governance, and resilience building.

The UNDP also provides advisory services to programming countries, engages in advocacy and raising of global awareness on anti-corruption, and tries to build synergies through synchronising global and regional activities.

In addition, the UNDP also addresses the costs of corruption by mainstreaming anti-corruption in its current work and other development processes.

Though it has a limited role, it tries to contribute to the global fight against corruption by supporting UNCAC's implementation and review, mainstreaming anti-corruption in its ongoing work programmes to achieve millennium development goals (MDGs) and advocacy and creating awareness.

5.1.6 International Anti-Corruption Conference (IACC)

The IACC is a global forum that brings together civil society, political heads and the private sector to tackle the challenges posed by corruption. It takes place every two years in a different geographic region of the world, most recently in Panama in December 2016. Up to 2,000 delegates from 135 countries attend the conference, which is overseen by the IACC Council and organised by Transparency International (TI).

According to its website, the IACC:

> *'advances the anti-corruption agenda by raising awareness and stimulating debate. It fosters networking, cross-fertilisation and the global exchange of experience that are indispensable for effective advocacy and action, on a global and national level. The conference also promotes international cooperation among government, civil society, the private sector, and citizens by providing the opportunity for face-to-face dialogue and direct liaison between representatives from the agencies and organisations taking part'.*

5.1.7 Transparency International (TI)

TI is a movement that aims to free the world of corruption. It now has more than 100 chapters and its secretariat is in Berlin. TI is a non-governmental organisation (NGO) that monitors and publicises corporate and political corruption in international development. It also publishes the annual *Global Corruption Barometer,* the very influential *Corruption Perceptions Index* and a comparative listing of corruption worldwide.

The mechanics and conduct of corruption differ from country to country. Chapters of TI are locally established and, therefore, well placed to address corruption in their respective countries ranging from small bribes to large-scale looting. As chapters are staffed with experts with local knowledge they are ideally placed to determine the priorities and approaches that are best suited to tackling the overall issues of corruption, along with the individual cases of mega corruption in their countries.

TI is an important think tank for the global fight against financial crime. Its biggest success has been to place the subject of corruption on the world's agenda. It has also played a vital role in the introduction of the UNCAC and the OECD's Anti-Bribery Convention.

5.1.8 Global Witness

Global Witness is an NGO that carries out research and investigations into the causes and effects of the exploitation of natural resources by public and private entities throughout the world, specifically in cases where such exploitation is used to fund conflict, human rights abuses and corruption. The organisation tries to create transparency in the mining, logging, oil and gas sectors so that citizens who own those resources can also benefit fairly from them. Global Witness also conducts geographical and sector-specific campaigns that expose the shadow systems that enable corruption and conflict.

Global Witness believes that the only way to protect peoples' rights to land, livelihoods and a fair share of their national wealth is to demand total transparency in the resources sector, sustainable and equitable resource management and by stopping the international financial system from propping up resource-related corruption. The Global Witness team draws on a wide range of skills, from undercover investigations and financial research, to information gathering on the ground and close cooperation with partners and activists all over the world.

5.2 Practical Application and Limitations of Quantitative Indicators

Learning Objective

4.5.2 Understand the practical application and limitations of quantitative indicators in combating corruption

Corruption is typically not done openly, and is unpredictable. It varies over time and by location, and takes many forms including bribery, collusion, abuse of power and nepotism. Corruption occurs at all levels (global, national and local), and is not restricted to a specific player but is undertaken by businesses, individuals and politicians. One of the main challenges with attempting to measure corruption is its continuously evolving nature. Measuring corruption, therefore, is not straight forward. Instead, what is usually measured is anti-corruption – the framework of what should happen to prevent or combat corruption, ie, transparency, accountability and integrity. Effective measurements rely on sufficient data being available, and is typically measured along four categories from 'soft' to 'hard':

- **Perception** – opinions by ordinary citizens, business owners, or experts on specific topics. They are not facts, and could be distorted. Data is typically collected via opinion polls and surveys.
- **Experience** – specific experiences including frequency, location and amount of bribes paid. Data is typically gathered in face-to-face interviews and surveys.
- **External assessments** – ratings, rankings and scores put together by experts using large-scale online surveys, administrative data and third-party reports.
- **Administrative** – 'hard measures' consisting of government laws, activities and performance data produced by governments.

The main drawbacks of quantitative methods are related to the quality and quantity of data, and the quality of the underlying inputs and survey responses. Data must be credible without the need for complex statistical techniques yet this is not always the case. Furthermore, there is no standard methodology in use, which makes the consequent ranking of countries particularly difficult.

6. Mutual Legal Assistance (MLA)

Learning Objective

4.6.1 Know how the concept of dual criminality may be applied in cases of corruption

Mutual legal assistance (MLA) is a method of cooperation between states to obtain assistance in the investigation or prosecution of criminal offences. MLA is generally used for obtaining material that cannot be obtained on a police-to-police cooperation basis, particularly with regards to enquiries that require coercive means. In civil law jurisdictions, like France, such assistance is usually requested by courts or prosecutors and is also referred to as 'judicial cooperation'.

MLA is normally used to obtain assistance in the investigation of the proceeds of crime and in the freezing and confiscation of proceeds. Proceeds of crime matters can be on a criminal (conviction) basis or a civil (non-conviction) basis. Due to the increasingly global nature of crime, MLA is critical to criminal investigations and serves as a vital tool in the pursuit of criminal finances, including the recovery of the proceeds of crime that may have been moved and hidden overseas.

There are now several bilateral and multilateral mutual legal assistance treaties (MLATs, commonly pronounced as 'M-Lats') which provide substantial help to counter financial crime. The US has signed more than 60 MLATs. These treaties are useful for gathering evidence and intelligence, taking the testimony of witnesses and obtaining certified documents that would be difficult for the officials of one nation to obtain without the cooperation of another country.

6.1 Dual Criminality

In the context of mutual legal assistance, dual criminality refers to the principle that the criminal offence underlying the request for assistance must be a crime in both the requesting state and the recipient state. Traditionally, the concept of dual criminality required that both the requesting and the recipient country had legislation on the same crime with the same elements. Over time, dual criminality requirements have gradually been loosened. Many countries nowadays take a 'conduct-based' approach to dual criminality, that is, if the underlying conduct is a crime in both countries, the requirement of dual criminality is met.

UNCAC takes a broad, conduct-based approach to dual criminality as follows:

> *'the conduct underlying the offence for which assistance is sought is a criminal offence under the laws of both states parties'. (Article 43.2 of the UNCAC)*

Take, for example, a situation in which a counterparty to UNCAC is investigating foreign bribery of an official of another UNCAC party. In this case, the dual criminality requirement is met if the bribery would be an offence under domestic regulation. Therefore, it is not necessary that the country under investigation recognises foreign bribery as an offence.

End of Chapter Questions

Think of an answer for each question and refer to the appropriate section for confirmation

1. Are bribery and corruption exactly the same things?
   Answer reference: Section 1.1

2. Does the UK Bribery Act 2010 cover the overseas associates of a parent UK-based company?
   Answer reference: Section 2.1

3. Are only acts of giving and taking a bribe offences under the Bribery Act?
   Answer reference: Section 2.2

4. What is meant by 'facilitation payments'?
   Answer reference: Section 2.2.1

5. Is an organisation liable for acts of associated persons?
   Answer reference: Section 2.4

6. What is meant by adequate procedures?
   Answer reference: Section 2.5

7. What are the six principles of bribery prevention?
   Answer reference: Section 2.6.1

8. Name four differences between the Bribery Act and the Foreign Corrupt Practices Act (FCPA).
   Answer reference: Section 3.2

9. What is embezzlement?
   Answer reference: Section 4.1.1

10. What is abuse of office by public office holders?
    Answer reference: Section 4.1.3

11. Is illicit enrichment a criminal act?
    Answer reference: Section 4.1.4

12. What are four aspects of United Nations Convention Against Corruption (UNCAC)?
    Answer reference: Section 5.1.1

13. Have only European countries adopted the Organisation for Economic Co-operation and Development (OECD) Anti-Bribery Convention?
    Answer reference: Section 5.1.2

14. What is the role of the United Nations Development Programme (UNDP) in combating corruption?
    Answer reference: Section 5.1.5

15. What is mutual legal assistance?
    Answer reference: Section 6

16. What is the concept of dual criminality?
    Answer reference: Section 6.1

Chapter Five
Fraud and Market Abuse

1. Fraud	97
2. Types of Fraud	98
3. Market Abuse	102
4. The Sarbanes-Oxley Act 2002	108

This syllabus area will provide approximately 4 of the 50 examination questions

1. Fraud

1.1 Three Classes of Fraud

Learning Objective

5.1.1 Know the three classes of fraud defined in the UK Fraud Act (2006): false representation; failing to disclose information; abuse of position

Section 1 of the Fraud Act 2006 creates a new general offence of fraud and introduces the three possible ways of committing it. The Act provides a statutory definition of the offence, defining it in practical terms that arise in three situations (Sections 2, 3 and 4) all of which are underpinned by some form of dishonest behaviour.

Under the Fraud Act, there is no need to prove that an actual gain or loss was achieved, making it primarily an offence of conduct rather than a result crime. It is important to note that the offences under the Act are almost entirely offender-focused as long as the requisite element of dishonest intention exists.

The three practical situations identified in the Act are; fraud by false representation, failing to disclose information and abuse of position:

- **Section 2: Fraud by false representation** is defined as being if a person dishonestly makes a false representation, and, by making the false representation intends to:
    - make a gain for themselves or another, or
    - cause loss to another or to expose another to a risk of loss.

  To commit an offence, the defendant must have not only dishonestly made a false representation but have made that representation intending to either make a gain or expose somebody to loss or risk of loss.
- **Section 3: Fraud by failing to disclose information** is defined as:
    a. a person failing to disclose any information to a third party when they are under a legal duty to disclose such information
    b. intending to make a gain for himself or another, or to cause loss to another or to expose another to a risk of loss.
- **Section 4: Fraud by abuse of position** applies to a person who occupies a position where he is expected to safeguard or not to act against, the financial interests of another person, abusing that position, with the intention to make a gain for themselves or another, or to cause loss to another or to expose another to a risk of loss. This includes cases where the abuse consisted of an omission rather than an overt act (Section 4 (2)).

In all three classes of fraud, the Act requires that for the person to be guilty of fraud, they must have acted dishonestly, and with the intent of making a gain for themselves or anyone else, or inflicting a loss (or a risk of loss) on another. The references to 'gain' and 'loss' in Sections 2 to 4 of the Fraud Act 2006 are to be read in conjunction with Section 5 of the Act where both terms are explained. The Act not only applies to both tangible and intangible property but also to services.

It also established two other indictable offences, which are; the possession of articles for use in frauds (Section 6) and the making or supplying of articles for use in frauds (Section 7). Sections 6 and 7 carry their own respective punishments that can lead to imprisonment of up to ten years or to a fine (or to both).

Section 11 makes it an offence to obtain services when it is known that payment cannot be made or where there is no intent to make payment for the services.

2. Types of Fraud

Learning Objective

5.2.1 Know common examples of types of fraudulent activity: identity fraud and identity theft; cyber attacks; computer hacks; malware; application fraud; 419 fraud; account takeover; money mules; authorised payment fraud; smurfing

5.2.2 Know the difference between internal and external fraud

In November 2018, the FCA published their first annual financial crime data analysis intended to provide intelligence on the threats and trends firms are facing. More than 2,000 firms including all UK-based banks and building societies were required to complete the survey which provides a collective industry view of the risk criminal activity poses to society and how firms are responding. The main types of fraud found in the analysis are included in this section.

2.1 Identity Theft and Identity Fraud

Identity theft occurs when a fraudster has sufficient information about a person's identity (eg, name, date of birth, current/previous addresses) to commit identity fraud. The person subject to identity theft can be alive or dead. Identity theft can lead to fraud which may have a direct impact on a person's finances and could make it difficult to obtain loans, credit cards, or mortgages.

Identity fraud is described as the use of a stolen identity in criminal activity to obtain goods or services by deception such as:

- opening bank accounts
- obtaining credit cards, loans and state benefits
- ordering goods
- taking over existing accounts
- taking out mobile phone contracts, or
- obtaining genuine documents, such as passports and driving licences.

Stealing a person's identity is not in itself identity fraud. Identity fraud only occurs when the stolen identity is used for any of the above activities.

2.2 Cyber Attacks

Cyber attacks occur in different ways, but all are aimed at obtaining access to valuable personal details. A cyber attack is an assault using one or more computers targeting other computers. It can be used to steal data or to use an infected computer to launch other attacks. Cyber crime includes the use of malware, phishing, ransomware and distributed denial-of-service (DDoS) attacks as explained in more detail below:

- **Malware** – any program or file that is harmful for the user. Malware includes viruses, worms, Trojan horses and spyware.
- **Phishing** – a means to access valuable personal details, such as usernames and passwords. Phishing attacks are counterfeit communications, such as emails, text messages, or letters purporting to be authentic communications originating from legitimate institutions. Embedded links within the communication direct to a hoax website where the recipient is to log in, thus, revealing their user-ID and password. Once personal details have been obtained, they can be used to commit fraud including identity theft and bank fraud.
- **Ransomware** – a form of malware that encrypts the victim's files and demands a ransom payment to restore access.
- **DDoS attack** – flooding of the target with traffic from multiple systems to attempt to disrupt normal traffic to a server.

2.3 Computer Hacks

Computer hackers break into computers and computer networks to be able to gain sensitive and personal information that can be used to commit fraud. It is worth noting fraud has been committed if money has been lost. The most common forms of computer hacking are DDoS attacks, phishing and malware.

2.4 Malware

Malware is software designed to be placed on someone's computer or other device to ensure that it does not work as it is supposed to be. In some cases, it may also collect information or data saved on the device to pass on for fraudulent use. Malware is also known as ransomware, viruses, worms, Trojan horses, adware, scareware and crimeware.

Ransomware is a specific type of malware which stops the owner or user from accessing their computer or device until the ransom demand is met.

2.5 Application Fraud

Application fraud occurs when an account is opened in another person's name using fake or stolen documents. The account is then used to withdraw cash, get credit, apply for loans or other fraudulent activities.

2.6 419 Fraud

419 frauds are one of the most common types of 'confidence trick' being used in the market. The scam typically involves promising the victim a significant share of a large sum of money, for which the fraudster requires a small upfront payment, ostensibly to pay for 'fees'. If a victim makes the payment, the fraudster either invents a series of further fees for the victim, or simply disappears. The scam has been promoted using fax and traditional mail but now use of the internet is more common.

The number '419' refers to the section of the Nigerian Criminal Code dealing with fraud; historically many of these schemes have originated in Nigeria. The nature of the scam also results in these schemes being known as 'advance fee frauds'.

More recently, fraudsters have also used fake but seemingly authentic/trustworthy accounts on social networks to coax potential victims to agree to the deal. The scammer often sends one or more false documents bearing official government stamps and seals. The use of fraudulent cheques and money orders is also common in many advance-fee frauds, such as lottery and inheritance scams.

2.7 Account Takeover

Account takeover occurs when someone poses as a genuine customer, gains control of their accounts and makes unauthorised transactions. This could relate to any type of account including bank accounts, credit cards, emails or other service providers.

Access to online bank accounts is typically gained via phishing, spyware or malware. It is worth noting that in the context of account takeover, fraud has only been committed if money has been lost.

2.8 Money Mules

Money mules are persons who agree to share their bank details so that cash can be deposited into their accounts. They are subsequently given instructions to transfer the vast majority of the money to another account. They will keep some of the funds as 'payment' for their services. The activity of money mules constitutes money laundering and permits the placement of funds into the financial system. They typically do not have a criminal background, and are often recruited via social media platforms. According to the 2018 annual fraud report of the UK's Fraud Prevention Service, 50% of money mules are under the age of 25.

2.9 Authorised Payment Fraud

Authorised payment fraud or authorised push payment (APP) fraud occurs when an individual is deceived into sending a payment to a bank account controlled by the fraudster under false pretences. Attacks on individuals include sending invoices that look exactly like an invoice the individual expects, account takeovers (see 2.7), or acting on a fake email from a tradesperson or contractor instead of the actual request for payment. Other forms of APP fraud include the targeting of property transactions by intercepting a solicitor's email, and fake invoice fraud.

2.10 Smurfing

Smurfing is used in the depositing of large amounts of illegitimate money by breaking them up into smaller transactions below the reporting threshold. Smurfing occurs in all three stages of money laundering. In the placement phase, examples of smurfing include depositing cash into bank accounts, gambling, or buying smaller amounts of other currencies. In the layering phase, smurfing occurs with the transfer of funds to other accounts or to invest in a variety of financial instruments. In the integration stage, smurfing can, for example, occur when the smurf purchases valuables and gives them to the criminal.

2.11 Internal and External Fraud

Fraud can originate either internally or externally. Internal fraud originates from inside the organisation and includes actions taken by employees such as:

- theft of cash or stock
- theft from other employees
- not charging (or undercharging) friends, family or accomplices
- not considering bad credit for friends, family or accomplices, or
- approving loans on favourable conditions to family, friends or others that would otherwise not have been approved.

Companies are most at risk of internal fraud from employees who work long hours, regularly return to work after hours, and are unusually inquisitive about the company's systems. Companies should be particularly concerned about employees that resist taking annual leave, avoid having others assist them, or suddenly resign.

External fraud originates from outside the organisation and is committed by, for example, customers, suppliers, impersonators or hackers. Examples of customer fraud include:

- credit card fraud
- cheque fraud, or
- obtaining loans on the basis of incorrect or incomplete information.

Fraud by suppliers include, for example:

- invoicing for services and goods that have not been supplied
- providing kickbacks in return for being selected to supply goods or services
- invoices submitted by non-existing vendors, or
- supplying lower quality than agreed.

3. Market Abuse

Learning Objective

5.3.1 Know the international legislation for combating market abuse: the EU Market Abuse Regulation (2014) (MAR): the Dodd-Frank Wall Street Reform and Consumer Protection Act (Dodd-Frank) and the Volcker Rule; FATF Risk-based Approach Guidance for the Securities Sector (2018); ESMA guidance

3.1 International Initiatives

3.1.1 The EU Market Abuse Regulation (MAR) 2014

The EU Market Abuse Regulation (MAR) came into effect on 3 July 2016. It aims to increase market integrity and investor protection, enhancing the attractiveness of securities markets (such as the London Stock Exchange (LSE)) for capital-raising. MAR applies to:

a. financial instruments admitted to trading on a regulated market or for which a request for admission to trading on a regulated market has been made
b. financial instruments traded on a multilateral trading facility (MTF), admitted to trading on an MTF, or for which a request for admission to trading on an MTF has been made
c. financial instruments traded on an organised trading facility (OTF)
d. financial instruments not covered by point (a), (b) or (c), the price or value of which depends on or has an effect on the price or value of a financial instrument referred to in those points, including, but not limited to, credit default swaps and contracts for difference.

According to the Financial Conduct Authority (FCA):

'MAR strengthens the previous UK market abuse framework by extending its scope to new markets, new platforms and new behaviours. It contains prohibitions of insider dealing, unlawful disclosure of inside information and market manipulation, and provisions to prevent and detect these'.

MAR contains disclosure obligations, which state that inside information must be made available publicly as soon as possible. Delays are allowed, subject to certain requirements and notification to the FCA. Issuers must also maintain 'insider lists' of those who have access to inside information.

Some participants in the markets are required to monitor, detect and report suspicious transactions and orders to the FCA. This is a separate requirement to report suspicious transactions to those contained in anti-money laundering and combating the financing of terrorism (AML/CFT) legislation. There is also a provision in MAR requiring firms and regulators (such as the FCA) to receive **whistleblowing** notifications about suspected market abuse. MAR allows members states to give financial incentives to whistleblowers in some circumstances, but the UK has not implemented such a scheme.

3.1.2 The Dodd-Frank Wall Street Reform and Consumer Protection Act (Dodd-Frank) and the Volcker Rule

Dodd-Frank Act

In 2010, after a lengthy legislative process, the US Senate approved the Dodd-Frank Wall Street Reform and Consumer Protection Act. The stated aim of the legislation was:

> '...to promote the financial stability of the United States by improving accountability and transparency in the financial system, to end "too big to fail", to protect the American taxpayer by ending bailouts, to protect consumers from abusive financial services practices, and for other purposes'.

It changed the existing regulatory structure in the US. It created a host of new agencies (while merging and removing others) in an effort to streamline the regulatory process.

It creates an extensive new regulatory framework for swaps and security-based swaps, capturing substantially all derivatives transactions that previously were exempt from regulation under the Commodity Futures Modernization Act (CFMA). Title VII sets forth the new legislative framework for derivatives. The Act contemplates mandatory clearing and trading on regulated facilities for many derivatives contracts, with an exception for non-financial end users.

Swap dealers and major swap participants are subject, among other things, to capital and margin requirements, business conduct rules and special duties in their dealings with governmental entities, the Employee Retirement Income Security Act (ERISA) and governmental plans and endowments. While many end users will not be directly regulated, they often will be affected indirectly as their counterparties become subject to new requirements, with respect to margin rules.

Other significant provisions include the swaps 'pushout' rule, collateral segregation and real-time swap transaction reporting requirements, position limits and large trader reporting, and the application of the securities laws to security-based swaps.

Dodd-Frank (Volcker Rule)

Financial regulators have been considering imposing restrictions on proprietary trading by financial institutions for a long time, The Dodd-Frank Wall Street Reform and Consumer Protection Act includes the Volcker Rule, which limits proprietary trading and sponsorship of hedge funds by banks.

This rule prohibits a bank, or institution that owns a bank, from engaging in proprietary trading that is not arrived at from a relationship with a client, or from owning or investing in a hedge fund or private equity fund, as well as limiting banks' liabilities. The implementation date of the rule was delayed until July 2014. Revisions to the Volcker Rule in the US meant that banks are permitted to invest up to 3% of their Tier 1 capital in private equity and hedge funds.

Proprietary trading in treasury bonds and bonds in other government-backed or municipal entities is also excluded. This was changed as the original idea would have caused problems globally as the US banks are active primary government bond dealers in markets around the globe. Proprietary trading is seen by many as a conflict of interest with clients, since the firm may be betting/taking positions which contradict client positions. Most banks, not just US ones, have scaled back their proprietary trading desks over the years since the financial crisis started in 2007.

3.1.3 FATF Risk-Based Approach Guidance for the Securities Sector

The FATF Recommendations follow a risk-based approach, which means that supervisors and institutions identify, assess and understand the risks to which they are exposed and implement the most appropriate risk mitigants. It permits firms and regulators to focus their attention and resources on areas where their risks are highest.

The guidance is specifically aimed at securities providers setting out key characteristics of securities transactions that can create opportunities for criminals, and measures that can be put in place to address such vulnerabilities. The measures that are implemented within a firm should be in line with the nature, size and complexity of the business, and the guidance highlights that it is the responsibility of senior management to implement a culture of compliance.

Within any securities business, the nature of the business relationship between securities provider, intermediaries, and underlying customers affects how risks will be managed. The guidance clarifies that it is the responsibility of the firm to take into consideration whether a customer acts on their own behalf or as an intermediary when assessing the type and extent of due diligence required. Understanding the customer base of an intermediary can provide useful insights into the risk associated with the intermediary itself.

The guidance emphasises the importance of ongoing transaction monitoring, and advocates a group-level approach to the assessment of risks.

3.1.4 European Securities and Markets Authority (ESMA) Guidance

The European Securities and Markets Authority (ESMA) has issued technical standards on the MAR, covering prospectus-related matters. The technical standards cover:

- contents of notification of financial instruments, as well as the timing, format and template of submissions
- conditions, restrictions, disclosure and reporting obligations for buyback programmes and stabilisation measures
- arrangements, procedures and record-keeping requirements related to market soundings
- establishment, maintenance and termination of accepted market practices
- arrangements, systems, procedures and notification templates to report suspicious orders and transactions
- technical means for the public disclosure of inside information and its delay
- format of insider lists and the format for updates
- format and template for the notification of managers' transactions, and
- technical arrangements for the objective presentation of recommendations.

3.2 Abusive Behaviours

Learning Objective

5.3.2 Know behaviours that constitute market abuse

5.3.3 Know the insider dealing provisions of the UK's Criminal Justice Act 1993 (Part 5, Section 52)

5.3.4 Know the offences relating to financial services provisions of the UK's Financial Services Act 2012 (Part 7, Sections 89, 90 and 91)

5.3.5 Know how market abuse is detected

3.2.1 Market Abuse

Firms and individuals participating in the financial markets are required to observe certain minimum standards of conduct, and should not be involved in market abuse. The types of behaviour that may constitute market abuse include but are not restricted to:

- unlawful disclosure
- manipulating transactions
- manipulating devices
- dissemination
- misleading behaviour and distortion.

Examples of these behaviours include:

1. **Insider dealing** – when an insider deals, or tries to deal, or encourages another to deal or not deal, on the basis of inside information.
2. **Unlawful disclosure** – where an insider improperly discloses inside information to another person.
3. **Manipulating transactions** – trading, or placing orders to trade, that gives a false or misleading impression of the supply of, or demand for, one or more investments, raising the price of the investment to an abnormal or artificial level. This is also known as 'spoofing'.
4. **Manipulating devices** – trading, or placing orders to trade, which employ fictitious devices or any other form of deception or contrivance.
5. **Dissemination** – giving out information that conveys a false or misleading impression about an investment or the issuer of an investment where the person doing this knows the information to be false or misleading.
6. **Misleading behaviour and distortion** – behaviour that gives a false or misleading impression of either the supply of, or demand for, an investment or behaviour that otherwise distorts the market in an investment.

In addition to the civil offences described under MAR, criminal market manipulation is an offence under Sections 89–91 of the Financial Service Act 2012, and the FCA will investigate these offences when appropriate.

3.2.2 Criminal Justice Act 1993

Despite the introduction of the MAR regime and the FCA Code of Conduct described above, previous insider dealing provisions remain on the statute book in the UK. Section 52 of the Criminal Justice Act 1993 creates two relevant offences. The first relates to dealing on the basis of inside information, the second to disclosing inside information or encouraging another to deal. The deals must either take place on a regulated market, or through, or by a professional intermediary.

Inside information is specific information relating to a particular security, which is not public and is such that if it were made public it would have a significant impact on the price. The individual dealing must 'know' that they are in possession of inside information from an inside source (a person who is a director, shareholder or employee of the firm in question, or has the information by virtue of some other employment, office or profession). The requirement for the prosecutor to prove knowledge makes the offence difficult to prove.

3.2.3 Offences Relating to Financial Services

The UK Financial Services Act of 2012, Part 7, considers misleading statements, misleading impressions and misleading statements in relation to benchmarks as offences related to financial services.

Misleading Statements

The offence of misleading statements applies if a person:

a. makes a statement which they know to be materially false or misleading
b. makes a statement which is materially false or misleading, being reckless as to whether it is, or
c. dishonestly conceals any material facts whether in connection with a statement made by them or otherwise.

The offence is committed when the person makes the statement or conceals the facts with the intention to induce another person to:

a. enter into or offer to enter into, or to refrain from entering or offering to enter into, a relevant agreement, or
b. exercise, or refrain from exercising, any rights conferred by a relevant investment.

In order for the offence to be committed, there has to be a link to the UK such that either the statement is made from the UK, the person to whom the inducement is intended is in the UK, or the agreement is or would be exercised in the UK.

It is a defence for a person to show the statement was made under the following circumstances:

a. price stabilising rules
b. control of information rules, or
c. the relevant provisions related to exemptions for buy-back programmes and stabilisation of financial instruments.

Misleading Impressions

Providing a false or misleading impression as to the market in, or price or value of any relevant investment is an offence if the person intends to create the impression, and the impression is intended to induce another person to acquire, dispose of, subscribe to, or underwrite the investments or to refrain from doing so; and/or the person:

1. knows the impression is false or misleading or is reckless as to whether it is, and
2. intends to produce a gain for themselves or another, or a loss to another person.

The terms gain and loss extend only to the gain or loss in money or property of any kind whether it be temporary or permanent. A gain includes a gain resulting from keeping something as well as obtaining something and a loss includes losing something one has as well as not getting something.

In order for the offence to be committed, the act is done or the course of conduct is engaged in the UK, or the false or misleading impression is created there.

The defence against the offence of misleading impressions may apply if the accused can show that they:

1. reasonably believed that their conduct would not create an impression that was false or misleading
2. acted on, or engaged in the conduct to stabilise the price of the investment and conform price stabilising rules
3. acted on, or engaged in the conduct conform the control of information rules, or
4. acted on, or engaged in the conduct conform the exemptions for buy-back programmes and stabilisation of financial instruments.

Misleading Statements in Relation to Benchmarks

An offence is committed in relation to a benchmark if the person making the statement to a second person does so:

1. in the course of arrangements for the setting of a relevant benchmark
2. intending for the statement to be used for the purpose of the setting of the relevant benchmark, and
3. knowing the statement is false or misleading or being reckless as to whether it is.

In order for the offence to be committed, the statement has to be made in or from the UK or to a person in the UK. It is a defence to show the statement was made in conformity with:

1. price stabilising rules
2. control of information rules, or
3. exemptions for buy-back programmes and stabilisation of financial instruments.

It is an offence to engage in a course of conduct which creates a false or misleading impression of the price or value of any investment or the interest appropriate to a transaction if:

1. the person intends to create the impression
2. the impression may affect the setting of a relevant benchmark
3. the person knows the impression is false or misleading or is reckless as to whether it is, and
4. the person knows the impression may affect the setting of a relevant benchmark.

In order for the offence to be committed, the act is done or the course of conduct is engaged in, the UK, or the false impression is created there. It is a defence to show that the person acted or engaged in the conduct:

1. for the purpose of stabilising the price of investments and in conformity with price stabilising rules
2. to confirm the control of information rules, or
3. to confirm the exemptions for buy-back programmes and stabilisation of financial instruments

3.2.4 Detecting Market Abuse

Firms have the responsibility to detect market abuse, and respond quickly to ensure it does not continue. Due to the fact that the financial markets are highly automated, the tools used to detect market abuse are also highly automated and include surveillance software and hardware to identify irregular patterns, unusual transaction sizes, and unusual price levels.

Regulators typically undertake independent surveillance of financial markets to identify market abuse. Their surveillance generally includes analysing transaction reporting data, order book data, benchmark submission and other market data to spot any potential market abuse.

4. The Sarbanes-Oxley Act 2002

Learning Objective

5.4.1 Know the main provisions of the Sarbanes-Oxley Act (2002)

4. The Main Provisions of the Sarbanes-Oxley Act (2002)

There are primarily two approaches to corporate governance which are followed throughout the world:

1. **Rules-based approach** – instils the code into law with appropriate penalties for transgression.
2. **Principles-based approach** – requires the company to adhere to the spirit rather than the letter of the code. The company must either comply with the code or explain why it has not, through reports to the appropriate body and to its shareholders.

The US follows a rules-based approach and that is enshrined into law by Sarbanes-Oxley (SOX) 2002. The UK and most other common law countries follow a principles-based approach where adherence is mostly part of the stock exchange's listing requirements and deviations, if any, have to be explained by the company through reporting requirements.

SOX is a US federal law and is also known as the *Public Company Accounting Reform and Investor Protection Act* (in the Senate) and *Corporate and Auditing Accountability and Responsibility Act* (in the House). The SEC implements SOX.

It was enacted against a backdrop of and as a reaction to a number of major corporate and accounting scandals, notably including those affecting Enron and WorldCom which cost investors billions of dollars and shook public confidence in the US securities markets. SOX set new or expanded requirements for all US public company boards, management and public accounting firms. Some provisions of the Act also apply to privately held companies, for example the wilful destruction of evidence to impede a Federal investigation.

The Act contains eleven titles, or sections, ranging from additional corporate board responsibilities to criminal penalties. The SEC created a new, quasi-public agency, the Public Company Accounting Oversight Board (PCAOB) charged with overseeing, regulating, inspecting, and disciplining accounting firms in their roles as auditors of public companies. The Act also covers issues such as auditor independence, corporate governance, internal control assessment, and enhanced financial disclosure.

1. **PCAOB – Title I** creates independent oversight of public accounting firms providing audit services ('auditors'). It also creates a central oversight board tasked with registering auditors, defining the specific processes and procedures for compliance audits, inspecting and policing conduct and quality control, and enforcing compliance with the specific mandates of SOX.
2. **Auditor Independence – Title II** establishes standards for external auditor independence, to limit conflicts of interest. It also addresses new auditor approval requirements, audit partner rotation, and auditor reporting requirements. It restricts auditing companies from providing non-audit services (eg, consulting) for the same clients.
3. **Corporate Responsibility – Title III** mandates senior executives to take responsibility for the accuracy and completeness of corporate financial reports. It defines the interaction of external auditors and corporate audit committees, and specifies the responsibility of corporate officers for the accuracy and validity of corporate financial reports.
4. **Enhanced Financial Disclosures – Title IV** describes enhanced reporting requirements for financial transactions, including off-balance-sheet transactions, proforma figures and stock transactions of corporate officers. It requires internal controls for ensuring the accuracy of financial reports and disclosures, and mandates both audits and reports on those controls.
5. **Analyst Conflicts of Interest – Title V** includes measures designed to help restore investor confidence in the reporting of securities analysts. It defines the codes of conduct for securities analysts and requires disclosure of knowable conflicts of interest.
6. **Commission Resources and Authority – Title VI** defines practices to restore investor confidence in securities analysts. It also defines the SEC's authority to censure or bar securities professionals from practice and defines conditions under which a person can be barred from practicing as a broker, adviser, or dealer.
7. **Studies and Reports – Title VII** requires the Comptroller General and the SEC to perform various studies and report their findings.
8. **Corporate and Criminal Fraud Accountability – Title VIII** is also referred to as the Corporate and Criminal Fraud Accountability Act of 2002. It describes specific criminal penalties for manipulation, destruction or alteration of financial records or other interference with investigations, while providing certain protections for whistleblowers.
9. **White Collar Crime Penalty Enhancement – Title IX** section is also called the *White Collar Crime Penalty Enhancement Act of 2002*. This section increases the criminal penalties associated with white-collar crimes and conspiracies. It recommends stronger sentencing guidelines and specifically adds failure to certify corporate financial reports as a criminal offence.

10. **Corporate Tax Returns – Title X** obliges the chief executive officer to sign the company tax return.
11. **Corporate Fraud Accountability – Title XI** identifies corporate fraud and records tampering as criminal offences and joins those offences to specific penalties. It also revises sentencing guidelines and strengthens their penalties.

SOX created the perception that stricter financial governance laws are needed, which prompted new SOX-type regulations also being enacted in other jurisdictions such as Canada (2002), Germany (2002), South Africa (2002), France (2003), Australia (2004), India (2005), Japan (2006) and Italy (2006).

End of Chapter Questions

Think of an answer for each question and refer to the appropriate section for confirmation

1. What are the three classes of fraud found in the Fraud Act 2006?
   Answer reference: Section 1.1

2. For an offence of fraud to have occurred, is an actual gain or loss necessary?
   Answer reference: Section 1.1

3. How are identity fraud and identity theft related?
   Answer reference: Section 2.1

4. What are the different types of cybercrime?
   Answer reference: Section 2.2

5. Describe an account takeover.
   Answer reference: Section 2.7

6. What is 'smurfing'?
   Answer reference: Section 2.10

7. What is the difference between internal and external fraud?
   Answer reference: Section 2.11

8. List the different international initiatives?
   Answer reference: Section 3.1

9. What types of conduct are regarded by the Financial Conduct Authority (FCA) as abusive behaviours?
   Answer reference: Section 3.2.1

10. What are the two insider dealing offences found in the Criminal Justice Act 1993?
    Answer reference: Section 3.2.1

11. What are the defences against misleading statements?
    Answer reference: Section 3.2.3

12. List the sections of the Sarbanes-Oxley Act 2002.
    Answer reference: Section 4.1

Chapter Six
Tax Evasion

1. Tax Evasion   115
2. Criminal Finances Act (2017)   120

This syllabus area will provide approximately 4 of the 50 examination questions

1. Tax Evasion

1.1 Tax Evasion and Tax Avoidance

Learning Objective

6.1.1 Know the difference between tax evasion and tax avoidance

6.1.2 Know international EU and US approaches to improving tax compliance: the Foreign Account Tax Compliance Act (FATCA); Crown Dependencies and Overseas Territories (CDOT) regulation; OECD's Common Reporting Standard (CRS) for the Automatic Exchange of Financial Information; EU's list of non-cooperative tax jurisdictions

6.1.3 Understand the difference between personal and corporate liability

6.1.4 Know how tax evasion is detected

Tax avoidance is defined as the use of legally permissible methods to modify an individual's or an organisation's financial situation to lower the amount of tax owed. This is generally accomplished by claiming the permissible deductions, credits and allowances.

Most taxpayers use this form of tax reduction. For example, in most countries individuals who contribute to pension plans with pre-tax funds are engaging in tax avoidance because the amount of taxes paid on the funds when they are withdrawn is usually less than the amount that the individual would otherwise owe at the time of contribution. Furthermore, retirement plans allow taxpayers to defer paying taxes until a much later date.

Tax evasion on the other hand is an illegal practice where a person, organisation or corporation intentionally avoids paying their true tax liability. Those caught evading taxes are generally subject to criminal charges and substantial penalties.

Tax-aggressive strategies fall into a grey area. Laws known as general anti-avoidance rule (GAAR) statutes which prohibit 'tax-aggressive' avoidance have been passed in several developed countries, including Canada, Australia, New Zealand, South Africa, Norway and Hong Kong. Though the specifics may vary according to jurisdiction, these rules invalidate tax avoidance which is technically legal but not for a business purpose or in violation of the spirit of the tax code.

1.2 International EU and US Approaches to Improving Tax Compliance

1.2.1 The Foreign Account Tax Compliance Act (FATCA)

Under US tax law, US persons (regardless of country of residence) are generally required to report and pay US federal income tax on income from all sources. Regardless of residence location and dual citizenships, they are simultaneously required to self-report their non-US assets.

The US is almost unique in taxing not only non-resident citizens but also non-resident 'US Persons for Tax Purposes'. The US law requires US citizens living abroad to pay US taxes on foreign income if the foreign tax is less than US tax.

The US's Internal Revenue Service defines the terms 'US citizen' and 'US person' as:

US citizen:

- an individual born in the US
- an individual whose parent is a US citizen
- a former alien who has been naturalised as a US citizen
- an individual born in Puerto Rico
- an individual born in Guam, or
- an individual born in the US Virgin Islands.

US person:

- a citizen or resident of the US
- a partnership created or organised in the US or under the law of the US or of any state, or the District of Columbia
- a corporation created or organised in the US or under the law of the US or of any state, or the District of Columbia
- any estate or trust other than a foreign estate or foreign trust, or
- any other person that is not a foreign person.

The Foreign Account Tax Compliance Act (FATCA) is a US federal law that is intended to detect and deter the evasion of tax by US persons who hide money outside the US. FATCA is also used by government to detect US persons and their assets and to enable cross-checking with self-reported assets. The data generated by FATCA reports is used to cross-check a US person's self-reported data at the Financial Crimes Enforcement Network (FinCEN). FATCA is intended to lead to detection of persons who have not self-reported their true assets or declared their incomes.

Under FATCA, non-US foreign financial institutions (FFIs) are required to report assets and identify information related to suspected US persons using them.

1.2.2 Crown Dependencies and Overseas Territories (CDOT)

All the crown dependencies and overseas territories (CDOT) entered into automatic tax information exchange agreements with the UK in the Autumn of 2013. On 13 March 2014, HMRC published the International Tax Compliance (Crown Dependencies and Gibraltar) Regulations 2014, outlining the obligations of reporting financial institutions in relation to the UK agreements with the Isle of Man, Jersey, Guernsey and Gibraltar. These regulations cover the definition of reporting financial institutions, reportable accounts, identification and reporting obligations, as well as penalties.

Financial institutions in Jersey, Guernsey and the Isle of Man (the Crown Dependencies) and the Overseas Territories of Anguilla, Bermuda, the British Virgin Islands, the Cayman Islands, Gibraltar, Montserrat and the Turks and Caicos Islands (the Overseas Territories) will automatically provide information relating to the financial affairs in respect of UK resident clients from 2014 onwards. This is sometimes referred to as 'UK FATCA', as its framework resembles the US's FATCA regime.

Following the model provided by the US FATCA, the UK Chancellor of the Exchequer announced enhanced automatic exchange of information agreements with the Crown Dependencies as part of a broader package of tax measures in the 2013 budget. The package that was agreed with the UK included:

- An **intergovernmental agreement** (IGA) providing for automatic exchange of information about UK residents with accounts in the Crown Dependencies (and residents of the Crown Dependencies with accounts in the UK).
- An **alternative reporting arrangement** (in the IGA) for UK resident non-domiciled individuals (RNDs).
- A **tax disclosure facility** to enable those with irregularities in their tax affairs to correct matters with HMRC in advance of the exchange of information.

The IGAs that the UK has entered into with the Crown Dependencies (and Gibraltar) are fully reciprocal and therefore require domestic legislation in both the UK and the Crown Dependencies to implement the agreements. For the UK, regulations implementing these IGAs, the *International Tax Compliance (Crown Dependencies and Gibraltar) Regulations 2014*, came into force on 31 March 2014.

The package of measures negotiated with the Overseas Territories closely follows those negotiated with the Crown dependencies, with respect to the information to be exchanged and the proposed reporting timelines.

Coverage

CDOT financial institutions will undertake due diligence to identify any reportable accounts in existence on or after 30 June 2014. These are financial accounts maintained by the institutions where the account holder is either a UK-specified person (essentially a UK-resident individual, partnership or unlisted company) or is a non-UK entity the controlling persons of which include one or more UK specified persons. Controlling persons are individuals who exercise control over an entity. In the case of a trust, this will mean the settlor, the trustees, the protector (if any), the beneficiaries or class of beneficiaries, and any other individual exercising ultimate effective control over the trust.

From 2016 onwards, the information will be exchanged by the tax authorities by 30 September following the end of the calendar year in question and financial institutions must provide the information on reportable accounts to their local tax office by 31 May/1 June following the end of the calendar year in question.

1.2.3 OECD Common Reporting Standards (CRS) for the Exchange of Financial Information

On 6 May 2014, 47 countries tentatively agreed on common reporting standards (CRSs) to share information on residents' assets and incomes automatically in conformation with the standard. Until now, the parties to most treaties which are in place for sharing information have shared information upon request, which has not proved effective in preventing tax evasion. The new system is supposed to automatically and systematically transfer all the relevant information. On 29 October 2014, 51 jurisdictions signed an agreement to automatically exchange information based on Article 6 of the Convention on Mutual Administrative Assistance in Tax Matters.

The OECD CRS is a major step towards an internationally coordinated approach to disclosure of income earned by individuals and organisations. As a measure to counter tax evasion, it builds upon other information sharing legislation, such as FATCA and the EU Savings Directive. However, crucially, FATCA is much narrower in scope than the OECD standard for automatic exchange of information (AEoI).

The CRS, that is formally referred to as the standard for automatic exchange of financial account information, is, in practical terms, a framework of an information standard for the AEoI, developed in the context of the OECD.

The aim of this framework is for jurisdictions to obtain information from their financial institutions and automatically exchange that information with other jurisdictions on an annual basis. It sets out the financial account information to be exchanged. The financial institutions are required to report the different types of accounts and taxpayers covered, as well as the common due diligence procedures to be followed. These initiatives involve governments obtaining information from their financial institutions and exchanging data automatically with other nations. Financial institutions (and other investment entities) will have significant additional reporting responsibilities, in order to disclose details of their account holders, with potential penalties for those unable or unwilling to comply fully.

The legal basis for exchange of data is the Convention on Mutual Administrative Assistance in Tax Matters and the idea is based on the FATCA implementation agreements.

The AEoI consists of two regulations or agreements:

- **OECD Competent Authority Agreement (CAA)** is the bilateral agreement between jurisdictions that have signed up to the AEoI. The agreement is what allows for the competent authorities (in most cases, this is the jurisdiction's tax authority) to exchange information.
- **OECD Common Reporting Standard (CRS)** sets out the baseline regulation to be adopted in the jurisdictions that have signed up to AEoI. It sets out who will be reporting, what will be reported and to some degree the format of the reporting. This could be seen as the minimal requirements for the regulations.

Financial information to be reported includes interest, dividends, account balance, income from certain insurance products and sales proceeds from financial assets. In gathering data, residency or tax residency within a country is the decisive factor, not citizenship. The CRS relies heavily on local anti-money laundering and KYC requirements, and on self-certification by account holders, although it includes some documentation remediation. The intention is to eventually have a single global standard.

1.2.4 EU List of Non-Cooperative Tax Jurisdictions

In order to promote good tax governance, the EU has compiled a list of non-cooperative tax jurisdictions. The list is the result of a thorough screening and dialogue process with non-EU countries to assess them against agreed criteria for good governance relating to tax transparency, fair taxation, the implementation of OECD Base Erosion Profit Shifting (BEPS) measures and substance requirements for zero-tax countries.

The list is not static, and as of 27 February 2020 contains the following jurisdictions:

- American Samoa
- Cayman Islands
- Fiji
- Guam
- Oman
- Palau
- Panama
- Samoa
- Seychelles
- Trinidad and Tobago
- US Virgin Islands, and
- Vanatu

1.2.5 Individual and Corporate Liability

The Criminal Finances Act 2017 amends the Proceeds of Crime Act (POCA) 2002. It includes the definition of terrorist property and creates two new corporate offences for tax evasion:

1. Failure to prevent facilitation of UK tax evasion offences.
2. Failure to prevent facilitation of foreign tax evasion offences.

The Act makes companies and partnerships criminally liable if they fail to prevent tax evasion either by a member of their staff or an external agent even if they were not involved or were not aware of it. The new rules target deliberate and dishonest behaviour, but do not introduce any new offences at the individual or personal level. Prosecution could result in both a conviction and unlimited penalties. Corporate liability is the extent to which a company is responsible for the actions of their employees, whereas personal liability refers to the extent to which a person is responsible. Under these rules, an associated person is defined as:

- an employee
- an agent, or
- any other person who performs services on behalf of the company

1.2.6 Detecting Tax Evasion

According to the OECD (www.oecd.org), two types of corporate tax evasion appear particularly wide spread: under-reporting of income and over-reporting of deductions. Although historically difficult to detect, advances in the technology used by tax authorities have resulted in increased detection.

Tax evasion by an individual follows from efforts to conceal assets by putting them in someone else's name, or depositing funds with banks in countries with strong secrecy laws such as Switzerland. In August 2013, the US Department of Justice (DOJ) and the Swiss Federal Department of Finance entered into a Non-Prosecution Agreement Programme providing Swiss banks with a way to resolve potential liabilities in the US for tax-related criminal offences, including tax evasion. Under the programme, banks are protected from prosecution in exchange for disclosing information related to undeclared accounts from US tax payers. Swiss banks were liable for penalties as a percentage of the maximum aggregate value of all US-related accounts held.

The penalty was calculated as the sum of:

- 20% of the aggregate value of all US-related accounts on 1 August 2008
- 30% of the aggregate value of all US-related accounts opened between 1 August 2008 and 28 February 2009, and
- 50% of the aggregate value of all US-related accounts opened after 28 February 2009.

The programme did not provide a better outcome than if banks would have worked directly with the DOJ. Around 25% of banks withdrew from the programme because the time given to make a decision was too short and the DOJ kept changing the requirements and the perception of bait-and-switch. Many banks exited US clients altogether, and the penalties did not correlate to the conduct of the bank.

Example

In December 2009, HSBC Swiss Private Bank announced they had paid a penalty to the US DOJ of $192m and admitted to helping US customers to hide more than $1bn in assets from taxation.

2. Criminal Finances Act (2017)

Learning Objective

6.2.1 Know the extra-territorial reach of the Act

6.2.2 Know the offences introduced by the Criminal Finances Act (2017)

6.2.3 Understand the liabilities corporate entities face from 'associated persons'

6.2.4 Understand strict liability and the meaning of 'reasonable procedures'

6.2.5 Understand the six principles for tax evasion prevention and their legal context

6.2.6 Know the maximum penalties under the Act

The Criminal Finances Act 2017 amends the POCA 2002. It has an extraterritorial reach and applies to all tax evasion activities, whether committed in the UK or elsewhere. The Act introduces the specific offence of strict liability.

In a legal context, strict liability refers to the liability that does not depend on actual negligence or intent to harm, but that is based on the breach of an absolute duty. It is an absolute duty of the directors and managers of any commercial organisation that undertakes a business or part of its business in the UK to ensure compliance with the Criminal Finances Act offence of failing to prevent tax evasion. It is a strict liability offence, which in practical terms means that if an associate, whether an employee or a third-party service provider, has failed to prevent tax evasion, the organisation concerned will be guilty of an offence. It is not a defence to say they were unaware of it.

2.1 Offences – UK Tax Evasion

A corporate or partnership is guilty of an offence if a person commits a UK tax evasion facilitation offence when acting in the capacity of a person associated with the corporate or partnership. A UK tax evasion offence is an offence:

a. of cheating the public revenue, or
b. under the law of any part of the UK consisting of being knowingly concerned in, or in taking steps with a view to, the fraudulent evasion of a tax.

A UK tax evasion facilitation offence is an offence under the law of any part of the UK consisting of:

a. being knowingly concerned in, or in taking steps with a view to, the fraudulent evasion of a tax by another person (but only when the other person has committed a UK tax evasion offence facilitated by that conduct)
b. aiding, abetting, counselling or procuring the commission of a UK tax evasion offence, or
c. being involved in the commission of an offence consisting of being knowingly concerned in, or in taking steps with a view to, the fraudulent evasion of a tax.

'Tax' means a tax imposed under the law of any part of the UK, including national insurance contributions under:

a. Part 1 of the Social Security Contributions and Benefits Act 1992, or
b. Part 1 of the Social Security Contributions and Benefits (Northern Ireland) Act 1992.

2.2 Offences – Foreign Tax Evasion

A foreign tax evasion offence relates to conduct which:

a. amounts to an offence under the law of a foreign country
b. relates to a breach of a duty relating to a tax imposed under the law of that country, and
c. would be regarded by the courts of any part of the UK as amounting to being knowingly concerned in, or in taking steps with a view to, the fraudulent evasion of that tax.

A foreign tax evasion facilitation offence relates to conduct which:

a. amounts to an offence under the law of a foreign country
b. relates to the commission by another person of a foreign tax evasion offence under that law, and
c. would, if the foreign tax evasion offence were a UK tax evasion offence, amount to a UK tax evasion facilitation offence.

A corporate or partnership is guilty of failing to prevent the facilitation of foreign tax evasion if, at any time, a person commits a foreign tax evasion facilitation offence when acting in the capacity of a person associated with the corporate or partnership, and any of they are:

a. incorporated, or formed, under the law of any part of the UK
b. carrying on business or part of a business in the UK (where business includes an undertaking)
c. any conduct constituting part of the foreign tax evasion facilitation offence takes place in the UK.

2.3 Defences and Penalties

The defence for the corporate or partnership is made by showing that:

- appropriate procedures are in place to prevent an associated person to commit a tax evasion facilitation offence, or
- it was not reasonable in all the circumstances to expect to have any prevention procedures in place.

The corporate or partnership, when found guilty, is liable to an unlimited fine and a criminal record:

- on conviction or indictment
- on summary conviction in England and Wales
- on summary conviction in Scotland or Northern Ireland, where the fine may not exceed the statutory maximum.

2.4 Guiding Principles to Prevent Tax Evasion

HMRC has formulated guidance around six principles for the prevention procedures a business should put in place. The six principles are defined as follows:

1. **Risk assessment** – assess the nature and extent of its exposure to the risk of associated persons.
2. **Proportionality** – risk-based prevention procedures will depend on the levels of control and supervision that a business is able to exercise over a person acting on its behalf and the proximity of that person.
3. **Top level commitment** – senior management should be committed to prevention and should foster a culture where facilitation of tax evasion is never acceptable.
4. **Due diligence** – procedures should take an appropriate and risk-based approach.
5. **Communication** (including training) – prevention policies and procedures are communicated throughout the business.
6. **Monitoring and review** – the business monitors and reviews prevention procedures and makes improvements where necessary.

Following these principles will assist a corporate or partnership in ensuring they have reasonable procedures in place to prevent an associated person committing a tax evasion facilitation offence.

End of Chapter Questions

Think of an answer for each question and refer to the appropriate section for confirmation

1. What is the difference between tax avoidance and tax evasion?
   Answer reference: Section 1.1

2. What is the US Foreign Account Tax Compliance Act (FATCA)?
   Answer reference: Section 1.2.1

3. Which countries are on the EU list of non-cooperative tax jurisdictions?
   Answer reference: Section 1.2.4

4. Which offences were introduced with the Criminal Finances Act 2017?
   Answer reference: Section 2

5. What are the six guiding principles to avoid tax evasion facilitation?
   Answer reference: Section 2.4

Chapter Seven
Financial Sanctions

1. Financial Sanctions   127

This syllabus area will provide approximately 4 of the 50 examination questions

1. Financial Sanctions

Learning Objective

7.1.1 Know the purpose and application of financial sanctions screening in relation to: terrorist financing; proliferation finance

7.1.2 Understand the impact of the financial sanctions listing process of the: United Nations; European Union; United Kingdom, including the role of OFSI; OFAC; other states

7.1.3 Know the range of legal financial sanctions related to 'designation': asset freeze; prohibitions; targeted sanctions

7.1.4 Know the potential criminal and civil penalties of dealing with designated persons and entities

---

Financial sanctions are economic and trade restrictions put in place by one or more countries against a targeted country, group or individual. Sanctions are imposed by governments, and international and multilateral bodies to meet their policy and security objectives against targeted foreign countries, regimes, terrorists and those engaged in the proliferation of weapons of mass destruction (WMDs). Financial sanctions can, for example, be issued by the United Nations (UN), the European Union (EU), or an individual government. A financial sanctions order prohibits a firm from carrying out transactions with the target and, in some cases, from providing financial services.

Financial Action Task Force (FATF) Recommendation 6 requires countries to implement targeted financial sanctions to comply with the United Nations Security Council Resolutions (UNSCRs). Financial sanctions are a strong tool in combating money laundering, terrorist financing, and proliferation finance.

Financial institutions need to maintain a robust sanctions and compliance programme with no margin for error. Identifying a potential violation of a sanctions list (terrorist financing or proliferation financing) requires constant attention of a firm since sanctions lists are changed on an almost continuous basis. The firm needs to ensure that it has a system in place for daily screening against different sanction lists in real time. Such a system consists of a combination of processes, systems and human expertise. It includes a reliable, robust filter mechanism to screen transactions against accurate and up-to-date sanctions lists. Due to the cost involved with implementing and maintaining these systems, many firms choose to use hosting services from third-party providers. However, the firm remains ultimately responsible for any failures of the process. Screening systems typically route messages in certain, predefined categories to centrally hosted filters where they are matched against the sanctions lists identified by the institution. Commonly used sanctions lists are those by the Office of Foreign Assets Control (OFAC), the UN, the EU and HM Treasury.

The screening process checks for possible matches using different tools and logical tests to detect anagrams, inversion of letters, missing letters, misspellings, abbreviations and even phonetic similarities (also known as 'fuzzy logic').

1.1 Terrorist Financing

The UNSC imposes various terrorist sanctions regimes. Consolidated lists of the targets of these sanctions are published and made available through national authorities, along with lists from other regimes (such as EU sanctions or those imposed at a national level). These lists of entities and individuals are published in a variety of formats to assist firms to incorporate them in their customer and transaction screening systems.

1.2 Proliferation Financing

In an international context, counter-proliferation controls comprise a framework of treaties and UN Resolutions, in particular UNSCR 1540 (2004), which primarily 'universalised' export controls that were previously implemented mainly on a voluntary and national basis. UNSCRs are addressed to member states, requiring them to take specific actions regarding the subject matter. They, therefore, do not in themselves directly impose obligations on firms. Member states are required to introduce domestic controls to prevent proliferation.

In the context of proliferation financing, UNSCR 1540 provides the following:

'3. Decides also that all States shall take and enforce effective measures to establish domestic controls to prevent the proliferation of nuclear, chemical, or biological weapons and their means of delivery, including by establishing appropriate controls over related materials and to this end shall:

... d) Establish, develop, review and maintain ... controls on providing funds and services related to such export and trans-shipment such as financing...'

'There are a variety of United Nations (UN) and national and regional sanctions in place. These include:

- *country-based financial sanctions that target specific individuals and entities*
- *trade-based sanctions, eg, embargoes on the provision of certain goods, services or expertise to certain countries.*

In recent years, there has also been a series of UN Security Council Resolutions which have, inter alia, introduced targeted financial sanctions and/or activity-based financial prohibitions in respect of certain countries which relate to the prevention of Weapons of Mass Destruction (WMDs) proliferation'.

Source: JMLSG Paper on Trade Finance

1.3 Sanctions Processes

1.3.1 United Nations (UN)

Under Chapter VII of the UN charter, the sanctions process of the UN typically starts with a matter of concern taken up by the UNSC. At an early stage, knowing the Security Council may impose sanctions can be sufficient to prevent escalation or outbreak of conflict. Sanctions are a last resort imposed in a variety of instances including in the combating of terrorist financing and proliferation finance.

The sanctions process can be depicted as follows[1]:

Sanctions are imposed by means of a UNSCR establishing a sanctions regime and a sanctions list. Names of countries, individuals and groups on a sanctions list may change over time with names added to, and removed from, the list.

Sanctions committees are subsidiary organs of the Council and are composed of all 15 of the Council's members. The role of the sanctions committees is to implement, monitor and provide recommendations to the Council on particular sanctions regimes. Committees meet regularly to consider reports from expert panels and to meet with Member states, UN actors and international organisations. Sanctions need to be implemented with due regard for human rights. The range of sanctions can vary from comprehensive financial and trade sanctions to more targeted measures such as arms embargoes, travel bans, financial or diplomatic restrictions.

Sanctions Measures

Travel bans	Asset freezes	Arms embargoes	Bans on export of luxury goods	Commodity bans, eg, diamonds	Bans on items, materials, equipment, goods and technology related to nuclear ballistic missiles and other WMD programmes

1.3.2 European Union (EU)

The EU imposes sanctions or restrictive measures to achieve the goals of its foreign policy. They are a tool of the Common Foreign and Security Policy (CFSP) and are used as part of an integrated and comprehensive policy approach. Sanctions in the CFSP framework include the interruption or reduction of financial relations with third countries and restrictions against specific individuals or entities. They also include the interruption or reduction of diplomatic relations, restrictions on admission and other measures not affecting financial relations with third countries. The key objectives when adopting sanctions are to:

- safeguard EU values, fundamental interests, and security
- preserve peace
- consolidate and support democracy, rule of law, human rights and principles of international law, and
- prevent conflicts and strengthen international security.

---

1 https://news.un.org/en/story/2016/05/528382-un-sanctions-what-they-are-how-they-work-and-who-uses-them

EU sanctions can target the following:

- governments of non-EU countries because of their policies
- companies providing the means to conduct the targeted policies
- groups or organisations such as terrorist groups, and
- individuals supporting the targeted policies, eg, involved in terrorist activities.

Sanctions are developed to minimise adverse consequences for anyone not responsible for the targeted policies or actions. All sanctions measures are fully compliant with obligations under international law. The basic principles on the use of sanctions, their implementation and measurement and control of the impact are included in the *Guidelines on the Implementation and Evaluation of Restrictive Measures*.

In addition to sanctions, the EU has introduced a blocking statute which is a unified EU action against the unlawful effects of extraterritorial legislation of third countries. In effect, it protects any EU operators who are engaged in lawful international trade, movement of capital, and commercial activities against the effects of specific legislation from other countries by nullifying the effect of a ruling based on specified foreign laws and allowing EU operators to recover damages. Take the 2018 US sanctions on Iran, for example. Those sanctions have wide extraterritorial reach and are imposed by the US on non-US persons. However, the amendment to the EU Blocking Statute means that any EU operator is exempt from complying with the US sanctions. The Statute only applies to the extraterritorial laws specifically included in its annex.

As well as the UN and EU, sanctions and embargoes may also be put in place by the Organization for Security and Co-operation in Europe (OSCE), who can also impose national arms embargoes. The EU implements UN regimes by means of a directly effective EU Regulation which immediately forms part of the UK's law upon its adoption. The UK enforces those measures by means of domestic regulations which impose criminal penalties for breaches of the EU Regulation.

1.3.3 Office of Financial Sanctions Implementation (OFSI) – UK

The UK applies financial sanctions either as part of international or European moves to bring pressure to bear on target groups or regimes (for example, because of measures adopted by the UN) or to meet domestic policy objectives. The Office of Financial Sanctions Implementation (OFSI), part of HM Treasury, helps to ensure financial sanctions are properly understood, implemented and enforced in the UK. Most financial sanctions are made through EU law which has direct effect under UK law. OFSI works closely with the EC and other member states in implementing sanctions and developing EU guidance in this area. Other financial sanctions are put in place by UK laws such as these pieces of legislation:

- Terrorist Asset-Freezing etc. Act 2010.
- Counter Terrorism Act 2008.
- Anti-Terrorism, Crime and Security Act 2001.

OFSI produces a consolidated list relating to all sanctions regimes currently in force in the UK. In addition, it produces lists specific to the terrorist financing regimes, such as the ISIL (Da'esh) and Al-Qaida organisations list; as well as comprehensive guidance on complying with sanctions regimes. Under new powers contained in the Policing and Courts Act 2017, the UK can now implement UN sanctions without delay, with no need to wait for action at EU level.

Financial Sanctions

1.3.4 Office of Foreign Assets Control (OFAC)

In the US, the different lists exist and derive powers from various laws (eg, Immigration and Nationality Act; PATRIOT Act 2001) and Executive Orders made by the President. The lists maintained by the US government include the 'state-sponsors of terrorism' list, the 'specially designated terrorists' (SDTs) list, the 'specially designated global terrorists' (SDGT) list and, the 'specially designated nationals (SDNs) and blocked persons' list. These lists are maintained by the OFAC, part of the US Treasury.

OFAC administers and enforces economic and trade sanctions based on US foreign policy and national security goals against targeted foreign countries and regimes, terrorists, international narcotics traffickers, those engaged in activities related to the proliferation of WMDs, and other threats to the national security, foreign policy or economy of the US. In the same way as the UK's OFSI, OFAC produces both a consolidated list and regime-specific lists.

1.3.5 Other States

Other states will also have mechanisms to implement relevant international sanctions (especially UN sanctions) in their legislation and will often also have systems for their own listings. The requirements placed on financial institutions may also differ from country to country. Institutions operating in more than one jurisdiction must ensure that they understand the different regimes and incorporate the relevant lists in their control systems.

1.4 Consequences of Designation – Asset Freezes, Prohibitions and Targeted Sanctions

Financial sanctions come in many forms and will be adapted to the individual circumstances, such as the intent behind the designations and the nature of the entities listed. Broadly speaking, they will involve some form of bans and/or asset freezing.

Sanctions generally may include bans on travel, but in terms of financial sanctions, the UK's OFSI describes restrictions on a wide variety of financial markets and services, which can apply to named individuals, entities and bodies, to specified groups or to entire sectors. These have taken the form of:

- investment bans
- restrictions on access to capital markets
- directions to cease banking relationships and activities
- requirements to notify or seek authorisation prior to certain payments being made or received; and restrictions on provision of financial, insurance, brokering, advisory services or other financial assistance, and
- directions to cease all business of a specified type with a specific person, group, sector or country.

The freezing of terrorist assets is mandated by international law as a means to 'prevent and suppress the financing of terrorist acts'. An effective asset freezing regime is critical to combating the terrorist financing and, as a preventive tool against terrorism.

UNSCR 1373 and the FATF Recommendation 6 see asset-freezing, together with seizure of terrorist funds, as:

> 'necessary to deprive terrorists and terrorist networks of the means to conduct future terrorist activity and maintain their infrastructure and operations'.

Targeted asset freezes, which are usually applied to named individuals, entities and bodies, restrict access to funds and economic resources. Asset freezes comprise two elements:

- a prohibition on dealing with the funds or economic resources belonging to or owned, held or controlled by a designated person, and
- a prohibition on making funds or economic resources available, directly or indirectly, to, or for the benefit of, a designated person.

It is also prohibited to engage in actions that, directly or indirectly, circumvent the financial sanctions and prohibitions.

1.5 Dealing with Designated Persons and Entities

The major consequence of being designated or listed is that the entity's property is subject to seizure/restraint and/or forfeiture. In addition, all financial institutions are subject to reporting requirements with respect to an entity's property and must not allow those entities to access the property. These institutions may not deal or otherwise dispose of the property, unless the authorities grant some form of licence.

It is an offence to knowingly participate in, or contribute to, directly or indirectly, any activity of a terrorist entity. This interaction with the designated entity is an offence because this dealing may enhance the ability of any terrorist entity/group to facilitate or carry out a terrorist activity.

It is a criminal offence to knowingly (or with reasonable cause to suspect) make funds or financial services available, directly or indirectly, to a designated person. Making funds or financial services indirectly available to a designated person would involve these being routed via a third party. So, for example, it would be a criminal offence to give funds to a designated person's friend knowing or suspecting that some or all of the funds will be given to the designated person.

The consequences of a breach of sanctions are potentially extremely serious for both the institution and individuals involved. They may face criminal or civil (regulatory) actions, including large fines, imprisonment and banning from the financial services sector. Fines imposed by US authorities on European and other banks have reached many hundreds of millions of dollars.

In 2017, Part 8 of the POCA 2017 strengthened the powers of OFSI through the creation of new civil powers to impose penalties on companies and individuals who breach UK, EU or UN sanctions. The maximum penalty that can be imposed is £1 million, unless the breach relates to particular funds, when the fine can be up to 50% of the amount of the funds, if greater than £1 million. The Act also increased the maximum penalty from two to seven years' imprisonment.

End of Chapter Questions

Think of an answer for each question and refer to the appropriate section for confirmation

1. List the range of United Nations (UN) sanctions.
   Answer reference: Section 1.3.1

2. For what reasons does the Europe Union (EU) impose sanctions?
   Answer reference: Section 1.3.2

3. What is the Office of Financial Sanctions Implementation (OFSI)?
   Answer reference: Section 1.3.3

4. What are the two components of an asset freeze?
   Answer reference: Section 1.4

Chapter Eight
Financial Crime Risk Management

1.	Considerations for the Financial Services Sector	137
2.	Risks	145
3.	Practical Business Safeguards	152

This syllabus area will provide approximately 8 of the 50 examination questions

1. Considerations for the Financial Services Sector

The categories of risks faced by any organisation in the financial services sector are very broad. They cover different components or factors of the basic **inherent risk**. These factors are derived from regulatory obligations, guidance and expectations, creating industry best practices and market dynamics.

In other words, inherent risk factors are all those imaginable underlying causes and circumstances where a financial institution (FI) may be used for purposes connected to financial crime.

Managing these inadequately can have disastrous consequences not only for individual firms but also for the entire system or market. In the case of a single firm, this can lead to damaging reputation, regulatory and legal sanctions and financial costs, including fines by the regulators.

In today's interdependent markets, the failure of a single firm or group can also cause contagion effects. Financial crime can lead to systemic risk, ie, the risk of damage to or collapse of the entire financial system.

Recent examples of financial crime that led to huge contagion losses and helped prompt a global financial crisis includes the Madoff Ponzi scheme and malfeasance at Lehman Brothers that helped prompt a global financial crisis.

Larger corporations may be able to survive a serious fraud and rebuild but for smaller companies the impact can be disastrous and too great to recover from.

Firms must have systems and controls for countering the risk that they may be used to further financial crime. These systems and controls must enable them to identify, assess, monitor and manage money laundering risk and be comprehensive and proportionate to the nature, scale and complexity of their activities.

1.1 The Direct Impact of Financial Crime on Firms

Learning Objective

8.1.1 Understand how financial crime can directly impact on firms: embezzlement; asset misappropriation; fraudulent customer activity; defrauded by organised criminals; limiting access to data; data compromise

1.1.1 Asset Misappropriation

Asset misappropriation including embezzlement, happens when people who are entrusted to manage the assets of an organisation steal from it. Asset misappropriation fraud involves third parties and/or employees in an organisation who abuse their position to steal from it through fraudulent activity. It is also known as 'insider fraud'.

At one end of the scale, asset misappropriation fraud may be limited to isolated cases of expense fiddling or an employee lying about their CV to get a job. At the other end, it may involve organised crime groups infiltrating organisations to take advantage of weak processes and inadequate internal systems and controls.

According to the UK's fraud reporting centre (Action Fraud), asset misappropriation fraud includes any of the following:

- embezzlement
- deception by the firm's employees
- false expense claims
- payroll fraud, where payments have been diverted or fictitious, ghost employees have been created
- data theft and/or intellectual property theft.

Embezzlement is one component of asset misappropriation and refers to the crime of misappropriating resources entrusted to a person's care. The difference between embezzlement and stealing is that embezzlement is stealing resources that one was hired to handle or protect 'done from inside' the firm or organisation.

Asset misappropriation is a common problem and can be very harmful to businesses that fall victim to it, especially new or small ones. It is not just business owners and shareholders who are affected; it can hurt a large group of different people. The affected businesses may be forced to raise prices on goods and services and may even have to lay off workers that they can no longer afford to pay.

The affected firm not only loses money but also its business reputation is spoiled because clients and the general public perceive embezzlement to be incompetence or outright criminal activity by the functionaries of the company. Another harmful effect of embezzlement is that it damages any evaluation of the company's economic standing. The initial reaction of some bosses can also indirectly damage the company because they may try to tackle embezzlement by withdrawing their trust in their employees and instituting stricter rules and even surveillance that, in turn, destroys staff morale.

If not tackled, opportunistic one-off deceptions can become systemic and spread throughout an organisation, creating a culture of theft and fraud. When this happens, fraudsters think their actions are acceptable and fail to make the distinction between company funds and their own funds.

This type of fraud may be committed by company directors, employees, or anyone else entrusted to hold and manage the assets and interests of an organisation. Typically, the assets stolen are cash or cash equivalents, such as credit notes or vouchers. However, the fraud can include company data and intellectual property.

In the UK, all asset misappropriation frauds including embezzlement must be reported to the UK's national fraud reporting centre, Action Fraud, irrespective of whether committed by an individual, a larger corporation or a financial institution.

1.1.2 Protecting Against Asset Misappropriation

Action Fraud recommends that organisations take steps to help to protect themselves from asset misappropriation fraud, by:

- vetting employees thoroughly, including checking employee CVs and references
- implementing a whistleblowing policy
- controlling access to buildings and systems, using unique identification and passwords
- restricting and closely monitoring access to sensitive information
- imposing clear segregation of duties
- considering job rotation
- using tiered authority and signature levels for payments
- regularly reconciling bank statements and other accounts
- periodically auditing processes and procedures
- promoting a culture of fraud awareness among staff
- adopting and rigorously implementing a zero-tolerance policy towards employee fraud, and
- having a clear response plan in place in case fraud is discovered.

It should be noted that the definition of asset misappropriation fraud does not include minor theft from an organisation by insiders, such as stealing stationery or other physical assets.

Organisations holding individuals' data must ensure that it is adequately protected from loss or theft. Getting data protection wrong can bring commercial, reputational, regulatory and legal penalties; getting it right earns the firm real rewards in terms of customer trust and confidence.

1.1.3 Customer Activity and Organised Criminals

Financial sector firms are exposed to numerous and diverse types of financial crimes. *The FCA Guide to Financial Crime* lists some examples:

- a firm is defrauded by customers (eg, mortgage fraud)
- a firm is defrauded by employees or contractors (insiders), eg, a staff member steals from their employer and amends the records to conceal the theft
- a firm's customers are defrauded by an insider, eg, a staff member steals customers' money
- a firm's customers are defrauded after a third party misleads the firm, eg, criminals evade security measures to gain access to a customer's account
- a firm's customers are defrauded by a third party because of the firm's actions, eg, the firm loses sensitive personal data, thereby allowing the customer's identity to be stolen
- a customer is defrauded, by a firm executing payments connected to fraud on the customer's instruction, eg, a customer asks their bank to transfer funds to what turns out to be a share sale scam.

Serious, complex and organised fraud and corruption can have a significant impact on financial institutions who have been defrauded by individuals, organised groups of criminals, companies and even individual members of staff.

The fraudulent activity can be internal or external to the firm, for example, forged transfer of assets and forged sale instructions or proceeds are directed to bank accounts set up by the fraudsters specifically for the purpose of laundering the proceeds.

The responsibility for combating financial crime (CFC) cannot be isolated but cuts across the organisation from the board and management via human resources and legal and auditing services to the various specialised officers for money laundering and fraud prevention, data protection and IT security.

Fraudulent activities such as embezzlement, corruption and falsification of official documents can cause considerable damage to the financial institutions. The impact of such activities can lead to:

- reduced profits and potential risks to the financial stability of the firm
- damage to the firm's reputation, which may arise from supervisory or other regulatory action, such as fines
- increased costs arising from the investigation of theft, forensic work by expert or specialist firms and remediation where required, such as new systems and controls.

The occurrence of such fraudulent activities can also lead to increased insurance costs following revised premiums and even the need to take out additional insurance cover because a risk was not previously identified.

1.1.4 Limiting Access to Data

The portability of data in large quantities, using the internet or small storage devices, has created a new dimension and risk factor to data security. This portability necessitates the introduction of proper controls to mitigate the risk by limiting the access to data.

Sophisticated criminals are increasingly targeting financial institutions to steal their customer data. Personal details, names, addresses, bank details and passwords are all attractive fraudsters. The data can be used for account takeovers and credit card fraud.

There are many ways that criminals can target financial firms with a view to stealing data, including:

- infiltrating firms and placing people as employees who download data onto USB sticks
- theft of computers, laptops and data-files on disk
- use of 'social engineering' to obtain customer and/or staff information.

Once criminals have personal details, including bank accounts and investments, they can try to steal customer assets. They may take over the accounts of their victims, changing the address and/or bank details and then sell investments or withdraw monies, having them paid into fraudulently opened bank accounts. They can then withdraw the cash and abscond with the proceeds.

Data theft can have very damaging consequences for the firm which may be left with angry customers and loss of reputation. The organisation may have to compensate their customers and reinstate their accounts.

Financial crime is estimated globally to cost the financial services sector around $20 billion pa.

1.2 Exploitation as a Vehicle for Financial Crime

Learning Objective

8.1.2 Understand how firms can be exploited as a vehicle for financial crime: criminals using the firm's services to launder the proceeds of crime; customer payments to terrorists; theft of customer data to facilitate identity fraud; trade-based money laundering

1.2.1 Laundering the Proceeds of Crime/Payments to Terrorists

Financial institutions can be exploited as vehicles for financial crime in a variety of ways. Criminals will seek to use a firm's services at various stages of the classic money laundering cycle:

- **Placement** – criminals can seek to place money derived from crime in accounts with institutions, for example by depositing cash over-the-counter (OTC). This is the most vulnerable stage for them and they may use front companies representing cash-intensive businesses to disguise the origin of the money.
- **Layering** – this involves moving money around the financial system to disguise its origins. This could involve many different transactions in financial institutions, such as moving between accounts at different banks in different jurisdictions or buying and selling investments.
- **Integration** – if 'cleaned', criminal money is being used in legitimate businesses or to fund a criminal's lifestyle, for example by buying property, vehicles or holidays. The funds will be passing through the financial system in the normal course of business, and will, therefore, be much harder for firms to detect.

Terrorist financing (TF) can be very difficult to detect as it may involve small sums of money, perhaps even deriving from legitimate income. In recent years, payments to terrorist fighters abroad have been noted, where banks or money transmission agents are used to send money to areas of conflict such as Syria. Terrorist attacks carried out by small groups in Europe have been self-financed, perhaps using benefits payments, legitimate income or small loans.

1.2.2 Theft of Customer Data

Customer data is any personal customer information held in any format by the financial institution. Examples include national insurance records, addresses, dates of birth, details of family circumstances, bank details and medical records. Information must be kept secure because criminals can use it to commit offences such as identity theft or account takeover which are an increasing threat to the financial services sector.

Customer data can be compromised in a number of ways. Data protection is not purely an IT issue: it is also available in hard copy format. Physical access to the records whether electronically stored or on paper has to be protected and monitored. Firms must, therefore, consider the physical safety of business premises and there should be a policy for access to data. Visitors should be logged and supervised while they are on the premises.

The firm should take a risk-based approach (RBA) to reducing financial crime and undertake enhanced recruitment checks where appropriate, such as enhanced vetting of staff who have access to customer data. Firms should carry out credit and criminal record checks on individuals with access to large amounts of customer data.

1.2.3 Trade-Based Money Laundering

Trade-based money laundering uses a legitimate trade to disguise criminal proceeds. It involves a number of schemes to complicate the documentation of the transaction which may include:

- moving illicit goods
- falsifying documents
- misrepresenting financial transactions, and
- under- or over-invoicing the value of goods.

Red flags identified by the US Immigration and Customs Enforcement (ICE) include:

- payments to a vendor by unrelated third parties
- false reporting, such as commodity misclassification, commodity over- or under-valuation
- repeated importation and exportation of the same high-value commodity, known as carousel transactions
- commodities being traded that do not match the business involved
- unusual shipping routes or transshipment points
- packaging inconsistent with the commodity or shipping method
- double invoicing.

1.3 Propagation of Financial Crime

Learning Objective

8.1.3 Understand how a firm or its representatives may collude in the propagation of financial crime: misstatement of financial circumstances; corporate malfeasance

1.3.1 Misstatement of Financial Circumstances

Misstatements of financial circumstances can either be deliberate, such as a clear breach of a requirement of a financial reporting standard, or judgmental, arising from unsuitable estimation techniques or the selection of inappropriate accounting policies. Misstatements in the financial statements can, in other words, arise from either fraud or error. The distinguishing factor between fraud and error is whether the underlying action that results in the misstatement of the financial statements is intentional or unintentional.

Fraud, in this context, will be:

> 'an intentional act by one or more individuals among management, those charged with governance, employees, or third parties, involving the use of deception to obtain an unjust or illegal advantage'.

The conduct will also be a violation of auditing standards prescribed by the supervisory bodies such as the US Public Company Accounting Oversight Board (PCAOB) created under SOX. In the UK and Ireland, auditors are obliged to apply international standards to risks of material misstatement due to fraud.

Misstatement of financial circumstances can be accomplished in many ways including:

- manipulation, falsification, or alteration of accounting records or supporting documents from which the financial statements are prepared
- misrepresentation in, or intentional omission from, the financial statements of events, transactions, or other significant information, and
- intentional misapplication of accounting principles relating to amounts, classification, manner of presentation, or disclosure.

Misstatement of financial circumstances can have severe consequences. In examining financial statements, professional investigators often focus their attention on certain red flags. Financial statement fraud is devastating to lenders, shareholders, boards of directors and employees who rely on these statements. Recent examples include Tesco, Shell and VW.

1.3.2 Corporate Malfeasance

Corporate malfeasance is a broad term that covers major and minor crimes that might be committed by a corporate officer or member of the executive management of a corporation. The acts of corporate malfeasance can take many forms and range from highly unethical to illegal. These acts can be attempts to defraud investors by issuing false financial reports or can be instances of corporate espionage.

For example, a fraudulent and regulatory violation or an accounting cover-up is illegal, while adherence to poor safety or work standards in foreign countries that are unacceptable in the company's home country is unethical. These acts while morally reprehensible, may be legal. This even affects employees through subtle discrimination against some individuals either on basis of race, gender, age or other characteristics.

1.4 Implications of Business Strategies

Learning Objective

8.1.4 Understand the relevant implications of business strategies: corporate structure; outsourcing and oversight; use of middlemen; FinTech; green finance

1.4.1 Corporate Structure

Corporate organisational structure refers to how the management and employees in a business take decisions and perform their required tasks. The proper structure of the organisation is important for it to optimise its productivity and achieve sustainable long-term growth. For a business to succeed and grow there must be a proper fit between its organisational structure, its size and the industry in which it operates. Evidence of bad organisational structure includes low productivity, high employee turnover and hiring problems, plus misalignment between technology and decision-making.

A bad organisational structure can also inhibit the business from growing. In a dynamic industry, prone to rapid change, it is important to move from a centralised organisational structure to a decentralised one, wherein decision-making power is shared among a larger informed group. Decentralised organisational structures tend to facilitate a competitive growth strategy for larger firms in these types of industries. Typically, businesses that cannot make this shift do not progress beyond the small business level.

A proper operational structure in a firm is a necessary prerequisite for the implementation of the risk-based approach to CFC. Senior management can only decide on the appropriate approach in the light of the firm's structure.

1.4.2 Outsourcing and Oversight

Outsourcing is a critical component of financial institutions' management of their business operations and control of their costs. Institutions are outsourcing increasingly complex and sensitive banking and financial operations to third parties. A company can delegate (eg, outsource) tasks to third parties but legally remains fully responsible and accountable for all decisions, actions undertaken, and data generated by its partners. Firms can delegate tasks but not responsibilities.

Outsourcing is an area of risk and concern to the regulators especially the outsourcing of critical activities that could result in poor outcomes for customers. The FCA has an obligation that:

> 'all firms must ensure they have appropriate oversight of outsourced arrangements and meet their wider responsibilities to deliver fair customer outcomes'.

Firms, therefore, need to create internal capacities and expertise to carry out this crucial oversight.

The FCA has undertaken a thematic review of firms in this context and issued guidance in this regard as *'Considerations for Firms Thinking of Using Third-Party…'* For the FCA, the aim of these regulatory obligations is to ensure that firms manage the operational risks that are associated with use of third parties appropriately and that the arrangements with these third parties do not in any way impair the regulator's ability to regulate the firm.

1.4.3 Use of Middlemen

If a firm wishes to place reliance on a third party or middleman for the provision of some services, this conduct should become part of the firm's overall risk-based assessment.

The FCA expects firms to take adequate and risk-sensitive measures to address the risk that a middleman acting on behalf of the firm may engage in corruption and ensure that these relationships are subject to thorough due diligence and management oversight.

If a firm has an appointed representative, it must ensure that the representative complies with the record-keeping obligations under Regulation 40 of MLR 2017. This principle applies equally to situations where the record-keeping is delegated in any way to a third party (such as to an administrator or an introducer).

1.4.4 FinTech

FinTech refers to the application of technology to innovative ways to provide financial services. For example, digital bank accounts and e-wallets. The main reasons for using FinTech are typically ease of use and account-opening process, competitive pricing, and quality of service. The ease of account opening, however, also leaves FinTech open to being used by criminals. Within the EU, for example, using the passporting mechanism, FinTech operators can apply for a licence in one country yet operate in all EU countries. Opening accounts with different providers in different jurisdictions is relatively easy, and does not require any travel to the varying locations. Once done, depositing amounts under the money laundering reporting limit in each of the jurisdictions is unlikely to raise any questions by regulators in each of the respective countries.

1.4.5 Green Finance

Green or sustainable finance has been growing for a number of years, but is still a relatively new development in finance. Similar to other new products, institutions typically introduce the new products before updating their financial crime guidance and other policies and procedures. In addition, systems and controls take time to be put in place. Meanwhile, the institution is potentially open to be used for financial crime.

2. Risks

2.1 Risk Assessment – Introduction

In January 2014, the BCBS issued *'Sound Management of Risks related to Money Laundering and Financing of Terrorism'* on the importance and conduct of risk assessments by a financial institution:

> *'Sound risk management requires the identification and analysis of ML/FT risks present within the bank and the design and effective implementation of policies and procedures that are commensurate with the identified risks. In conducting a comprehensive risk assessment to evaluate ML/FT risks, a bank should consider all the relevant inherent and residual risk factors at the country, sectoral, bank and business relationship level, among others, in order to determine its risk profile and the appropriate level of mitigation to be applied'.*

The Wolfsberg Group in its paper, *'Risk Assessments for ML, Sanctions and Bribery & Corruption 2015'* clarified that when money laundering risk assessment is referred to, it is generally understood to include terrorist financing, sanctions and bribery and corruption, as there are significant commonalities in the factors used to conduct money laundering and bribery, and corruption risk assessments. However, bribery and corruption risk assessment involves some additional components such as third parties who act on behalf of a financial institution, hiring practices, charitable giving and business gifts and entertainment. These, can potentially be used inappropriately to bestow a benefit and can, therefore, pose bribery risks.

In the UK, the Joint Money Laundering Steering Group (JMLSG) Guidance also outlines some of the considerations that should be taken into account when conducting a risk assessment, the application of an RBA being a core theme (Chapter 4 of the Guidance).

The basic objective of any financial crime risk assessment is to improve the firm's financial crime risk management through a thorough identification of the risks a financial institution is facing, determining how these risks are mitigated by a firm's financial crime controls and establishing the **residual risk** that remains with the financial institution in the conduct of its business.

The results of a financial crime risk assessment by a firm can be used for different purposes, such as to:

- identify gaps or opportunities for improvement in anti-money laundering policies, procedures and processes
- make informed decisions about risk appetite and the implementation of control efforts, allocation of resources and procurement of technology
- develop risk mitigation strategies, including applicable internal controls and, therefore, lower residual risk exposure
- ensure senior management are aware of the key risks, control gaps and remediation efforts, and
- assist management in ensuring that resources and priorities are aligned with its risks.

There are numerous ways to conduct risk assessments. The risk assessment process can be divided into three distinct sequential phases:

- determine the inherent risk
- assess the internal control environment (both design and operating effectiveness), and
- derive the residual risk.

Inherent risk represents the exposure to money laundering, sanctions or bribery and corruption risk in the absence of any control environment being applied. As no two financial institutions are exactly the same, inherent risk ratings may vary for each financial institution depending on the size and scope of its businesses and the risks involved.

Senior management is the overall owner of the risk environment. They may delegate the assessment of risk to the legal/financial crime compliance/anti-money laundering unit), which may have primary responsibility for the initiation and delivery aspects of the money laundering risk assessment. This will include tasks such as methodology development, maintenance, periodic refresh process/activity initiation and completed assessments record-keeping.

2.2 National Risk Assessments

Learning Objective

8.2.1 Know the role, significance, and utilisation of national risk assessments

In 2013, the FATF issued the National Money Laundering and Terrorist Financing Risk Assessment Guide that provides guidance on the conduct of risk assessment at both country or national level. National risk assessments are required under Recommendation 1: assessing risks and applying a risk-based approach. The guidance is not a standard and does not specify rules or actions.

National risk assessments assist in the prioritisation and efficient allocation of resources in combating money laundering and the financing of terrorism. The way in which countries assess this risk is up to the individual supervisory authority, and will ensure money laundering and terrorist financing risks are properly understood. The results of the assessment will be used by, among others, supervisory authorities, policy makers, law enforcement, financial intelligence units (FIUs), and financial institutions as a basis for their approach to AML/CFT.

2.3 Assess and Manage the Impact of Risks on a Firm's Business Activities

Learning Objective

8.2.2 Understand how to identify, assess and manage the impact of risks posed on a firm's business activities by the following: products and services customers; sectors; countries; delivery channels

All financial institutions are different and will face different threats and vulnerabilities. Therefore, the inherent risk ratings also vary for every institution, depending upon the size and scope of its businesses and the risks involved.

A risk assessment covering different categories of risk will be carried out to inform the firm's management of the risks they face and the mitigations they need to put in place.

2.3.1 Customers

To assess the inherent money laundering risk of any business the customer base and business relationship must be assessed. A number of factors affect the quality of risks such as client types, industries involved, activities, professions and businesses, alongside other considerations, such as the length of a relationship.

Depending upon the expected amount of money laundering risk, each type is assigned a risk score. The volume of clients that fall within each client type should be determined and this data utilised to determine the percentages of each risk classification, eg, low risk versus moderate or high versus higher risk, to determine the overall inherent client risk.

2.3.2 Products and Services

The Wolfsberg Group paper *Risk Assessments for ML, Sanctions and Bribery & Corruption (2015)* explains the risks details for clients, one of the other major risk components that can be found when considering products and services risks. A financial institution should identify its portfolio of main products/account types and assign an inherent score (for example, low, moderate, high or higher) to each, based on its general inherent characteristics and the degree of financial crime risk present for each product or service. The volume of identified products/account types offered by the business, and if relevant, associated account balances and turnover, should be determined.

This data can be utilised to determine the percentage of each of the products/account types that are rated according to the risk classification to determine the overall inherent product risk.

2.3.3 Sectors

Different industry sectors pose different anti-money laundering/combating financing for terrorism (AML/CFT) risks to financial institutions, who will include a sector risk score as part of their overall customer risk assessment. Different institutions will have different risk appetites and tolerances, but commonly cash-intensive businesses, such as casinos, taxi firms, bars and takeaway restaurants, may be regarded as high risk. Money service businesses, such as bureaux de change and money transmitters, are frequently regarded as high risk, because of the roles they play in many money laundering schemes, and computer and mobile phone sales/distribution firms have been regarded as high risk because of the occurrence of tax (VAT) fraud in the sector. Some charities, particularly those providing services in high-risk or conflict areas may be regarded as a higher risk from a terrorist financing point of view.

2.3.4 Countries

Identifying countries that pose a higher risk of financial crime is a core component of any inherent risk assessment undertaken by an financial institution. Country risk must be considered alongside the other risk factors in other risk categories, for example, in clients, products and services and for transactions. For example, the percentages of business transactions with a high-risk country can provide an indication of the inherent risks originating from a country.

The Wolfsberg Group's paper, *Risk Assessments for ML, Sanctions and Bribery & Corruption 2015* contains an example of a country's risk ratings, developed on a four-point rating scale. However, depending on the rating scale chosen, the ratings assigned by the financial institution can differ.

Country (or geographical) risk is also important in any sanctions risk assessment, not only with respect to the sanctioned countries themselves, but also with respect to those countries which have well-known or other significant connections to territories. These could include territories bordering, or in close proximity to, sanctioned countries, or those countries which present potential opportunities for the diversion of funds with the intent to violate or circumvent sanctions regulations.

Financial Crime Risk Management

The current ability of money launderers and other criminals to penetrate financial systems makes many jurisdictions vulnerable to money laundering. The countries named by the Financial Action Task Force (FATF) in regular public statements of countries with strategic AML/CFT deficiencies may be regarded as higher risk by institutions. In the EU, the European Commission (EC) has an obligation to publish its own list of higher-risk countries. In October 2016, it adopted the same list as the FATF, but this process was rejected as inadequate by the European Parliament in January 2017. The Commission will publish a revised list in due course and this will be taken into account by firms carrying out their risk assessments (for example, as required by the MLRs in the UK). Following the Fourth Anti-Money Laundering Directive (4MLD), the EC, partly based on the FATF's high-risk and non-cooperative jurisdictions list, identifies and publishes their own list of high-risk third countries.

A checklist of factors that contribute to making a country or jurisdiction particularly vulnerable to money laundering or other illicit financial activity, however, can provide a basic guide. The checklist developed by some regulators includes risk factors such as:

- countries with bank secrecy rules that obstruct law enforcement investigations or that prohibits large value, or suspicious or unusual transaction reporting by both banks and non-bank financial institutions
- a lack of, or inadequate, know your customer (KYC) requirements to open accounts or conduct financial transactions, including the permitted use of anonymous, nominee, numbered or trustee accounts
- a lack of effective monitoring of cross-border currency movements
- no reporting requirements for large cash transactions
- no requirement to maintain financial records over a specific period of time
- use of bearer monetary instruments
- patterns of evasion of exchange controls by legitimate businesses
- ease of incorporation, in particular, where ownership can be held through nominees or **bearer shares**, or where off-the-shelf corporations can be acquired
- a lack of, or weak, bank regulatory controls, or failure to adopt or adhere to the BCBS's Core Principles for Effective Banking Supervision, especially in jurisdictions where the monetary or bank supervisory authority lacks skills or is simply uncommitted
- well-established offshore financial centres or tax-haven banking systems, especially jurisdictions where such banks and accounts can be readily established with minimal background investigations
- countries where charitable organisations or alternative remittance systems, because of their unregulated and unsupervised nature, are used as avenues for money laundering or terrorist financing
- limited narcotics, money laundering, and financial crime enforcement because of lack of skills or simply because of no commitment to do so
- patterns of official corruption at political or public official level and permissive attitudes towards corruption of business and banking communities
- countries where international currencies such the US dollar, pound and/or euro are readily accepted, especially where banks and other financial institutions freely allow deposits of these currencies
- where there is significant trade in, or export of gold, diamonds, and other gems in countries with large parallel or black market economies.

In addition, country risk is also applicable in any anti-bribery and corruption risk assessments. Some countries carry increased levels of bribery and corruption risk, usually to do with how those in power are able to abuse their positions for personal financial gain. If financial institutions are dealing with countries with corrupt reputations the bribery and corruption risks must be given due consideration when country risk assessments are being undertaken.

2.3.5 Delivery Channels

Delivery channel risk relates to the way that the financial institution delivers its services to its clients. These can be face to face, such as customers coming into premises and interacting with the institution's staff; or non-face to face, where the institution never actually meets its customers or they can operate remotely using FinTech.

The latter way is generally regarded as being higher-risk, particularly when it comes to customer due diligence. Firms have to rely on alternative methods of verifying identification, by checking against electronic records, for example. That said, monitoring of activity may be easier if all interactions are carried out on a digital platform, where the data is available in real time. The UK's JMLSG's guidance identifies the following risk factors relating to delivery channels:

- private banking
- anonymous transactions (which may include cash)
- non face-to-face business relationships or transactions
- payment received from unknown or unassociated third parties.

2.4 Risks Associated with Non-Compliance for the Private Sector

Learning Objective

8.2.3 Understand the risks associated with non-compliance for regulated firms: financial; reputational; legal; operational; systemic; regulatory; criminal; prudential

2.4.1 Financial and Reputational

The categories of financial crime risks faced by regulated firms are diverse. Managing these risk factors inadequately can be catastrophic and lead to reputation risk, regulatory or legal sanctions and consequent financial costs. The impact of financial crimes on firms are both financial and reputational, as a result of supervisory reprimand or other regulatory actions.

Reputational damage can arise in numerous ways which affect the good reputation of a financial institution. A financial institution's reputation is negatively affected by the announcement of a serious investigation into financial crime in connection with client accounts, which has, or is likely to have, a significant financial impact through regulatory, civil or criminal monetary fines and penalties.

Reputation can also be negatively affected by existing and prospective clients, where negative allegations, including criminal allegations, are made, for example, providing banking services to corrupt politically exposed persons (PEPs), facilitating terrorist finance transactions or dealing with dirty money and questionable regimes.

Some significant fines have been levied by the regulators on companies for failing to put in place AML procedures, training and controls.

2.4.2 Legal

Legal risk arises from different sources but is primarily rooted in uncertainty due to legal actions and in the applicability or interpretation of contracts, laws or regulations.

Laws, regulations and guidance are constantly evolving. The expectations of the regulators are also rising as to what a reasonable risk-based AML programme should look like. Examination and testing experiences are also increasing in number, frequency, depth and intensity. The standards expected by regulators have largely shifted from accepting good or common practice to expecting the highest implemented standards as the norm.

As these expectations have increased, it has become more difficult to implement a true risk-based approach if judgements are made on a rules-based approach.

The costs of developing any meaningful risk-based systems and controls and keeping them under review may appear to be substantial but in the case of regulatory censure the costs to the firm are much higher and can be disastrous. Regulatory fines and heavy penalties are levied for any regulatory violations, along with commitments to undertake ongoing actions such as having a team appointed by regulators for ongoing monitoring. The censures often also involve several regulatory agencies who take simultaneous actions for the same or similar issues.

2.4.3 Operational

The Bank for International Settlements (BIS) defines operational risk as:

> 'The risk of loss resulting from inadequate or failed internal processes, people and systems or from external events'.

This definition covers legal risk (exposure to fines, penalties and punitive damage resulting from supervisory actions as well as private settlements) but excludes business and reputation risk. The BIS requires banks to hold capital for operational risk, but the BCBS recognises that the approach for operational risk management chosen by an individual firm will depend on a range of factors. These include its size and sophistication, and the nature and complexity of its activities.

At a high level, the BIS believes that for banks of all sizes, the following are crucial elements of an effective operational risk management framework:

- clear risk oversight by the board and senior management
- a strong operational risk culture

- a strong internal control culture including:
  - clear lines of responsibility
  - segregation of duties
  - effective internal reporting
  - contingency planning.

2.4.4 Systemic, Regulatory, Criminal and Prudential

Non-compliance enhances systemic risk since it may trigger instability or the collapse of an entire industry or economy. The interlinked nature of financial services only enhances the systemic risk levels.

Firms which fail to manage their financial crime risk may face a range of repercussions, including criminal prosecution resulting in penalties and/or imprisonment if found guilty, and regulatory restrictions in the form or limitations or withdrawal of their licence.

Financial firms must have sufficient capital in place at all times, as well as adequate risk controls. These requirements are incorporated in the prudential regulations. It is the role of the supervisory authority to ensure the firms under their supervision meet the requirements and are run in a safe and sound way. Non-compliance rules can result in intervention by the regulator and include variation, suspension, or loss of licence, as well as penalties.

3. Practical Business Safeguards

Learning Objectives

8.3.1 Know the relevant risk factors firms may consider before commencing business relationships: nature and purpose of the relationship; source of introductions; company structure; political connections; country risk; establishing beneficial ownership; the customer's or beneficial owner's reputation; source of funds/wealth; expected account activity; sector risk; involvement in public contracts; charities, voluntary and not-for-profit bodies

3.1 Considerations for Business Relationships

3.1.1 Nature and Purpose of Relationship and Source of Introduction

The source via which a new business relationship is introduced to a financial institution may mean additional risk assessments are required. A client introduced by an existing, long-term client of good standing will pose a lower risk than a customer who has come to the financial institution via an internet search, for example.

The nature and intended purpose of the business relationship will give a firm indication of the potential risk for the institution to be used for money laundering and terrorist financing. Where applicable, information must be obtained about the beneficial owner. Understanding the nature and purpose of a relationship will enable a firm to determine whether additional measures for enhanced due diligence (EDD) are required.

3.1.2 Company Structure

Linking the beneficial owner to the proceeds of corruption is critical to CFC but the causal linkages are at times difficult to establish. Most of the billions in corrupt assets that are moving around in the world are through complex money trails and it eventually takes refuge in shell companies and other spurious legal structures. These structures form the most important component of the complex web of instruments of deception in corruption cases, behind which the beneficiaries of it all hide.

With sizeable wealth and resources, the corrupt exploit transnational corporate constructions that are hard to penetrate. Nearly all cases of grand corruption have one thing in common – there is a reliance on corporate vehicles, legal structures such as companies, foundations and trusts, to conceal ownership and control of tainted assets.

The World Bank report of 2011 titled *Puppet Masters: How the Corrupt Use Legal Structures to Hide Stolen Assets and What to Do About it* takes these specialised corporate vehicles as its angle of investigation. This comprehensive report examined over 150 cases of large-scale corruption and found that most cases involve the use of one or more corporate vehicles to conceal beneficial ownership. The report examined the use of legal structures to hide stolen assets, outlined in detail how corporate vehicles can be used to facilitate corruption, identified significant challenges that countries face when seeking to implement measures to prevent corporate vehicles being misused in corruption schemes, and provided recommendations to countries on how to address these challenges.

The Misuse of Legal Persons and Arrangements

A number of studies by the FATF, the World Bank's Stolen Asset Recovery Initiative (StAR) and United Nations Office on Drugs and Crime (UNODC) have explored the misuse of corporate vehicles for illicit purposes, including money laundering and terrorist financing. In general, it has been seen that a lack of adequate, accurate and timely beneficial ownership information facilitates the crimes of money laundering and terrorist financing by disguising the:

- identity of known or suspected criminals
- true purpose of an account or property held by a corporate vehicle, and/or
- source or use of funds or property associated with a corporate vehicle.

The information and full identity details of the beneficial owner are the key to combating the menace of money laundering/terrorist financing. The information about the beneficial ownership can be obscured in many ways as explained in the FATF's *Guidance Transparency and Beneficial Ownership (October 2014)*. The real truth is not easy to extract especially in the case of:

a. shell companies (which can be established with various forms of ownership structure), especially in cases where there is foreign ownership which is spread across jurisdictions
b. complex ownership and control structures involving many layers of shares registered in the name of other legal persons
c. bearer shares and bearer share warrants
d. unrestricted use of legal persons as directors
e. formal nominee shareholders and directors where the identity of the nominator is undisclosed
f. informal nominee shareholders and directors, such as close associates and family

g. trusts and other legal arrangements which enable a separation of legal ownership and beneficial ownership of assets
h. use of intermediaries in forming legal persons, including professional intermediaries.

These problems are exacerbated when various countries are involved in different aspects of a corporate vehicle. Criminals create and operate corporate vehicles from different countries, thereby preventing competent authorities in any one jurisdiction from obtaining all the relevant information about a corporate vehicle which is being investigated either for money laundering/terrorist financing or associated predicate offences such as corruption or tax crimes.

Case Studies

If we look at different cases, it is interesting to note that virtually all grand corruption cases involve a company, trust, or foundation ('corporate vehicles' in the StAR report's terminology) that has been created to conceal the beneficial owner's identity.

- Diepreye Alamieyeseigha, former governor of Nigeria's Bayelsa State used companies with innocuous sounding names: *Santolina Investment Corporation* (incorporated in the Seychelles) and *Salomon and Peters* (incorporated in the British Virgin Islands) in order to conceal his beneficial interest in, and ownership of, monetary and real estate assets he acquired through bribery and corruption.
- Bruce Rappaport, former Ambassador of Antigua and Barbuda to Israel and Russia, bought an 'off-the-shelf' company called *Offshore Services ltd*, renamed it *IHI Debt Settlement*, and used that entity to defraud his government of US$ 14 million.
- US lobbyists Jack Abramoff and Michael Scanlon set up the *American International Center* (incorporated in Delaware), a supposed think tank that in reality was a sham created to divert funds to entities they owned and controlled.

3.1.3 Political Connections

The dangers of customers with political connections, and therefore a heightened risk of corruption or involvement in the extraction of national assets, was recognised by the FATF from the first version of its Recommendations. The risk extends to immediate family members and associates, who may be used by a politically exposed person (PEP) to disguise their ownership of looted assets. The FATF introduced the concept of a PEP, which is defined as:

- ***Foreign PEPs*** *are individuals who are or have been entrusted with prominent public functions by a foreign country, for example heads of state or of government, senior politicians, senior government, judicial or military officials, senior executives of state owned corporations, important political party officials.*
- ***Domestic PEPs*** *are individuals who are or have been entrusted domestically with prominent public functions, for example heads of state or of government, senior politicians, senior government, judicial or military officials, senior executives of state owned corporations, important political party officials.*

Of course, PEP status does not mean an individual is corrupt – most will not be – but is an indication of risk that financial institutions must mitigate. Until 2012, the Recommendations only applied to foreign politically exposed persons, but domestic politically exposed persons must now be considered, and 4MLD contains provisions relating to them.

3.1.4 Establishing Beneficial Ownership

The FATF defines a **beneficial owner** as the natural person(s) who ultimately owns or controls a customer and/or natural person on whose behalf a transaction is being conducted. It also includes those persons who exercise ultimate effective control over a legal person or arrangement.

MLR 2017 Regulation 5(1)(b) provides that as part of the standard evidence, the firm should know the names of all individual beneficial owners owning or controlling more than 25% of the company's shares or voting rights, (even where these interests are held indirectly) or who otherwise exercise control over the management of the company.

The firm, for operational purposes, is likely to have a list of those authorised to give instructions for the movement of funds or assets, along with an appropriate instrument authorising one or more directors (or equivalent) to give the firm such instructions. The firm must take risk-based and adequate measures to verify the identity of those individuals.

The FATF recognises the problem in Section E of its 2012 Recommendations (24 and 25). The FATF provides guidance to the regulators on how to create transparency in the beneficial ownership in different structural arrangements. The EU's 4AMLD also addresses the issues of PEP corruption and the complicated legal arrangements that conceal the beneficial ownerships.

The two FATF Recommendations in this regard are:

1. *Recommendation 24: Transparency and beneficial ownership of legal persons – countries should take measures to prevent the misuse of legal persons for money laundering or terrorist financing. Countries should ensure that there is adequate, accurate and timely information on the beneficial ownership and control of legal persons that can be obtained or accessed in a timely fashion by competent authorities. In particular, countries that have legal persons that are able to issue bearer shares or bearer share warrants, or which allow nominee shareholders or nominee directors, should take effective measures to ensure that they are not misused for money laundering or terrorist financing. Countries should consider measures to facilitate access to beneficial ownership and control information by financial institutions and designated non-financial businesses and professions (DNFBPs) undertaking the requirements set out in Recommendations 10 and 22.*
2. *Recommendation 25: Transparency and beneficial ownership of legal arrangements – countries should take measures to prevent the misuse of legal arrangements for money laundering or terrorist financing. In particular, countries should ensure that there is adequate, accurate and timely information on express trusts, including information on the settlor, trustee and beneficiaries, which can be obtained or accessed in a timely fashion by competent authorities. Countries should consider measures to facilitate access to beneficial ownership and control information by financial institutions and (DNFBPs) undertaking the requirements set out in Recommendations 10 and 22.*

MLR 6, 5(b) read in conjunction with the JMLSG Guidance defines a beneficial owner as:

'Normally an individual who ultimately owns or controls the customer or on whose behalf a transaction or activity is being conducted'.

In respect of private individuals, the customer is the beneficial owner, unless there are features of the transaction, or surrounding circumstances, that indicate otherwise. Therefore, there is no requirement on firms to make proactive searches for beneficial owners in such cases, but they should make appropriate enquiries where it appears that the customer is not acting on their own behalf.

However, in the case of companies, MLR 6 defines beneficial owners as individuals either owning or controlling more than 25% of body corporates or partnerships (or at least 25% of trusts) or otherwise owning or controlling the customer. These individuals must be identified, and risk-based and adequate measures must be taken to verify their identities.

Verification requirements differ for customers and beneficial owners. The identity of a customer must be verified on the basis of documents, data or information obtained from a reliable and independent source.

The obligation to verify the identity of a beneficial owner the firm must take risk-based and adopt adequate measures so that it is satisfied that it knows who the real beneficial owner is.

The firm, in view of the money laundering or terrorist financing risk associated with the business relationship, to make use of records of beneficial owners in the public domain (if any exist), will ask its customers for relevant data; require evidence of the beneficial owner's identity on the basis of documents, data and information obtained from a reliable and independent source; or obtain the information otherwise, such as electronic databases and other sourced web applications.

3.1.5 Other Risk Factors

The financial firm in the context of CFC must assess its risks of how it might most likely be involved in money laundering or terrorist financing and the exercise should include factors which indicate these risks such as the following:

Source of Funds and Wealth

Obtaining information on the source of funds or source of wealth of the customer is an integral component of EDD measures that are applied by the financial firms for higher risk business relationships.

These measures are undertaken by the financial firm as part of its AML/CFT risk management exercise. Situations where the origin of wealth and/or source of funds of a beneficial owner cannot be easily verified or where the audit trail has been deliberately broken and/or unnecessarily layered pose as high risk of financial crime.

Expected Account Activity

Activities which can make it easier to conceal underlying beneficiaries or have no legitimate commercial rationale pose higher risks for the possibility of conduct of financial crime. Such activities include:

- customers (not necessarily PEPs) based in, or conducting business in or through, a high-risk jurisdiction, or a jurisdiction with known higher levels of corruption or organised crime, or drug production/distribution

- customers engaged in businesses which involves significant amounts of cash, or which are associated with higher levels of corruption (eg, arms dealing, extractive industries, scrap metal dealing, construction)
- customers engaged in industries that might relate to proliferation activities.

As part of the customer take-on process, firms will establish the expected account activity (the types of transactions, their frequency and size) and will then monitor the account against those expectations and against peer groups of similar customers. This will help identify unusual activity that may turn out to be suspicious. A money launderer may use an account in an innocuous way at the beginning of the relationship and then gradually increase the funds being placed through the account, until the relationship bears no resemblance to the one outlined at the point of CDD.

Public Contracts

The process of government contracting and procurement poses a risk of corruption. An obvious example is a contract for government procurement awarded to an enterprise in response to a bribe. Corruption can occur at any point in the process, starting from design and preparation, when selecting the technical criteria, the due date for submission of offers, the time of delivery of the project, and the parties invited to tender may distort the process.

In the UK, the Public Contracts Regulations 2015 (Statutory Instrument 2015 No. 102) came into force on 26 February 2015. The new rules apply to new procurement exercises after 26 February, subject to a small number of exceptions listed in the Regulations.

Charities, Voluntary and Not-for-Profit Bodies

Charities, voluntary and not-for-profit bodies range in size and scope from very small local groups to large multinational organisations. The risks are clearly not uniform across the sector, but there is a recognition that the activities of some of the organisations are vulnerable to abuse and that fake charities can be established to facilitate criminal activity, and at worst, terrorist financing. The FATF introduced a Special Recommendation in relation to non-profit organisations (NPOs) in 2001 (now Recommendation 8 in the current standards). This Recommendation highlighted the potential vulnerability to terrorist financing, but was criticised, particularly by civil sector organisations for being responsible for a cautious attitude, including removing services, towards charities by banks.

After much consultation, Recommendation 8 was revised in 2016. The revision was intended to clarify that not all NPOs are high risk and was intended to be addressed by the Recommendation and better align the implementation of it with the risk-based approach. The FATF has also published two relevant papers, *Risk of Terrorist Abuse of NPOs (June 2014)* and the *FATF Best Practices on Combating the Abuse of NPOs (June 2015).*

3.2 Opaque Corporate and Ownership Structures

Learning Objective

8.3.2 Understand the risks from counterparties with opaque corporate and ownership structures

Corporate and ownership structures are rendered opaque in more than one way. Some of the more popular ways of creating opaque structures are through having:

1. capital in the form of bearer shares
2. shell banks, and
3. anonymous accounts.

Regulations provide that extra care must be taken in the case of companies with capital in the form of bearer shares, because in such cases it is often difficult to identify the beneficial owner(s) of the firm. Companies that issue bearer shares are also frequently incorporated in high-risk jurisdictions. Firms should adopt procedures to establish the identities of the holders and material beneficial owners of such shares and to ensure that the financial firm is notified whenever there is a change of holder and/or beneficial owner.

As a minimum, these procedures should require a firm to obtain an undertaking in writing from the beneficial owner which states that immediate notification will be given to the firm if the shares are transferred to another party. Depending on its risk assessment of the client, the firm may consider it appropriate to have this undertaking certified by an accountant, lawyer or equivalent, or even to require that the shares be held by a named custodian, with an undertaking from that custodian that the firm will be notified of any changes to records relating to these shares and the custodian.

A **shell bank** is an entity incorporated in a jurisdiction where it has no physical presence involving meaningful decision-making and management, and which is not part of a financial conglomerate. Firms are not allowed to enter into, or continue, a correspondent banking relationship with a shell bank (Regulation 16 (1), (2), (5) and FATF Recommendation 13) and must take appropriate measures to ensure that they do not enter into or continue a correspondent relationship with a bank that is known to permit its accounts to be used by a shell bank.

Similarly, firms are also not allowed to set up an anonymous account or an anonymous passbook for any new or existing customer. All firms must apply CDD measures to all existing anonymous accounts and passbooks before such accounts or passbooks are used in any way (Regulation 16 (3), (4) and FATF Recommendation 10).

3.3 Measures to Minimise Financial Crime Opportunities within a Firm

Learning Objective

8.3.3 Understand what measures can be adopted to minimise financial crime opportunities within a firm: conflicts of interest policies; compliance monitoring; information barriers/Chinese walls; restricting physical access; limiting access to data; effective sign-off protocols; gifts and entertainment policies; remuneration policies; objective audit processes; IT security; whistleblowing; employee vetting; penetration testing and vulnerability assessment; secure disposal; staff training; segregation of duties

3.3.1 Conflicts of Interest Policies

In a financial institution, conflicts of interest can arise in many ways such as between:

- the institution and a client
- two or more clients in the context of the provision of services by the bank to those clients
- a bank vendor and a client.

Principle 8 of the FCA's *Principles for Businesses* requires that a firm must manage conflicts of interest fairly, both between itself and its customers and between a customer and another customer. The principle also requires the boards of directors and senior management to establish effective frameworks to identify, control and review conflicts of interest.

Senior management of a financial institution is basically responsible for ensuring that its systems, controls and procedures are adequate to identify and manage conflicts of interest. The compliance and legal departments normally assist in the identification and monitoring of actual and potential conflicts of interests in the workings of the institution.

The aim of any conflict of interest policy is to protect the integrity of the organisation's decision-making process, to enable the stakeholders to have confidence in it and to protect the integrity and reputation of the institution, management, employees and clients. The policy needs to be designed in such a manner that the management, employees and clients of the firm should avoid any actual conflicts of interest as well as the perception of conflicts of interest.

There are some basic key principles that are common to most of the conflict of interest policies:

1. definition of a conflict of interest in the specific context of the organisation
2. possibilities of such conflicts in future
3. criteria of declaring a conflict of interest situation, and
4. addressing a situation of actual or potential conflict of interest.

3.3.2 Compliance Monitoring

Monitoring compliance provides quality assurance and applies to the day-to-day activities of the operations of an institution. Compliance monitoring is typically undertaken by an independent function in the second line of defence. The compliance-monitoring team may report directly to the board.

3.3.3 Information Barriers

'**Chinese wall**' is a business term describing an information barrier within an organisation that is erected to prevent unnecessary information exchanges or communication flows that could lead to situations of conflicts of interest. A Chinese wall is employed in a variety of functional environments, including the financial sector, business, software development, project management, network security, law and journalism.

The FCA's Handbook glossary defines it as an:

> *'arrangement that requires information held by a person in the course of carrying on one part of its business to be withheld from, or not to be used for, persons with or for whom it acts in the course of carrying on another part of its business'.*

A Chinese wall (also now called an 'ethics wall') in a financial firm may be erected to separate and isolate people who make investments from those who are privy to confidential information that could influence the investment decisions. The wall is created to prevent leaks of corporate inside information as firms are generally required by law to safeguard insider information and ensure that improper trading does not occur.

A Chinese wall is most commonly employed in investment banks, between the corporate-advisory area and the brokering department to separate those giving corporate advice on takeovers from those advising clients about buying shares.

3.3.4 Restricting Physical Access

Data security should be considered as a specific fixed-risk responsibility. Data security is not only an IT issue but concerns key staff across the business (such as those with responsibility for human resources, security and countering financial crime) in their data security work.

The FCA in its *Financial Crime Guide* regards it as a good practice for senior management to assess data security risk and put in place appropriate policies, procedures and controls to reduce it. The importance of data security and how to keep it safe should also be understood by the staff. The risk of unauthorised access to premises and restricted areas, such as computer servers, record rooms and filing cabinets where customer data may exist must be assessed and a commensurate level of security must be provided by the management of the firm. The assessment should consider factors such as the vulnerability of premises; controls, filing and storing of records.

The limiting of physical access may involve measure such as:

1. installing alarms or CCTV
2. restricting access to the office with the use of door buzzers or key pad entry

3. monitoring visitors at all times
4. liaising with law enforcement agencies
5. raising staff awareness of the risks of poor physical security.

3.3.5 Limiting Access to Data

The portability of data in large quantities, using the internet or small storage devices has created a new dimension and risk factor to data security. This portability necessitates the introduction of proper controls to mitigate the risk by limiting the access to data.

Sophisticated criminals are increasingly targeting financial institutions to steal the data these institutions hold on their customers. Theft of personal customer details, such as names, addresses, bank details and passwords are attractive to organised criminals who want to undertake fraud. This data can be used for criminal activities such as, account takeovers and credit card fraud.

There are many ways that criminals can target financial firms to steal data, including:

- placing people as employees who download data onto USB sticks
- theft of computers, laptops and data files on disk
- phishing, vishing and other social engineering techniques.

Once criminals have the personal details, including bank accounts and investments, they can try to steal customer assets. They may take over the accounts of their victims, changing the address and/or bank details and then sell investments or withdraw monies, having them paid into fraudulently opened bank accounts. They can then withdraw and abscond with the cash.

Data theft can have very damaging consequences for the financial firm which may be left with angry customers and loss of reputation. Depending on the circumstances, the organisation may have to compensate their customers and reinstate their accounts.

Financial crime is estimated globally to cost the financial services sector around $20 billion pa.

3.3.6 Effective Sign-Off Protocols

Every staff member of the organisation has a responsibility to know, to understand and to abide by standards and also the workplace expectations. There are some almost universally accepted good computing practices and protocols that apply to computer users and now form part of most workplace expectations.

These 'best practices' or expectations from a computer user include:

- use of two-factor log-in plus use of passwords that cannot be easily guessed
- protection of these passwords
- protection of information when using the internet and email
- securing access to laptops, computers and mobile devices at all times, and
- effective sign off protocols.

The effective sign off protocol basically requires the computer users to shut down, lock, log off their computer before leaving them unattended, and also to make sure that these devices require a secure password to start up again.

The protocol also requires that the computers and portable devices should automatically log off when they are not being used. An automatic log-off process ensures that if a staff member has left the computer or has forgotten to log off, the opportunity for anyone else to access the computer is minimised.

In short, the protocol ensures that staff never leave their computers terminals unattended while logged on or never leave their computer unattended without first logging off.

3.3.7 Gifts, Entertainment and Remuneration Policies

Gifts and entertainment on a modest scale are commonly used to build goodwill and strengthen working relationships among business associates. Providing or accepting occasional meals, small company mementoes and even tickets to sporting and cultural events may be appropriate in certain circumstances. However, if offers of gifts, entertainment or travel are frequent and/or of substantial value, they may create the appearance of, or an actual, conflict of interest or be regarded as illicit payment.

Organisations in the financial sector do not subscribe to a common approach and some firms are more careful and have stricter gift policies, where staff are not allowed to accept directly or indirectly any discount, gift, entertainment (including meals, cultural events and tourist visits) or favours (referred to as gifts) that may influence, or be perceived to influence, the exercise of their function, or the performance of their duties or their judgement. Most other organisations also do not encourage corporate gifts or entertainment of any nature and do set high ethical and acceptable standards of behaviour which employees are obliged to follow in relation to any corporate gifts and entertainment.

Low-value items, for example, key rings, mugs, mouse mats and pens are allowed, providing that they have been given to employees as a goodwill gesture. High-value items, money or vouchers need to be passed to a designated person in the firm who decides if these gifts should be accepted or returned to the sender. Any offer or receipt of corporate entertainment or hospitality is referred to senior management before being offered or accepted. This includes and is not limited to, all corporate hospitality and invitations to lunch, dinner or other meals.

The FCA's *Financial Crime Guide* regards it as example of good practice if a firm has:

1. policies and procedures that clearly define the approval process and the limits applicable to gifts and hospitality (G&H)
2. processes for filtering G&H by employee, client and type of hospitality for analysis
3. processes to identify unusual or unauthorised G&H and deviations from approval limits for G&H
4. ensured that staff are trained on G&H policies to an extent appropriate to their role, in terms of both content and frequency, and regularly reminded to disclose G&H in line with policy
5. prohibited cash or cash-equivalent gifts.

The *Guide* considers examples of poor practice, which can be held against the firm such as:

1. senior management do not set a good example to staff on G&H policies or define acceptable limits and the approval of the process are not clearly defined
2. the G&H policy is not kept up to date
3. no steps are taken to minimise the risk of gifts going unrecorded, and
4. G&H and levels of staff compliance with related policies are not monitored.

Financial institutions must establish their remuneration policies to ensure that they can attract, develop, retain and reward employees. Remuneration includes salaries, bonus payments as well as additional payments including pensions and health insurance, and is a key driver of behaviour. Supervisory authorities establish remuneration guidelines that specifically focus on senior and risk-taking staff with an aim to:

- ensure risk and reward are aligned
- discourage excessive risk taking and short-term actions
- encourage effective risk management, and
- support positive behaviour.

3.3.8 Objective Audit Processes

Management is primarily responsible for identifying and complying with laws and regulations and for preventing and detecting acts of financial crime that affect the organisation.

The objective of an audit is to express an opinion as to whether the financial statements present fairly, in all material respects, the financial position, the results of operations, and the cash flows of the organisation. The auditor is responsible for detecting material misstatements from errors or fraud to achieve the objective of the audit. The auditors must observe the professional standards and code of ethics laid down by their professional body. Where serious discrepancies are identified, the auditors are under obligation to make an appropriate report, including where required to the law enforcement agencies.

Internal audit is an important part of the corporate governance structure within an organisation. It helps an organisation accomplish its objectives by bringing a systematic, disciplined approach to evaluate and improve the effectiveness of risk management, control, and governance processes. In other words, internal audit's basic role is to deal with issues such as compliance, fraud and is the crucial third line of defence in the fight against bribery, corruption and other financial crime.

Internal audit reviews the means used by the organisation to protect its assets, and assesses whether the appropriate safeguards are in place. If these are not well protected, then internal audit must recommend how to address the issue identified. Audit is not an extension of, or a substitute for good management, but can have a role in advising management and providing control with assurance to the board or executive.

Every audit begins with a planning phase that formulates its scope and audit plan, on which the auditors base their work plan. Depending on the management and special requests an audit work plan may include management audits, fraud and combating financial crime reviews and other special services. The auditors must design their audit procedures in such a manner that the audit should meet the objectives of the audit, which for a financial institution includes CFC.

3.3.9　IT Security

Financial sector firms are required to have appropriate governance, systems and controls in place to manage risk and minimise any threat to data security. The FCA expects firms to adopt a risk-based, proactive monitoring of staff to ensure that they are accessing or changing data for genuine business reasons. The FCA *Financial Crime Guide* regards it as a good practice to conduct regular reviews of individuals' IT access rights including for those staff who change roles but still retain access rights that they no longer need. In this context, random checks and assessments to ensure that staff are only accessing customer records for genuine business reasons are important.

Each staff member should have their own username and password for the organisation's IT systems. Firms must ensure that staff do not share usernames and passwords, or write them down and that they observe good password standards. In this context, it is recommended that the passwords should be a combination of letters, numbers and keyboard symbols, at least seven characters in length and changed regularly. Memory sticks and CDs may be good business tools but these devices can be easily concealed and used largely undetected. Therefore, firms should consider the risk of data loss or theft that can arise if portable devices are used without authorisation or in breach of procedures.

It will be appropriate to:

1. disable USB ports and CD writers, and
2. issue encrypted memory sticks to staff who need them.

It is good practice to maintain a clear record of who owns laptops and memory sticks to ensure that the firm will notice if one is lost or stolen. In addition, random checks of laptops may be helpful to ensure that only staff authorised to hold customer data on their laptops are doing so.

The FCA recommends that there should be clear procedures for backing up data. The threats to customer data throughout the whole backup process from the production of the backup tape or disk, through the transit process, to the ultimate place of storage should be considered. Firms should also consider encrypting their backup data, and when held offsite by a third party, proper due diligence on the third party is necessary. Disaster recovery procedures and remote backup should be given due consideration.

Internet and email facilities should only be provided to the staff with a genuine business need and firms should consider carefully the risks arising from allowing staff to access web-based communication facilities, examples of which include:

- web-based email (eg, Gmail)
- social networking sites (eg, Twitter)
- instant messaging (eg, Messenger), and
- file-sharing software (eg, Dropbox).

Use of these facilities, poses an increased risk that data may be lost or stolen and it will be appropriate to completely block access to these types of internet facilities, especially for staff that have access to customer data. It is also important to ensure that all customer data is securely disposed of, regardless of its format, whether it is in paper or electronic format.

3.3.10 Whistleblowing

Learning Objective

8.3.6 Know the additional measures financial services firms can take to manage the risk of financial crime originated or enabled by an employee: implementing whistleblowing procedures

Whistleblowing is when an employee reports suspected wrongdoing at work. Officially this is called *'making a disclosure in the public interest'*. An employee can report things that are not right, are illegal or if anyone at work is neglecting their duties, particularly if these pose health and safety risks.

The FCA has issued guidelines for the possible whistleblowers working in the financial sectors and the FCA is the 'prescribed person' under the Public Interest Disclosure Act (PIDA) 1998, which provides the statutory framework for protecting employees from detriment if they blow the whistle on their employer.

The Anti-Corruption Plan 2014 recognises the need to support those who help to identify and disrupt corruption. The plan reiterates the UK government's commitment to ensure a strong legislative framework to encourage workers to speak up about incidents of bribery and corruption without fear of reprisal. The Plan also intends to continue to explore whether there is more that can be done to incentivise and support whistleblowers in cases of bribery and corruption.

The FCA, alongside the PRA, on 6 October 2015 has published new rules in relation to whistleblowing. These new FCA rules aim to encourage a culture where individuals feel able to raise concerns and challenge poor practice and behaviour. The rules on whistleblowing took full effect in September 2016. The rules apply to deposit-takers (banks, building societies, credit unions) with over £250 million in assets, and to insurers subject to the Solvency II Directive.

The new key rules on whistleblowing require a firm to:

- appoint a senior manager as their whistleblowers' champion
- put in place internal whistleblowing arrangements able to handle all types of disclosure from all types of person
- put text in settlement agreements explaining that workers have a legal right to blow the whistle
- tell UK-based employees about the FCA and PRA whistleblowing services
- present a report on whistleblowing to the board at least annually
- inform the FCA if it loses an employment tribunal with a whistleblower
- require its appointed representatives and tied agents to tell their UK-based employees about the FCA whistleblowing service.

These rules are, however, also a non-binding guidance for all other firms that are supervised by the FCA and PRA.

3.3.11 Employee Vetting

There are requirements that staff in FCA-approved roles meet fit and proper criteria. The firm recruiting staff is expected to carry out various checks to determine this, including credit and criminal record checks. In most firms, junior staff also tend to have access to most customer data and present a higher risk in terms of potential conduct of financial crime. Firms should, therefore, be applying a risk-based approach to reducing financial crime and enhancing recruitment checks where appropriate.

The recruitment process should cover normal checks like ID checks, county court judgements (CCJs), bankruptcy, credit referencing, directorships, property ownership search, professional memberships, professional qualifications, validation of education and Disclosure and Barring Service (DBS) checks. The Criminal Records Bureau (CRB) and the Independent Safeguarding Authority (ISA) were merged to become the DBS in 2012.

The FCA's *Financial Crime Guide* views it as good practice if in a firm:

- staff in higher risk roles are subject to more thorough vetting
- temporary staff in higher risk roles are subject to the same level of vetting as permanent members of staff in similar roles
- where employment agencies are used, the firm periodically satisfies itself that the agency is adhering to the agreed vetting standard.

The FCA prescribes a simple basic level 'fit and proper' criterion for most grades of staff and an enhanced criterion for more senior levels.

In short, firms should be satisfied that the people they are recruiting have the honesty and integrity to handle customer data and other financial crime risks.

3.3.12 Penetration Testing and Vulnerability Assessment

A penetration test is defined as the process of systematically and actively testing a network deployed in a financial institution to determine what vulnerabilities may be present in it and to create a report with recommendations to mitigate or resolve these vulnerabilities.

Security measures commonly deployed in a network include systems like firewalls, intrusion detection and anti-virus software. To protect themselves from criminals, financial organisations need to go one step further by trying to understand the possible weaknesses of their deployed network.

Penetration Testing

A penetration test simulates the actions of an external and/or internal cyber attacker that aims to breach the information security of the organisation. The tools and methods employed by the penetration tester are similar to those utilised by hackers but it is only a probe of the network. It is conducted by skilled security specialists to attempt to break-in to the network and related systems to identify any vulnerabilities.

Vulnerability Assessment

A vulnerability assessment is the process of identifying and quantifying security vulnerabilities in a system. It is an in-depth evaluation of firm's information security system posture, indicating weaknesses as well as providing the appropriate mitigation procedures required to either eliminate those weaknesses or reduce them to an acceptable level of risk. A vulnerability assessment usually includes a mapping of the network and the systems connected to it, an identification of the services and versions of services running and the creation of a catalogue of vulnerable systems.

A vulnerability assessment forms the first part of a penetration test. An additional step in a penetration test is the exploitation of any detected vulnerabilities, to confirm their existence and to determine the damage that might result due to the vulnerability being exploited and the resulting impact on the organisation.

Penetration Testing versus Vulnerability Assessment

The difference between a penetration test and a vulnerability assessment is significant. In comparison to a penetration test, a vulnerability assessment is not so intrusive and does not always require the same technical capabilities. However, vulnerability assessments and penetration testing are both valuable tools and integral components of a threat and vulnerability management process.

3.3.13 Secure Disposal

Customer data is held by the firm either in paper and/or electronic format. It is important that firms should ensure that all customer data is securely disposed of regardless of its format.

There have been media reports in the recent past of financial institutions disposing of paper-based customer data insecurely. The reputational and regulatory risks of doing so are high, and so is the financial crime risk to customers. Many small firms tend to dispose of paper records by shredding all confidential waste in-house and some use a specialist secure disposal company. Using these methods is regarded as a good practice by the FCA.

On the electronic side, computer disks and any other data storage devices should be destroyed or shredded before disposal. In addition, firms should securely dispose of computers and hard drives when no longer needed.

It is poor practice simply to dispose of a computer at a rubbish dump, donate it to a charity or sell it to the staff, without first removing, destroying or wiping the hard drive. If the firm chooses to wipe the hard drive, specialist software should be used and an IT specialist should be consulted.

The policy of the firm on the disposal of customer data should be known to the staff, and where a third party is used, proper knowledge of its systems and possible monitoring of the process is preferable.

3.3.14 Staff Training

With regards to qualifications and training, the FCA regards it as good practice that firms should ensure that their employees' training needs are assessed at the outset and at regular intervals (including if their role changes). Appropriate training and support be provided and it should be ensured that any relevant training needs of the employees are satisfied. Firms should also review at regular intervals the quality and effectiveness of such training.

A firm must review, on a regular basis, employees' competence and take appropriate action to ensure that they remain competent for their role. It should also be ensured that maintaining competence for an employee takes into account such matters as:

1. technical knowledge and its application
2. skills and expertise, and
3. changes in the market and to products, legislation and regulation.

A firm must ensure that an employee who has been assessed as competent also remains competent by completing appropriate continuing professional development (CPD) programmes.

3.3.15 Segregation of Duties

Segregation of duties is implemented to ensure no single person has sole control over a transaction. Ideally, the persons initiating, recording, authorising, and reconciling transactions should not be the same. Segregation of duties ensures that (un)intentional mistakes are discovered early and that fraud does not go undetected.

In a small organisation, it is not always possible to implement segregation of duties due to the small number of employees, with employees often undertaking multiple tasks. As the organisation grows, segregation of duties will need to be implemented as soon as practicable and, in the mean time, checks and controls need to be in place to reduce the risks of mistakes, and to ensure the early discovery of any errors.

3.4   Internal Policies and Procedures

Learning Objective

8.3.4   Understand how internal policies and procedures on CFC are formulated: laws and regulations; regulators' handbooks; relevant codes of conduct; sector and regulatory guidance

3.4.1   Regulators' Handbooks

The FCA requires that all regulated firms and even some unregulated entities should produce:

> 'appropriate documentation of [its] risk management policies and risk profile in relation to money laundering, including documentation of that firm's application of those policies'.

A statement of the firm's AML/CTF policy and the procedures to implement it should necessarily clarify how the firm's senior management intends to discharge its responsibility for the prevention of money laundering and terrorist financing. This provides a framework of direction to the firm and its staff, and identifies the individuals and functions responsible for implementing particular aspects of the policy.

The firm's policy on CFC should also set out how senior management will undertake its assessment of the money laundering and terrorist financing risks the firm faces, and how these risks are to be managed. These policies are essential even for a small firm, as a summary of its high-level AML/CTF policy will focus the minds of staff on the need to be constantly aware of such risks and how they are to be managed.

Considering the extra-territorial applicability of laws for CFC firms must also communicate their policies and procedures established within the UK to prevent activities related to money laundering and terrorist financing to their branches and subsidiaries located outside the UK.

3.4.2 Laws and Regulations

Regulations are mandatory requirements made under enabling provisions/powers given in the law and have the same enforceability as laws. They are primarily rules and are designed to fill in the details of the broader concepts mandated by parliament in laws/statutes. Rulemaking is designed to ensure that a reasonable course of action is taken to meet a requirement given in law.

Regulations are also referred to as 'delegated legislation' or 'secondary legislation' and are made by a minister, or occasionally by a public body, under powers conferred by a law enacted by the parliament (primary law). There is a long list of different types of delegated legislation which may be called orders, rules, regulations, schemes or codes, depending on what the parent act calls them.

The UK's Cabinet Office *Guide to Making Legislation* (July 2015), in its one of the notes defines regulation as:

> 'A rule with which failure to comply would result into conflict with law or being ineligible for funding and other applied for schemes. This includes EU regulations, Acts of Parliament, statutory instruments, rules, orders, schemes and regulations etc made under statutory powers by minister or agencies, licences and permits issued under government authority, codes of practice with statutory force, guidance with statutory force, codes of practice, guidance, self-regulation, partnership agreements with government backing, approved codes of practice or bye-laws made by government'.

Simply put, the legislations establish the general governing 'laws' while the 'regulations' provide the specific ways in which those laws are interpreted and applied. Regulations have the same legal effect as primary laws.

3.4.3 Relevant Codes of Conduct

A code of conduct, in general terms, is explained as a set of rules that outline the norms and rules and responsibilities of, or proper practices for, an individual, party or organisation. Codes of conduct basically set benchmarks for behaviour in the marketplace and provide visible guidelines for behaviour. Codes in a way are an open disclosure by an organisation of the way it operates.

Codes can have different structures such as a general statement of principles and obligations, as well as technical agreements pertaining to specific operational aspects such as reporting requirements and even some dispute-resolution powers. However, in essence, there are primarily two types of codes of conduct – voluntary and mandatory codes.

Voluntary Code

Voluntary codes encourage organisations to conduct themselves in a manner that is beneficial both to the organisation and to the community in which they operate. They can also serve as a sign to consumers that the organisation's product, service or activity meets certain standards.

Voluntary codes exist for a range of industries, products and services, and address many aspects of marketplace behaviour. Voluntary codes are referred to by different names, including codes of conduct, codes of practice, voluntary initiatives and guidelines. Irrespective of what they are called, all such codes have certain commonalities:

- They are a set of non-legislatively mandated commitments.
- One or more individuals or organisations subscribe to them.
- They are designed to influence, shape and control or benchmark behaviour.
- They are to be applied in a consistent manner.
- They all try to reach a consistent outcome.

Mandatory Code

The mandatory codes also have different shapes and may comprise of either broad principles or of more specific provisions or they can be a combination of both.

All mandatory codes are prescribed and drive their validity from some legislation, regulation or rule. For example, the UK Corporate Governance Code that sets out standards of good practice in relation to board leadership and effectiveness, accountability and relations with shareholders. All companies with a premium listing of equity shares in the UK are required under the Listing Rules (mandated by the FCA) to report in their annual report and accounts on their application of the Code of Corporate Governance.

A code is meant to complement relevant standards, policies and rules, not to substitute for them.

3.4.4 Sector and Regulatory Guidance

The JMLSG is made up of the leading UK trade associations in the financial services sector. Its aim is to promulgate good practices in countering money laundering and to give practical assistance in interpreting the UK MLRs.

This is primarily achieved through publication of industry guidance for the financial sector which the JMLSG has been producing since 1990. The JMLSG Guidance sets out what is expected of firms and their staff in relation to the prevention of money laundering and terrorist financing, but allows them some discretion as to how they apply the requirements of the UK AML/CTF regime to products, services, transactions and customers.

Coverage

The Guidance covers money laundering and terrorist financing prevention. These are closely related to the risks of other financial crime, such as fraud. Fraud and market abuse, as separate offences, are not dealt with in the Guidance. It does, however, apply to dealing with any proceeds of crime that arise from these activities.

It is not to be applied unthinkingly, as a checklist of steps to take but financial institutions should encourage their staff to 'think risk' as they carry out their duties within the legal and regulatory framework governing AML/CTF. For example, production of the required evidence of identity should not automatically qualify the customers for access to the product or service they may be seeking.

Legal Status

The Proceeds of Crime Act (POCA) 2002 requires a court to take account of industry guidance that has been approved by an HM Treasury Minister when considering whether a person within the regulated sector has committed the offence of failing to report. Similarly, the Terrorism Act requires a court to take account of such approved industry guidance when considering whether a person within the financial sector has failed to report. MLRs 42 and 45 also provide that a court must take account of similar industry guidance in determining whether a person or institution within the regulated sector has complied with any of the requirements of the MLRs. The JMLSG Guidance is approved, with the exception of Chapter 4 of Part III, which deals with sanctions (a topic covered more comprehensively by Wolfsberg Group guidance and the FCA guide for firms).

When considering whether to take disciplinary action against an FCA-regulated firm in respect of a breach of the relevant provisions of the Systems and Controls Sourcebook (SYSC), the FCA also has regard to whether a firm has followed relevant provisions in JMLSG Guidance. When considering whether to bring a criminal prosecution in relation to a breach of the MLRs, the FCA may also have regard to whether the person concerned has followed this Guidance. In short, the FCA expects financial institutions to address their management of risk in a thoughtful and considered way, and establish and maintain systems and procedures that are appropriate, and proportionate to the risks identified. The JMLSG Guidance assists firms precisely to do this.

3.5   Effective Due Diligence Techniques

Learning Objective

8.3.5   Know effective techniques for conducting due diligence on: directors, employees; contractors; service providers

Most financial institutions and other businesses do background checks, screenings and due diligence reviews of new employees, directors and contractors. Background and integrity checks are an important feature of today's fast-paced, globalised business environment. However, in most cases, the due diligence process with respect to employees is finished at entry level.

Firms are required to employ staff who possess the skills, knowledge and expertise to carry out their functions effectively. Staff in higher-risk roles should be subject to more thorough vetting and temporary staff in higher-risk roles should be subject to the same level of vetting as permanent members of staff in similar roles. The firms must also review the competence of employees, directors and contractors, and take appropriate action to ensure they remain competent for their roles.

The ability to effectively pre-empt internal security issues and corporate crimes can save businesses from huge potential losses and reputational damage. Proper background checks must be repeated periodically to ensure that staff in financial difficulties, who may be more susceptible to bribery or committing fraud, are appropriately managed and regular meetings should be held with staff and attempts made to identify changes in their personal circumstances which might make them more susceptible to financial crime. There have been cases where junior staff have been bribed or threatened by criminals who wished to obtain customer data to commit fraud.

3.6 Employee Risk

Learning Objective

8.3.6 Know the additional measures financial services firms can take to manage the risk of financial crime originated or enabled by an employee: raising awareness; improving the management of IT privileges for joiners, movers and leavers; classifying and segmenting data; embedding ethical practice in relation to data security

3.6.1 Raising Awareness

All employees must be made aware of laws relating to money laundering and terrorist financing and the policies and procedures of their firm (including whistleblowing procedures). Employees must be given training relevant to their role (see chapter 9, section 3.1.6).

3.6.2 Identity and Access Management (IAM)

In large organisations, there is a continual flow of people joining, transferring between and leaving departments. One of the biggest challenges businesses face in the modern era is ensuring that those with access to information systems have appropriate access and that access levels are changed or removed when they leave or move within the organisation.

An identity and access management (IAM) system provides the framework and technology to support the business processes that facilitate the management of electronic identities. IAM solutions automate the initiation, capture, recording and management of user identities and their related permissions. The IAM will typically include a centralised directory service that scales appropriately as the organisation grows or shrinks. This central directory prevents credentials from being recorded haphazardly or insecurely as employees try to manage the burden of having multiple passwords or other authentication mechanisms for different systems.

IAM systems also facilitate the process of user enrolment and setup. If implemented correctly, they can decrease the time required for these processes by delivering a smooth workflow that reduces errors and the potential for abuse on misconfiguration.

A modern IAM system should automatically match employees' job titles, locations and business unit IDs to access rights. Depending on an employee's profile, some privileges may be automatically provisioned, while others may require special authorisation. All deviations to the standard should be subject to management approval to prevent 'privilege creep'.

3.7 Facilitating Practical Solutions for Business

Learning Objective

8.3.7 Know the role industry groups and guidance bodies play in facilitating practical solutions for business

Industry groups, trade associations and guidance bodies primarily are founded and funded by businesses that operate in a specific industry. These associations play a useful role, by providing a forum that enables businesses to meet and discuss industry-wide issues and practices. These bodies also provide a structured platform to share knowledge and technical information on common issues of interest.

These associations are not simple discussion groups but carry out many valuable and lawful functions which are not only beneficial to the industry but also to the public and regulators. The benefits include performing some critical functions such as setting common ethical and technical standards for products and developing mutual interfaces, thus providing practical solutions for businesses. These bodies are becoming increasingly important in the contemporary interdependent and technologically-linked markets. The Society for Worldwide Interbank Financial Telecommunication (SWIFT), a member-owned cooperative is one of the many examples of industry-driven initiatives.

These groups also set the standards for:

- admission to membership of a profession
- arranging education and training for those wishing to join the industry
- paying for and encouraging research into new techniques.

Industry groups, guidance bodies and similar associations have a crucial role to play in promoting best practices, helping companies become more ethical and competitive and helping the regulators to formulate effective policies.

Business associations provide a structure that enables private-sector leaders to find one voice and coordinate efforts. They provide the opportunity and leverage to influence lawmakers in an ethical and democratic manner.

Industry self-regulation schemes often arise out of an industry group which also normally provides a code of practice devised by members. A code prepared by the industry group can be better suited to a particular sector than having a code that is drafted in general terms for a whole industry. Such codes can acquire the force of regulatory law if approved by a statutory body or legislation authorises a self-regulatory body to regulate (eg, Lloyd's of London insurance market). Legislation may also prompt the adoption of codes, for example the JMLSG's Guidance for the prevention of money laundering/combating the financing of terrorism.

However, members of trade or industry associations are usually competitors and need to guard against the risk that their activities do not breach competition law.

3.8 Auditing

Learning Objective

8.3.8 Understand how auditing contributes to corporate governance, accounting and reporting requirements: audit committees; internal audit; external auditors

Firms are obligated to establish internal controls and systems to implement and maintain adequate policies and procedures sufficient to ensure compliance, including their managers, employees and appointed representatives (or where applicable, tied agents), with obligations under the regulatory system and for countering any risk that they may be used to further financial crime.

Accounting controls must be incorporated in the routine accounting processes of the business.

3.8.1 Audit Committees

Depending on the nature, scale and complexity of its business, it may be appropriate for a firm to form an audit committee. The audit committee arrangements of a firm must be structured to be proportionate to the task. The tasks expected from the audit committee vary according to the size, complexity and risk profile of the company.

An audit committee should typically examine management's process for ensuring the appropriateness and effectiveness of systems and controls, the arrangements made by management to ensure compliance with requirements and standards under the regulatory system, and oversee the functioning of the internal audit.

In short, the functions of the audit committee can be summarised as to:

- monitor the integrity of the financial statements of the company
- review the company's internal financial controls and monitor and review the effectiveness of the company's internal audit function
- make recommendations in relation to the appointment of the external auditor
- review and monitor the external auditor's independence and objectivity and the effectiveness of the audit process, taking into consideration the regulatory requirements.

Public limited companies listed on stock exchanges are obliged to have an audit committee that comprises of at least three, or in the case of smaller companies two, independent non-executive directors.

3.8.2 Internal Audit

The internal audit function assesses adherence to and the effectiveness of internal systems and controls, procedures and policies. The internal audit function is part of the overall systems and controls functions of an organisation.

All financial institutions are required to have an internal audit function. This function has responsibility for assessing the adequacy and controls within the organisation.

Internal audit must be an independent function and its independence must also be ensured to enable it to perform. The function must have direct reporting line either to the audit committee of the board or the board of directors depending on the structure of the company.

Internal audit plays an important role in the risk control framework. It provides an independent, internal assessment of the effectiveness of the firm's processes, controls and procedures. It also independently assesses the effectiveness of the risk management and CFC systems within the organisation. By performing regular business reviews, internal audit assesses whether the firm's processes and procedures are adequately controlled, up to date and performed in accordance with manuals and documentations.

In short, an internal audit function should have clear responsibilities and reporting lines to an audit committee or appropriate senior manager, be adequately resourced and staffed by competent individuals, be independent of the day-to-day activities of the firm and have appropriate access to a firm's records.

3.8.3 External Audit

External audit is an independent appraisal function of the financial statements of an organisation. It is carried out by a professionally qualified accountant of a recognised auditing firm authorised to conduct such an audit. All financial institutions are required to appoint external auditors. Not all businesses have a similar requirement: in the UK, the Companies Act exempts small companies (based on criteria relating to turnover, balance sheet and number of employees).

External auditors are required to audit the annual accounts and to report to the shareholders of the company whether, in their opinion, the annual accounts:

1. have been prepared in accordance with the Companies Act 2006, and
2. give a 'true and fair view' of the state of affairs of the company at the end of the financial year.

The external auditors have a limited role in CFC. Their role is to make assessment and pass an opinion. However, they are helpful in the fight against financial crime by:

- assessing procedures and making recommendations for improvement
- identifying weaknesses
- making appropriate reports in case of any discrepancies.

Discussions by the management with external auditors can be helpful as they have broader experience by virtue of having audited the customer and other firms. The external auditors are often well-placed to give advice even on potential areas of business risk that their auditing activities do not require them to focus on.

Moreover, and of great assistance to the risk oversight function, a firm's external auditors may produce specialised reports for the board and external clients that give assurance that the firm's control environment works as designed.

End of Chapter Questions

Think of an answer for each question and refer to the appropriate section for confirmation

1. How can financial crime like embezzlement impact a firm?
   Answer reference: Section 1.1.1

2. Why is limiting access to data important?
   Answer reference: Section 1.1.4

3. Explain misstatement of financial circumstances?
   Answer reference: Section 1.3.1

4. What is corporate malfeasance?
   Answer reference: Section 1.3.2

5. What risks must be looked into when outsourcing an activity?
   Answer reference: Section 1.4.2

6. What are the objectives of a financial crime risk assessment?
   Answer reference: Section 2.1

7. What are five examples of risk factors relating to country risk?
   Answer reference: Section 2.2.4

8. Why is establishing 'beneficial ownership' important?
   Answer reference: Section 3.1.3

9. What are possible opaque corporate and ownership structures?
   Answer reference: Section 3.2

10. What is whistleblowing?
    Answer reference: Section 3.3.9

Chapter Nine
The Role of the Financial Services Sector

1. Relations with Regulators	**181**
2. Specific Responsibilities	**185**
3. Compliance	**191**
4. FinTech	**195**
5. Customer Due Diligence (CDD)	**198**
6. Reporting Obligations	**212**
7. Consent Regimes	**214**
8. Record-Keeping Obligations	**215**

This syllabus area will provide approximately 7 of the 50 examination questions

1. Relations with Regulators

Learning Objective

9.1.1 Know financial services firms' responsibilities for dealing with regulatory and other relevant authorities: protection of customer confidentiality; responses to information requests; responses to investigation orders; civil recovery, forfeiture and confiscation; global investigation, prosecution and confiscation; presentation of evidence in court; transparency with the regulator

1.1 The Protection of Customer Confidentiality

The Data Protection Act 1998 controls how personal information is used by organisations, businesses and the UK government. Everyone responsible for using data must follow strict rules called the Data Protection Principles. Organisations must make sure that the information is:

- used fairly and lawfully
- used for limited, specifically stated purposes
- used in a way that is adequate, relevant and not excessive
- accurate
- kept for no longer than is absolutely necessary
- handled according to people's data protection rights
- kept safe and secure
- not transferred outside the UK without adequate protection.

Firms have a duty of confidentiality to their clients, former clients and in some cases, prospective clients. Financial institutions (FIs) are accordingly required to keep the affairs of their clients confidential unless disclosure is required or permitted by law or there is client consent. There is stronger legal protection for more sensitive personal information, such as ethnic background, political and religious beliefs.

Some of the customer information held by financial firms can even be privileged. Firms should be alert to the financial crime risks associated with holding customer data and should have written data security policies and procedures which are proportionate, accurate, up to date and relevant to the day-to-day work of staff.

The General Data Protection Regulation (GDPR), which is an EU legislation, became enforceable on 25 May 2018. The UK's decision to leave the EU has not affected the commencement of the GDPR.

Like the Data Protection Act, the GDPR applies to data controllers and processors in organisations. It will apply if either the organisation holding and processing the personal information is in the EU or if the data subject is based in the EU. It applies to organisations outside the EU who process the personal data of EU residents or who offer goods or services to individuals in the EU. The GDPR will harmonise rules across the EU for data protection and includes data protection principles similar to those in the Data Protection Act.

The GDPR expands the definition of personal data to include things such as genetic, mental, cultural, economic and social identities. Individuals are given increased rights over the use of their data, including the 'right to be forgotten', ie, to have their data erased from the records. Data controllers are made more accountable and will need to be able to demonstrate compliance, including in some cases the appointment of a data protection officer.

1.2 Responses to Information Requests and Investigation Orders, and Transparency

Regulators expect their firms to cooperate with them. The FCA states that:

'A firm must deal with its regulators in an open and cooperative way, and must disclose to the appropriate regulator appropriately anything relating to the firm of which that regulator would reasonably expect notice'.

The FCA has wide statutory powers to require information and documents from the subject of an investigation and other persons. Its powers and how it uses them are explained in the Enforcement Guide part of the Handbook. In any particular case, the FCA will decide which powers, or combination of powers, are most appropriate to use having regard to all the circumstances. It may use its power found in Section 165 of Financial Services and Markets Act (FSMA) to require information and documents from firms to support both its supervisory and its enforcement functions. Where the FCA has decided that an investigation is appropriate, the FCA will normally appoint investigators pursuant to FSMA Section 168. The FCA can also request information or carry out an investigation on behalf of overseas regulators. The MLRs also provide powers for statutory bodies such as the FCA and HMRC to require information from regulated firms.

1.3 Civil Recovery, Forfeiture and Confiscation

The Proceeds of Crime Act (POCA) 2002 primarily creates three asset recovery regimes each of which has its own features which are relevant in considering the best approach that may be taken in any particular case.

1.3.1 Civil Recovery

Civil recovery is a form of non-conviction-based asset forfeiture which allows for the recovery in civil proceedings before the High Court of property which is, or represents, property obtained through unlawful conduct. Importantly, the proceedings are against the property itself rather than against an individual.

These proceedings are civil litigation and the civil standard of proof (the balance of probabilities) applies. The court, however, will still require cogent evidence in order to be satisfied that property is on balance more likely to be the proceeds of unlawful conduct than not. To prove that property was obtained through unlawful conduct, it is not necessary to prove the commission of a particular criminal offence by a particular person on a particular occasion. It is sufficient to prove that the property was obtained through offending of a particular type (eg, drug trafficking, fraud and bribery).

Civil Recovery Orders are commonly sought by the law enforcement agency in the High Court under the POCA 2002, or the cash forfeiture proceedings may be brought in the Magistrates' Court following seizure by the police or HMRC under the Drug Trafficking Act 1994 or the POCA.

1.3.2 Cash Forfeiture

Cash forfeiture generally provides a simple and speedy non-conviction-based Magistrates' Court procedure for recovering criminal cash seized by the law enforcement agency. Any party wishing to contest the forfeiture must demonstrate to the court that the cash comes from a legitimate source.

Cash forfeiture is usually placed outside criminal proceedings. However, a person knowingly having possession of criminal property commits a money laundering offence, so a cash seizure creates the potential for a criminal investigation which may result in the making of a confiscation order in a larger sum than the seized cash.

In any case, where proceeds of crime have been identified but it is not feasible to secure a conviction, or a conviction has been secured but no confiscation order made, relevant authorities invariably consider using the non-conviction-based powers available under the Act.

1.3.3 Confiscation

Confiscation normally follows conviction for an offence. In making an order the court must decide whether the defendant has a 'criminal lifestyle', based on a number of legislative triggers, including specific types of offences. Where the court decides that the offender does not have a criminal lifestyle the court has to decide whether the offender has benefited from their particular criminal conduct; the specific crime for which they were convicted.

Where the offender fails to pay the confiscation order they may be subject to a sentence of imprisonment (the 'default sentence'). This imprisonment is not an alternative to paying the order, and the order remains 'extant' despite the serving of the default sentence.

Confiscation proceedings can take place under different laws including under the Criminal Justice Act (CJA) 1988, Drug Trafficking Act 1994, or POCA.

1.3.4 Transparency with the Regulator

Transparency, in this context, is usually taken to mean clear, open and honest communications. This means that financial institutions must report any significant issues in relation to financial crime to the regulators as soon as possible and not try to hide any information.

1.4 Global Investigation, Prosecution and Confiscation

The FATF paper on *Best Practices on Confiscation (Recommendations 4 and 38) and a Framework for Ongoing Work on Asset Recovery (October 2012)* stated that a robust system of provisional measures and confiscation is an important part of any effective anti-money laundering and combating the financing of terrorism regime. Confiscation prevents criminal property from being laundered or reinvested either to facilitate other forms of crime or to conceal illicit proceeds.

The FATF paper provides best practices and other helpful guidance to help countries strengthen their legal frameworks and to ensure that asset tracing and international financial investigations, prosecutions and confiscations can be conducted effectively. Some of the best practices listed are as follows:

a. Ensure that appropriate procedures and legal frameworks are in place to allow informal exchanges of information to take place, including prior to the letter of request for mutual legal assistance being submitted.
b. Competent authorities should engage with foreign counterparts, from a bilateral or regional perspective, and utilise appropriate international bodies such as the Egmont Group, INTERPOL, Europol and Eurojust.
c. Ensure that appropriate procedures and legal frameworks are in place to allow information deemed to be useful to be shared on a spontaneous basis. The practice of spontaneously exchanging information relating to asset tracing and financial investigation helps to facilitate a culture of reciprocity.
d. Enter into general arrangements, including formal bilateral asset sharing agreements, with other countries.

FATF Recommendation 4 obliges countries to adopt measures that allow laundered property, proceeds or instrumentalities to be confiscated without requiring a criminal conviction (non-conviction based confiscation) to the extent that such a requirement is consistent with the principles of their domestic law.

In the international context, Recommendation 38 mandates countries to have authority to take expeditious action in response to requests by foreign countries, and for arrangements for coordinating freezing, seizure and confiscation proceedings, which should include the sharing of confiscated assets, particularly when confiscation is directly or indirectly a result of coordinated law enforcement actions.

The UNCAC also creates the internationally accepted understandings for civil forfeiture, confiscation and recovery of property.

Article 31 of UNCAC titled as *Freezing, Seizure and Confiscation* requires states that are party to the Convention to have in place in their respective national laws a comprehensive framework for the restraint and confiscation of criminal proceeds. Chapter IV of the Convention covers the 'International Cooperation' on the issue (Articles 43–50) and its Chapter V covers the specific issues relating to Asset Recovery (Articles 52–57).

Article 43 of the Convention on 'International Cooperation' mandates that:

> '1. States parties shall cooperate in criminal matters in accordance with Articles 44 to 50 of this Convention. Where appropriate and consistent with their domestic legal system, states parties shall consider assisting each other in investigations of and proceedings in civil and administrative matters relating to corruption'.

1.5 Presentation of Evidence in Court

Black's Law Dictionary defines evidence as *'something (including testimony, documents and tangible objects) that tend to prove or disprove the existence of an alleged fact'*. The two most important constituent elements of an evidence for presentation in any court are that it is relevant (admissible and competent) and has weight'.

Financial firms will be able to provide evidence of transactions and other matters relating to their customers. Their regulators will expect them to cooperate with investigations and provide such evidence, where it is necessary. However, suspicious activity reports (SARs) made under AML/CFT legislation should be kept confidential, to protect both the reporting institution and the individual reporter. Normally, the matters contained in SARs can be produced in evidence through witness statements or production order procedures, but in some cases there may be an apparent need to disclose the SAR.

The Home Office guidance states that *'where disclosure is likely to be ordered in such a case, the prosecution has to carefully weigh the options as to whether it should proceed with the prosecution or withdraw proceedings'.*

2. Specific Responsibilities

2.1 The Role of the Money Laundering Reporting Officer (MLRO), Nominated Officer (NO) or Equivalent

Learning Objective

9.2.1 Know the role of the Money Laundering Reporting Officer (MLRO) and the Nominated Officer (NO) or equivalent

Firms that are subject to the MLR provisions (except for sole traders who have no employees), whether or not they are regulated by the FCA, are legally obliged to appoint an individual as a money laundering reporting officer (MLRO).

The MLRO should be able to act on their own authority and should also act as a focal point for the firm's anti-money laundering (AML) activity. The FCA specifically requires the MLRO to have responsibility for oversight of the firm's AML systems and controls, which include appropriate training for the firm's employees in relation to money laundering. The MLRO will need to be involved in establishing the basis on which an RBA to the prevention of money laundering/terrorist financing is put into practice. If the firm's staff suspects that it is being used for the purpose of money laundering or terrorist financing they are required to notify their MLRO. The regulatory provisions require that a firm's records should include reports by the MLRO to senior management.

Approval by the FCA is required for the appointment of the MLRO.

Firms are also obliged to appoint a nominated officer (NO) or equivalent who is responsible for receiving internal reports of suspicion, assessing them using their experience and access to information, and, if necessary, ensuring SARs under POCA and the Terrorism Act are made to the NCA.

The obligations under the MLRs and data protection legislation are not exactly mutually aligned; the NO and the MLRO must have due regard to both sets of obligations.

In many FCA-regulated firms it is likely that the MLRO and the NO will be one and the same person. When, therefore, discharging different legal and regulatory functions, it is important that the individual working in the dual role is aware which role they are acting in when performing their functions, making a notification or sending reports.

2.2 The Responsibilities of Directors and Senior Management

Learning Objective

9.2.2 Understand the responsibilities of directors and senior management in relation to CFC under the Senior Managers and Certification Regime (SM&CR) or equivalent individual accountability regimes

From a practical perspective, firms should consider how best they should assess and manage their overall exposure to financial crime. For financial institutions to have an effective risk-based approach, it is essential that the risk-based process is embedded in the internal controls of the institutions. The board of directors is ultimately responsible for ensuring that a designated person maintains an effective internal control structure, including suspicious activity monitoring and reporting. Strong senior management leadership and its engagement in combating financial crime (CFC) are crucial components of the design and implementation of an approach. Individual responsibility regimes such as the UK's Senior Management and Certification Regime (SM&CR), Australia's Banking Executive Accountability Regime (BEAR), or Hong Kong's Manager in Charge Regime all attempt to shape conduct, culture and governance across the financial sectors. Similar regimes have been implemented, or are in the course of being implemented across all major financial centres.

The board of directors and senior management must create a culture of compliance, ensuring that the firm's policies, procedures and processes, designed to limit and control risks of money laundering and terrorist financing, are fully consistent with the law and that staff adhere to them. The board of directors and senior management should be fully engaged in decision-making processes and should take ownership of the risk-based measures adopted, since they will be held accountable if the approach is found to be inadequate.

Firms should look at fraud and money laundering as part of an overall strategy to tackle financial crime, and there are many similarities – as well as differences – between procedures to tackle the two. When considering money laundering and terrorist financing issues, firms should consider their procedures against other financial crimes and market abuse and how these might reinforce each other. If responsibilities are allocated to different departments, there will also need to be strong links between those in the firm who are responsible for managing and reporting on these various areas of risk. When measures involving the public are taken specifically as an anti-fraud measure, the distinction should be made clear. Management has a responsibility to ensure that the processes and procedures are appropriately designed and implemented, and are effectively operated to reduce the risk of the firm being used in connection with conduct of any financial crime.

It is the responsibility of senior management to:

- establish procedures to ensure that there is objective validation of risk assessment and management processes and of related internal controls
- obtain appropriate assurance that the adopted risk-based methodology reflects the risk profile of the financial institution, and
- carry out regular assessments of the adequacy of the systems in place to prevent the firm from being used to further financial crime.

The extent and timing of this independent testing should take into account the size, nature and complexity of the firm and reporting should be conducted by, for example, the internal audit department, external auditors, compliance monitoring, specialist consultants or other qualified parties who are not involved in the implementation and operation of the financial institution's CFC programme.

UK – Senior Managers & Certification Regime (SM&CR)

The SM&CR in the UK, is designed and monitored by the FCA, which expects the senior management of the firm to take clear responsibility for managing financial crime risks, which should be treated in the same manner as other risks faced by the business. There should also be evidence that the senior management is actively engaged in the firm's approach to addressing the risks. Although SM&CR is a UK-specific regime, others that are in force or are being developed largely follow the same structure and rules.

Examples

- In 2008, the FSA fined Sindicatum Holdings ltd £49,000 and its MLRO, Michael Wheelhouse, £17,500 for not having adequate AML systems and controls in place for verifying and recording clients' identities. This was the first time the FSA had fined an MLRO.

- In 2011, the FSA imposed a financial penalty of £140,000 on Alpari (UK) ltd, an online provider of foreign exchange services for speculative trading, for failing to have in place adequate AML systems and controls. Its former MLRO, Sudipto Chattopadhyay also received a financial penalty of £14,000.

- In 2012, the FSA fined Habib Bank AG Zurich £525,000 and its former MLRO Syed Itrat Hussain £17,500 for failure to take reasonable care to establish and maintain adequate AML systems and controls.

- In 2017, the FCA fined Deutsche Bank £163,076,224 for breaches related to culture/governance and financial crime.

- In late 2019, Hong Kong's financial regulator levied a penalty of HK$3.5 million on Fidelty for conducting futures trades without the correct licence for 11 years. The fine was relatively low since the misconduct was not deliberate and no customers had lost money.

- During 2019, global fines for AML exceeded USD 8 billion.

In its *Financial Crime: A Guide for Firms* the FCA highlights its expectations that:

1. senior management should set the right tone and demonstrate leadership on financial crime issues
2. the firm should take active steps to prevent criminals taking advantage of its services
3. the firm has a strategy for self-improvement on financial crime, and that
4. the firm should have clearly laid down criteria to its functionaries for escalating any financial crime issues.

The FCA regards it as example of poor practice if:

1. there is little evidence of senior staff involvement
2. the firm concentrates on narrow compliance with minimum regulatory standards and has little engagement with the issues
3. financial crime issues are dealt with on a purely reactive basis, and
4. there is no meaningful record or evidence of senior management considering financial crime risks.

2.2.1 FCA – Senior Managers and Certification Regime (SM&CR)

In March 2016, the FCA's SM&CR came into force. The SM&CR focuses on the most senior individuals in a firm who either hold key individual positions or have overall responsibility for whole areas of the firm.

Under the SM&CR, firms must:

- ensure each senior manager has a statement of responsibilities setting out the areas for which they are personally accountable
- produce a firm responsibilities map that knits these together, and
- ensure that all senior managers are preapproved by the regulators before carrying out their roles.

One of the prescribed senior manager roles is overall responsibility for the establishment and maintenance of effective anti-money laundering systems and controls. In some firms, this responsibility may be given to the MLRO; if it is not, the relevant senior manager must have responsibility for supervision of the MLRO.

In 2018, the SM&CR was extended to include FCA firms, with changes to the regime including:

- newly prescribed responsibility for the conduct rules
- changes to the 12-week rule allowing for the temporary appointment of senior managers, and
- extending the partner senior management function to banks.

2.2.2 Management Information (MI)

The UK's FCA has issued amendments to *Financial Crime: A Guide for Firms* to reflect the importance of management information (MI) in combating financial crime. With respect to financial crime systems and controls, MI should provide senior management with 'sufficient information' to understand the financial crime risks to which their firm is exposed. This will help them effectively manage those risks and adhere to the firm's own risk appetite. MI should be provided regularly and ad hoc, as risk dictates.

Examples of financial crime MI include:

- an overview of the financial crime risks to which the firm is exposed, including information about emerging risks and any changes to the firm's risk assessment
- legal and regulatory developments and the impact these have on the firm's approach
- an overview of the effectiveness of the firm's financial crime systems and controls
- an overview of staff expenses, gifts and hospitality and charitable donations, including claims that were rejected, and
- relevant information about individual business relationships, for example:
    - the number and nature of new business relationships, in particular those that are high risk
    - the number and nature of business relationships that were terminated due to financial crime concerns
    - the number of transaction monitoring alerts
    - details of any true sanction hits, and
    - information and trend analysis from other parts of the business about suspicious activity reports considered or submitted.

MI may come from more than one source, for example customer-facing staff, the compliance department, internal audit, the MLRO and the NO or equivalent.

2.2.3 Structure

The FCA expects that with respect to CFC all financial institutions should have a governance structure that is appropriate to the size and nature of their business.

To be effective, a governance structure should enable the firm to:

- clearly allocate responsibilities for financial crime issues
- establish clear reporting lines and escalation paths
- identify and manage conflicts of interest, in particular where staff hold several functions cumulatively
- record and retain key decisions relating to the management of money laundering and sanctions risks, including, where appropriate, decisions resulting from informal conversations.

In *Financial Crime: A Guide for Firms*, the FCA considers it an example of good structure for CFC in a firm if:

1. financial crime risks are addressed in a coordinated manner across the business and information is shared readily
2. management responsible for financial crime are sufficiently senior as well as being credible, independent and experienced
3. it has considered how counter-fraud and anti-money laundering efforts can complement each other, and
4. it bolsters insufficient in-house knowledge or resource with external expertise, for example in relation to assessing financial crime risk or monitoring compliance with standards.

2.2.4 Risk Assessment

A thorough understanding of financial crime risks is key if a firm is to apply proportionate and effective systems and controls to combat crime.

A firm should identify and assess the financial crime risks to which it is exposed because of, for example, the products and services it offers, the jurisdictions it operates in, the types of customer it attracts, the complexity and volume of transactions, and the distribution channels it uses to service its customers. Firms can then target their financial crime resources towards the areas of greatest risk.

A business-wide risk assessment should be comprehensive and consider a wide range of factors – it is not normally enough to consider just one factor. It should draw on a wide range of relevant information – it is not enough to consider just one source and it should be proportionate to the nature, scale and complexity of the firm's activities.

Firms should build on their business-wide risk assessment to determine the level of risk associated with individual relationships.

This should enable the firm to take a holistic view of the risk associated with the relationship, considering all relevant risk factors, and apply the appropriate level of due diligence to manage the risks identified.

2.3 Adequate Management Systems and Controls

Learning Objective

9.2.3 Know the regulator's expectations from firms with respect to adequate management systems and controls to combat financial crime

Preventing and combating financial crime is a vital element of the overall remit and one of the FCA's key regulatory objectives of protecting and enhancing the integrity of the UK financial system. This includes ensuring that the system is not being used for purposes connected with financial crime. To achieve this, regulators impose specific requirements on financial services firms encapsulated in their regulations. In addition, they may also provide relevant guidance.

Best practices exist for the development of systems and controls to combat financial crime and, in some cases, an overview of financial crime risks and good and poor management practices. In combination, these can assist firms to adopt a more effective, risk-based and outcomes-focused approach to mitigating financial crime risk and enhances the understanding of the regulator's expectations. It helps firms to assess the adequacy of their financial crime systems and controls and remedy the deficiencies. Firms have a legal and regulatory obligation to establish and maintain robust defences and risk management frameworks that identify and mitigate risks. Regulators often provide firms with best practice information to improve their ability to combat all types of financial crime.

When supervising firms, the focus is on whether the firms are complying with rules and other legal obligations. Best practice information and guidance is for firms to consider when establishing, implementing and maintaining their anti-financial crime systems and controls, but is not directly enforced.

3. Compliance

3.1 Compliance Risk

Learning Objective

9.3.1 Know the Basel Committee on Banking Supervision's (BCBS's) definition of the term 'compliance risk'

9.3.2 Understand how a compliance culture may be created and maintained, including: tone from the top, performance management process, appointment of compliance/anti-MLROs; information gathering and analysis; application in routine operations; raising awareness; training; updates

The Basel Committee on Banking Supervision (BCBS) defines compliance risk as:

> 'the risk of legal or regulatory sanctions, material financial loss, or loss to reputation a bank may suffer as a result of its failure to comply with laws, regulations, rules, related self-regulatory organisation standards, and codes of conduct applicable to its banking activities'.

Prudent management of the compliance risks, together with effective supervisory oversight, is critical in protecting the safety and soundness of banks as well as the integrity of the financial system. Failure to manage these risks can expose banks to serious reputational, operational, compliance and other risks. The BCBS has also issued a set of guidelines (January 2014) to describe how banks should include risks related to money laundering and terrorist financing within their overall risk management framework.

These guidelines are consistent with the International Standards on Combating Money Laundering and the Financing of Terrorism and Proliferation, issued by the FATF in 2012 and supplement their goals and objectives. The risk management guidelines published by the BCBS include cross-references to FATF standards to help banks comply with national requirements based on those standards.

The general ethical climate of an organisation is typically called 'tone from the top' reflecting that ethics start with the board and work their way down the organisation from there. When the board displays good ethical behaviour, this sets an example to all other employees of the organisation. Equally, bad behaviour at the top is typically reflected in the behaviour displayed by other members of staff. In addition to the tone from the top, management of staff performance and remuneration are important tools for an institution to reward ethical behaviour and penalise bad behaviour.

3.1.1 Compliance Culture

The culture of an organisation defines and characterises shared attitudes, values, goals, and practices prevailing within the organisation. It shapes judgements, ethics and behaviours that are displayed at key moments that matter to the performance and reputation of firms and the services that they provide.

The FCA views culture from the perspective of a conduct regulator and regards an effective culture as one that supports the business model and business practices that should have at their core, the fair treatment of customers and behaviours that do not harm market integrity.

Ensuring the right outcomes is the responsibility of everyone at the firm, led by senior management, and not something delegated to compliance or control functions.

The key drivers of culture at a firm include:

- setting the tone from the top
- translating this into easily understood business practices
- supporting the right behaviours through performance management, employee development, and reinforcing through reward programmes.

'The FCA evaluates culture at a firm from what is observed. This can be through a range of different measures such as how a firm responds to, and deals with, regulatory issues; what customers are actually experiencing when they buy a product or service from front-line staff; how a firm runs its product approval process and the considerations around these; the manner in which decisions are made or escalated; the behaviour of that firm on certain markets; and even the remuneration structures'.

The FCA also looks at how a board of directors engages in those issues (Clive Adamson, Former Director of Supervision, the FCA, at the CFA Society – UK Professionalism Conference, London, 18 August 2013).

However, the challenge for many firms is that culture is hard to change and requires dedicated and persistent focus over several years to embed different approaches and ways of behaving.

When compliance is made a part of everyday routine, it becomes a culture. In a compliance culture, everyone works towards the same goals of achieving and maintaining compliance. The process starts with induction, with compliance requirements forming part of the initial induction process to ensure staff understand and follow organisational culture right from the beginning.

3.1.2 Appointment of Compliance/Anti-Money Laundering Reporting Officers

The FCA Handbook and Guide provide that the MLRO must have sufficient resources, experience, access and seniority to carry out the role effectively. The firm's staff, including its senior management should consult the MLRO on matters relating to ML; the MLRO should be aware and have oversight of the firm's highest-risk relationships. It is also the responsibility of the senior management to actively support the MLRO and ensure that the MLRO is independent, has adequate resources and has access to all relevant information. The MLRO should be able to escalate relevant matters to senior management and, where appropriate, the board. The MLRO has sole discretion and authority to review internal SARs and make reports to the NCA.

The MLRO in turn must monitor the effectiveness of systems and controls and ensure that they have continuing competence that enables them to discharge their duties efficiently. An MLRO also has to ensure that the firm obtains, and makes appropriate use of, any government or FATF findings concerning the approach to money laundering prevention in countries or jurisdictions with which the firm interacts.

This is especially relevant when the firms are dealing with countries where the approach to money laundering disciplines has been found to be materially deficient by the FATF (assessment reports can be found at www.fatf-gafi.org).

3.1.3 Information Gathering and Analysis

Information gathering is one of the crucial determining factors for compliance professionals to be able to meaningfully analyse data received through the institution's different reporting systems. The manner in which the data is structured basically creates the scope to analyse it and determines whether the problems, if any existing in the systems, can be identified at an early stage.

A substantive knowledge of a company's culture and effectiveness of its compliance programmes can be seen through analysis of reports that allege misconduct and the questions posed about company policies.

The challenge, however, in data analysis and reporting is that there is no right number of total reports or information gathering about specific incident types. Each organisation in the industry faces different risks. Financial institutions intending to use the information gathered through reporting data as a diagnostic tool should also compare their data to that of their peer industries since data within industries can vary.

The analysis of the data gathered over time has now enabled different segments of the industry to develop some industry benchmarks and historical trends. These benchmarks do assist ethics and compliance programmes in making informed decisions about programme effectiveness, potential problem areas, need for corrective interventions and necessary resource allocations.

3.1.4 Application in Routine Operations

Compliance has to be built into the culture of an organisation by prioritising it including by measures such as the following:

> 'compliance records are reflected in staff appraisals and remuneration…and internal audit and compliance departments routinely test the firm's defences against financial crime, including specific financial crime threats' (FCA's *Financial Crime Guide*).

If an organisation ensures that most of the important decisions are taken through consultation with those who are affected by these decisions, then the group dynamics so created also helps taking ownership of the decisions by the entire organisation and helps to embed compliance and control in the normal routine of the staff of the firm.

In short, it is only the creation of a well-rooted compliance culture that enables the continuous and automatic application in routine of compliance requirements within an organisation.

3.1.5 Raising Awareness

It is essential for firms to recognise the importance of staff awareness and alertness. Such factors as staff intuition, direct exposure to a customer face-to-face or on the telephone, and the ability, through practical experience, to recognise transactions that do not seem to make sense for that customer, cannot be automated and can only be achieved through proper staff awareness, training and alertness.

The obligations on senior management and the firm in relation to staff awareness and staff training address each requirement separately. The MLRs require firms to take appropriate measures so that all relevant employees are made aware of the law relating to money laundering and terrorist financing, and that they are regularly given training in how to recognise and deal with transactions which may be related to a financial crime.

The relevant director or senior manager has overall responsibility for the establishment and maintenance of effective training arrangements (Regulation 20). Awareness and training arrangements specifically for senior management, the MLRO and the NOs are equally important and should, therefore, also be considered by firms.

Importantly, a successful defence by a staff member under POCA may leave the firm open to prosecution or regulatory sanction for not having adequate training and awareness arrangements.

3.1.6 Training

Firms have an obligation under the MLRs (Regulation 21) to take appropriate measures so that all relevant employees are made aware of the laws relating to money laundering and terrorist financing. Staff should be given appropriate training on money laundering and other financial crimes to ensure that employees are aware of, and understand, their legal and regulatory responsibilities and their role in handling criminal property and money laundering/terrorist financing risk management.

Firms must employ staff who possess the skills, knowledge and expertise to carry out their functions effectively. They should review employees' competence and take appropriate action to ensure they remain competent for their role. Vetting and training should be appropriate to employees' roles.

It is important that firms ensure that:

1. tailored training is in place to ensure staff knowledge is adequate and up to date
2. new staff in customer-facing positions receive financial crime training tailored to their role before interacting with customers
3. training has a strong practical dimension (eg, case studies) and some form of testing which should always be used
4. the firm satisfies itself that staff understand their responsibilities (eg, computerised training and tests)
5. whistleblowing procedures are clear and accessible, and staff members know that the firm respects their confidentiality.

3.1.7 Updates

A culture of compliance is an essential part of the organisation's proper functioning. If implemented correctly, it lays out the basics of compliance to everyone within the firm as well as setting clear expectations as to what role everyone should play in ensuring the firms adherence to the code of conduct.

Compliance training at all levels starting from induction also forms part of the culture. This compliance training irrespective of methods of delivery must always be up to date. Any formal learning created, must be regularly reviewed and updated to reflect any changes to laws and legislation or to internal policies and procedures.

Outside the formal learning process, the firms must also keep their teams updated with any changes to regulations. This could be done by email, internal newsletters, the intranet or even posters and leaflets around the office building. By making compliance topical, it becomes a point of discussion like other news stories, rather than just another piece of training that the employees have to think about once or twice a year.

4. FinTech

Learning Objective

9.4.1 Know the benefits of utilising technology to support a compliance culture and the limitations of over-reliance on systems

9.4.2 Know how distributed ledger technology (DLT) and advanced/objective blockchain ID can be utilised for customer due diligence (CDD)

9.4.3 Know how the following technological solutions can be used for CDD: digital recognition, face recognition

9.4.4 Know how artificial intelligence (AI) can be utilised for detecting financial crime

9.4.5 Know how data sources can be utilised by firms to detect financial crime: customer complaints; trade and transaction monitoring; suspicious transaction reports (STRs); internet and website usage patterns; customer device profiles; employee turnover statistics

9.4.6 Know the challenges associated with fast-paced electronic markets (FPM)

9.4.7 Know the role of the Global Financial Innovation Network (GFIN)

4.1 The Utilisation of Technology and Reliance on Systems

IT-based control monitoring tools help simplify the consolidation of an organisation's various compliance requirements and facilitate the coordination of distinct and, at times, unrelated documentation requirements and testing efforts. The effective implementation and subsequent embedding of an organisation's compliance programmes into its culture is important for integration with system-based processes. It can be achieved by building compliance activities and procedures into existing business processes and technology so that heads of different businesses can start to share responsibility for compliance.

However, real problems arise when organisations acquire and install system-based compliance programmes that are separate and distinct from their own system of internal controls or its culture. These expensive moves invariably result in organisations burdened with fragmented programmes that are not only difficult to manage and expensive but also almost impossible to monitor.

These automated programmes are ineffective in supporting comprehensive and timely decision-making by managing and supporting the development of a meaningful compliance culture within the organisation.

In short, compliance is more an issue of culture and requires a solution that goes beyond the software. However, technology can help to embed compliance into the culture of an organisation.

4.2 Technological Solutions for Customer Due Diligence (CDD)

Distributed ledger technology (DLT) or blockchain is a digital record or database stored on multiple computers in a network of trusted participants. Each of the participants can make different entries on a record, and the information is not controlled by any individual participant. Information is registered and distributed without the need to have a middleman to facilitate a transaction. Transaction validity is ensured by the use of mathematical verification of the entries between the participants. The larger the number of participants, the higher the number of validations and, therefore, the more secure the network. One of the main challenges with the current CDD processes is that they rely heavily on manual intervention, and are prone to mistakes and data errors. A centralised identity management function using blockchain with multiple participants within a firm will improve efficiency as well as the accuracy of the CDD. It will reduce duplication of efforts and allow for a variation of information to be used across the institution.

Further accuracy of the CDD can be achieved by the incorporation of facial or iris scans, as well as scanned ID information. Particularly if this information can then be used to digitally verify the identity of the (prospective) customer. Digital ID, facial and iris scans can all be incorporated in the process and the information can be saved as part of the blockchain.

4.3 Artificial Intelligence (AI)

Financial institutions inherently have significant amounts of data related to transactions, financial behaviour, and customers. AI can be applied to identify early warning signals for financial crime, highlight irregular or unusual patterns in transactions, and to reduce reliance on manual processes. The use of AI in financial institutions is not yet widespread, but is expected to increase in the near future.

4.4 Data Sources

Different forms of data are collected by an enterprise. These can be divided into three broad categories:

1. Traditional enterprise data from customer information systems, enterprise resource planning (ERP) data, online transactions and financial data (general ledger, accounts payable, accounts receivable).
2. Machine, or sensor-generated data from sources such as call detail records (CDRs), weblogs, smart meters, manufacturing sensors, equipment log and trading system data.
3. Social data from customer feedback streams, blogging sites and social media platforms such as Facebook and LinkedIn.

Over the last decade, there has been an increase in the use of data analytics to mine big data and identify the patterns, trends and anomalies that are often indicators of fraud or other types of financial crime.

In the past, there were isolated and excessively circumscribed efforts to make use of this data, but this was more in response to some particular incidents or investigations than as a systemic effort. Now there are much more concerted efforts to detect, deter and prevent financial crimes and analytics have a major influence in shaping how firms approach these efforts. For example, systems like Enterprise Fraud Management (EFM) are becoming more widespread as they allow organisations to integrate technology platforms, methodologies and analytics approaches to identify the indicators of fraud. Active monitoring of customer complaints, trades and transactions, and suspicious transaction reports (SARs) provides invaluable information to detect financial crime.

As an example, a US federal agency was faced with processing and analysing massive amounts of structured and unstructured data to continue its oversight and monitoring functions. Implementing an EFM infrastructure allowed it to explore the data efficiently, develop models and then refine those models to predict and provide alerts about potential fraudulent behaviour. Case management was incorporated to manage alerts to resolution and then those results were fed back into the models to identify positives and false positives to improve the models' effectiveness. Social network analysis was utilised to identify previously unknown relationships and expand the network of potentially fraudulent actors and activity.

4.5 Fast-Paced Electronic Markets (FPM)

Fast-paced electronic markets (FPM) such as, for example, foreign exchange markets, are expanding significantly. Trading in financial instruments is becoming increasingly electronic, and new participants specifically focused on FPM have entered the market.

These markets and their participants provide challenges for supervisory authorities due to the range of participants, types of data, tools and technology. Supervisory authorities need to understand the new market developments and ensure they have an accurate view of market conditions and how they impact new markets and their participants. Due to their nature, FPMs are fast moving and subject to quick market movements. As such, they require close monitoring and timely analysis of underlying drivers. The BIS identified the following structural trends that have affected the approach to market monitoring as a result of technological advances:

- Change in nature and location of trading, including fragmentation of trading across a large range of new venues.
- Change in the nature of participation with liquidity provision becoming more centralised and non-banking financial institutions entering the market and becoming established.
- Creation and commoditisation of large quantities of high-frequency data may increase barriers to entry, but also opens new opportunities.

4.6 Global Financial Innovation Network (GFIN)

Launched in January 2019 by an international group of financial regulators and related organisations, the Global Financial Innovation Network (GFIN) is committed to supporting financial innovation in the interests of customers. The GFIN aims to provide a more efficient way to support financial innovation firms in their interaction with regulators in scaling their ideas. In addition, they aim to create a platform for financial regulators to share experiences and approaches on innovation in financial services.

5. Customer Due Diligence (CDD)

5.1 The Implementation of Customer Due Diligence (CDD) Procedures

Learning Objective

9.5.1 Know how regulated financial institutions implement customer due diligence (CDD) procedures: know your customer (KYC); ongoing monitoring; non-face-to-face; correspondent banking; politically exposed persons (PEPs); reliance on others

9.5.2 Understand how firms implement a risk-based approach

Customer due diligence (CDD) forms the backbone of any efforts to combat financial crime by any financial institution. FATF Recommendation 10 provides a comprehensive regime of CDD that financial institutions are obliged to observe.

FATF Recommendation 10 prohibits financial institutions from keeping anonymous accounts or accounts in obviously fictitious names.

Financial institutions should be required to undertake CDD measures when:

1. establishing business relations
2. carrying out occasional transactions:
    - above the applicable designated threshold (€15,000), or
    - that are wire transfers in the circumstances covered by the Interpretive Note to Recommendation 16
3. there is a suspicion of money laundering or terrorist financing, or
4. the financial institution has doubts about the veracity or adequacy of previously obtained customer identification data.

The FATF requires countries to ensure by law that financial institutions must conduct CDD. However, countries have the flexibility to determine how to impose specific customer due diligence obligations, either through law or other enforceable means.

5.1.1 Customer Due Diligence (CDD)

A financial institution is required to establish a systematic procedure for identifying and verifying its customers and, where applicable, any person acting on their behalf and any beneficial owner(s). Generally, a financial institution should not establish any relationship, or carry out any transactions, until the identity of the customer has been satisfactorily established and verified in accordance with FATF Recommendations.

Consistent with the FATF standards, the procedures adopted by the financial institutions should include the taking of reasonable measures to verify the identity of the beneficial owner of corporate and trust clients.

When dealing with a representative of the customer it is important that the institution should verify that any person acting on behalf of the customer is so authorised, and should also verify the identity of that person.

The identity of customers, beneficial owners and persons acting on their behalf, should be verified by using reliable, independent source documents, data or information. When relying on documents, an financial institution should be aware that the best documents for the verification of identity are those documents that are most difficult to obtain illicitly or to counterfeit such as passports and driving licences. When relying on sources other than such documents, the financial institution must ensure that the methods (which may include checking references with other financial institutions and obtaining financial statements) and sources of information are appropriate, and in accordance with the financial institution's policies and procedures and risk profile of the customer.

As for all elements of the CDD process, an financial institution should necessarily consider the nature and level of risk presented by a customer when determining the extent of the applicable due diligence measures. In no case, should an financial institution disregard its customer identification and verification procedures just because the customer is unable to be present for an interview (non-face to face customer). The financial institution should also take into account risk factors such as why the customer has chosen to open an account far away from their base/office, in particular in a foreign jurisdiction. It is also important to consider the relevant risks associated with customers from jurisdictions that are known to have AML/CFT strategic deficiencies and apply enhanced due diligence when this is called for by the FATF, other international bodies or national authorities.

Using CDD information, a financial institution should be able to identify transactions that do not appear to make economic sense, that involve large cash deposits or that are not consistent with the customer's normal and expected transactions.

5.1.2 Know Your Customer (KYC)

Know your customer (KYC) is a part of CDD and is a process by which banks obtain information about the identity and activities of customers. This process helps to ensure that bank services are not misused. The KYC procedure must be completed by the financial institutions while opening accounts and should also be periodically updated. KYC involves the verification of identity and residence.

The adoption of effective KYC standards is an essential part of any financial institution's risk management practices. Banks with inadequate KYC risk management programmes may be subject to significant risks, including legal and reputational risk. Sound KYC policies and procedures not only contribute to a bank's overall safety and soundness; they also protect the integrity of the financial system by reducing the likelihood of financial institutions becoming vehicles for money laundering, terrorist financing and other unlawful activities. Recent initiatives to reinforce actions against terrorism have underlined the importance of firms' ability to monitor their customers wherever they conduct business.

In October 2001, the BCBS issued a CDD paper for banks, subsequently followed by a guide in 2003 and a consolidated KYC risk management paper in October 2004. The CDD paper outlines four essential elements necessary for a sound KYC programme.

These elements are:

- customer acceptance policy
- customer identification
- ongoing monitoring of higher risk accounts, and
- risk management.

The principles laid down have been accepted and widely adopted by jurisdictions throughout the world as a benchmark for commercial banks and a good practice guideline for other categories of financial institution.

KYC is the primary tool to establish the identity of the client. This covers identifying the customer and verifying their identity by using reliable, independent source documents, data and information. For individuals, firms should obtain data to verify the identity of the customer, their address/location and a recent photograph. This should also be done for the joint holders and mandate holders.

For non-individuals, banks will obtain identification data to verify the following:

- legal status of the entity
- identity of the authorised signatories, and
- identity of the beneficial owners/controllers of the account.

The KYC process must ensure that sufficient information is obtained on the nature of employment/business that the customer does/expects to undertake and the purpose of the account opening.

5.1.3 Ongoing Monitoring of Due Diligence

The essential sequential outcomes of any system of ongoing monitoring are that:

- it flags up transactions and/or activities for further examination
- these reports are reviewed promptly by the right person(s), and
- appropriate action is taken on the findings of any further examination.

Monitoring can be either in real time, when transactions and/or activities can be reviewed as they take place or are about to take place; or after the event, through some independent review of the transactions and/or activities that a customer has undertaken.

In either case, unusual transactions or activities will be flagged for further examination. Monitoring may be by reference to specific types of transactions, to the profile of the customer, or by comparing their activity or profile with that of a similar, peer group of customers, or through a combination of these approaches. Effective and real-time monitoring is primarily systems-based on a considered identification of transaction characteristics, such as:

- the unusual nature of a transaction – eg, abnormal size or frequency for that customer or peer group
- the early surrender of an insurance policy
- the nature of a series of transactions – eg, a number of cash credits
- the geographic destination or origin of a payment – eg, to or from a high-risk country, and
- the parties concerned – eg, a request to make a payment to or from a person on a sanctions list.

Under Regulation 28 of MLR 2017, firms must conduct ongoing monitoring of the business relationships with their customers. This is a separate and independent, but related, obligation from the requirement to apply CDD measures.

Money Laundering Regulation 8(2) explains that:

'Ongoing monitoring' of a business relationship means:

1. *scrutiny of transactions undertaken throughout the course of the relationship (including, where necessary, the source of funds) to ensure that the transactions are consistent with the relevant person's knowledge of the customer, his business and risk profile, and*
2. *keeping the documents, data or information obtained for the purpose of applying customer due diligence measures up-to-date.*

Firms need to know who their customers are to guard against fraud, including impersonation fraud, and the risk of committing offences under POCA and the Terrorism Act, relating to money laundering and terrorist financing. POCA Sections 327–334 and the Terrorism Act Section 21(A).

Firms need to carry out CDD and monitoring, for two broad reasons:

1. to help the firm, at the time due diligence is carried out, to be reasonably satisfied that customers are who they say they are, to know whether they are acting on behalf of another, and that there is no legal barrier (eg, sanctions) to providing them with the product or service requested, and
2. to enable the firm to assist law enforcement, by providing available information on customers or activities being investigated.

The JMLSG in its Guidance on AML/CFT is of the view that it may often be appropriate for the firm to know rather more about the customer than their identity: it will, for example, often need to be aware of the nature of the customer's business to assess the extent to which their transactions and activity undertaken with, or through, the firm are consistent with that business.

Schedule 7 to the Counter-Terrorism Act 2008 gives HM Treasury power to require firms, in certain circumstances, to carry out enhanced CDD and monitoring (JMLSG Guidance has provided further elaboration of this in Part 3 of its Guidance).

5.1.4 Non Face-to-Face Customer Due Diligence (Enhanced Due Diligence (EDD))

Account opening using a non face-to-face approach refers to a situation where the customer is not interviewed and the signing of account opening documentation and sighting of identity documents of the customer is not conducted in the presence of an employee of a regulated entity, eg, where the account is opened via the internet or by post or telephone.

The MLRs prescribe three specific types of relationship in respect of which enhanced due diligence (EDD) measures must be applied.

These are:

1. where the customer has not been physically present for identification purposes (non-face to face)
2. in respect of a correspondent banking relationship, and
3. in respect of a business relationship or occasional transaction with a politically exposed person (PEP).

The extent of verification in respect of non face-to-face customers basically depends on the nature and characteristics of the product or service requested and the assessed money laundering risk presented by the customer. A firm should take account of such cases in developing their systems and procedures.

MLR 14(2) provides that:

'Where the customer has not been physically present for identification purposes, a firm must take specific and adequate measures to compensate for the higher risk, for example by applying one or more of the following measures:

   a. ensuring that the customer's identity is established by additional documents, data or information;
   b. supplementary measures to verify or certify the documents supplied, or requiring confirmatory certification by a credit or financial institution which is subject to the money laundering directive;
   c. ensuring that the first payment is carried out through an account opened in the customer's name with a credit institution (bank)'.

If a customer approaches a firm remotely (by post, telephone or over the internet), the firm should carry out non face-to-face verification, either electronically, or by reference to documents. The organisation should consider taking additional measures that include assessing the possibility that the customer is deliberately avoiding face-to-face contact. It is, therefore, important to be clear on the appropriate approach in these circumstances.

Non face-to-face identification and verification carries an inherent risk of impersonation fraud, and firms should apply additional verification checks to manage the risk of impersonation fraud. The additional check may consist of robust anti-fraud checks that the firm routinely undertakes as part of its existing procedures, or may include:

- requiring the first payment to be carried out through an account in the customer's name with a UK or EU-regulated credit institution or one from an equivalent jurisdiction
- verifying additional aspects of the customer's identity, or of their electronic footprint
- telephone contact with the customer prior to opening the account on a home or business number which has been verified (electronically or otherwise), or a welcome call to the customer before transactions are permitted, using it to verify additional aspects of personal identity information that have been previously provided during the setting up of the account
- communicating with the customer at an address that has been verified (such communication may take the form of a direct mailing of account opening documentation to him, which, in full or in part, may be required to be returned completed or acknowledged without alteration)
- internet sign-on following verification procedures where the customer uses security codes, tokens, and/or other passwords which have been set up during account opening and provided by mail (or secure delivery) to the named individual at an independently verified address
- other card or account activation procedures, and
- requiring copy documents to be certified by an appropriate person.

5.1.5 Due Diligence in Correspondent Banking

The JMLSG Guidance for the UK financial sector issued on 19 November 2014 defines correspondent banking as:

'the provision of banking services by one bank (the correspondent) to an overseas bank (the respondent) to enable the respondent to provide its own customers with cross-border products and services that it cannot provide itself, typically because it lacks an international network'.

Examples of these services include:

- inter-bank deposit activities
- international electronic funds transfers
- cash management
- cheque clearing and payment services
- collections
- payment for foreign exchange services
- processing client payments (in either domestic or foreign currency), and
- payable-through accounts.

Correspondent banking relationships are vulnerable to money laundering and terrorist financing because they involve a bank carrying out transactions on behalf of another bank's customers where information on those customers is very limited. The UK's MLR 2017 provide that all correspondent banking relationships with respondents from non-EEA states must be subject to an enhanced CDD and ongoing monitoring which should, as a minimum, meet the requirements that are laid down in Regulation 34 of MLR 2017.

The FATF also regards correspondent banks as 'high risk' and in Recommendation 13 obliges that financial institutions should be required, in relation to cross-border correspondent banking and other similar relationships, in addition to performing normal CDD measures, to:

a. gather sufficient information about a respondent institution to understand fully the nature of the respondent's business and to determine from publicly available information the reputation of the institution and the quality of supervision, including whether it has been subject to a money laundering or terrorist financing investigation or regulatory action
b. assess the respondent institution's AML/CFT controls
c. obtain approval from senior management before establishing new correspondent relationships
d. clearly understand the respective responsibilities of each institution, and
e. with respect to payable-through accounts, be satisfied that the respondent bank has conducted CDD on the customers having direct access to accounts of the correspondent bank, which can provide relevant CDD information upon request to the correspondent bank.

Some of the important risks faced when dealing with a correspondent bank are:

- **Geographic risks** – correspondent banking activity deals with transactions all around the globe, therefore, transactions may originate from, terminate in or pass through high-risk jurisdictions. In some cases, multiple high-risk jurisdictions may be involved. Some jurisdictions have inadequate AML standards, insufficient regulatory supervision, greater risk for crime, corruption, drug trafficking or terrorist financing. There is also a potential risk of inadvertently dealing with a shell bank. Transactions with shell banks and anonymous accounts beneficiaries are prohibited under UK MLR 16 and in the US by the Bank Secrecy Act.

- **Risks** are also posed by payable-through accounts; foreign correspondent banking transactions can potentially facilitate and be conduits for financing or laundering the proceeds of different international crimes including terrorist financing, drug trafficking and other underlying offences. Similarly, there is potentially a risk of sanctions violations in correspondent banking relationships with banks located in irresponsible countries that do not honour sanctions.

A correspondent bank's risk profile should, therefore, be developed, based on the location, ownership, management structure, customer base, AML policies and strength of the AML enforcement systems. The challenges of identification of the bank's customers and a full picture of transactions needs to be dealt with when dealing with a respondent.

Transactions involving high-risk corridors (from one or more high-risk countries to another high-risk country) need to be examined very carefully. For example, transactions originating from countries with high corruption indices to tax havens or transactions from a drug consumption jurisdiction to drug production jurisdiction are high risk and must be monitored for suspicious activity.

5.1.6 Due Diligence for Politically Exposed Persons (PEPs)

Individuals who have, or have had, a high political profile, or hold, or have held, public office, can pose a higher money laundering risk to firms as their position may make them vulnerable to corruption. This risk also extends to members of their immediate families and to their known close associates. PEP status itself does not incriminate individuals or entities. It does, however, put the customer, or the beneficial owner, into a higher risk category.

Regulation 35(1) of MLR 2017 requires firms to have appropriate risk-based procedures to:

- determine whether a customer is a PEP
- obtain appropriate senior management approval for establishing a business relationship with such a customer
- take adequate measures to establish the source of wealth and source of funds which are involved in the business relationship or occasional transaction, and
- conduct-enhanced ongoing monitoring of the business relationship.

Firms should, in any case, take adequate and meaningful measures to establish the source of funds and source of wealth. Firms should note that not all declarations are publicly available and that a PEP customer may have legitimate reasons for not providing a copy.

If firms need to carry out specific checks, they may be able to rely on an internet search engine, or consult relevant reports and databases on corruption risk published by specialised organisations such as the Transparency International Corruption Perceptions Index. If there is a need to conduct more thorough checks, or if there is a high likelihood of a firm having PEPs for customers, subscription to a specialist PEP database may be an adequate risk mitigation tool.

Firms should, in any case, take adequate and meaningful measures to establish the source of funds and source of wealth and approval from senior management for establishing a business relationship should be obtained. The firm should, as far as practicable, be alert to public information relating to possible changes in the status of its customers with regard to political exposure. When an existing customer is identified as a PEP, then EDD must be applied to them.

5.1.7 Reliance on Others for Due Diligence

MLR 17 expressly permits a firm to rely on another person to apply any or all of the CDD measures, providing that the other person is listed in Regulation 17(2), and that consent to being relied on has been given. The relying firm, however, retains responsibility for any failure to comply with a requirement of the Regulations, as this responsibility cannot be delegated. The firm relied on must be of a certain regulated type.

The regulatory provision is best explained by a working example.

Example

- Firm A enters into a business relationship with, or undertakes an occasional transaction for, the underlying customer of Firm B, for example by accepting instructions from the customer (given through Firm B).
- Firms A and B both act for the same customer in respect of a transaction (eg, Firm A as executing broker and Firm B as clearing broker).
- Firm A may rely on firm B to carry out CDD measures, while remaining ultimately liable for compliance with the MLRs as under most regulatory frameworks firms can delegate the work but not the responsibility.

In this context, in terms of MLRs, if Firm B is in the UK it must be an FCA-authorised credit or financial institution (excluding a money service business) or an auditor, insolvency practitioner, external accountant, tax adviser or independent legal professional, who is supervised for the purposes of anti-money laundering. If Firm B is in the European Economic Area (EEA) it must be a similar organisation and be supervised for AML. Outside the EEA, Firm A must be satisfied that Firm B is subject to requirements equivalent to the Money Laundering Directive and supervised for compliance with them in an equivalent manner to firms in the EEA.

5.1.8 Risk-Based Approach to Due Diligence

MLR 2017 and other regulations require CDD to be implemented on a risk-based approach which implies that the CDD implemented by a firm should not be rigidly applied, but that the measures should be applied on a risk-sensitive basis depending on the type of customer, business relationship, or nature of the transaction or activity. Lower risk categories will require less information to be gathered than highly complex, high risk categories which would be subject to EDD. A risk assessment will need to be in place to determine the level and extent of information to be collected and independently verified.

5.2 Enhanced Due Diligence (EDD) Requirements for Higher-Risk Situations

Learning Objective

9.5.3 Know enhanced due diligence (EDD) requirements for higher-risk situations

The term enhanced customer due diligence refers to the more rigorous verification processes that must be applied to higher-risk business relationships. The grounds on which enhanced customer due diligence must be applied are set out in Part 1, Chapter 2 (Enhanced Customer Due Diligence) and Regulation 28(11) (ongoing monitoring) of MLR 2017.

A financial institution should also establish EDD policies and procedures for customers who have been identified as higher risk by them. In addition to established policies and procedures relating to appropriate approvals for account opening, a financial institution should also have specific policies regarding the extent and nature of EDD, the frequency of ongoing account monitoring and updating of CDD information and other records.

The FCA in its revised guidance requires that the extent of EDD must be 'commensurate to the risk' associated with the business relationship or occasional transaction but firms can decide, in most cases, which aspects of CDD they should enhance. This will depend on the reason why a relationship or occasional transaction was classified as high risk.

Examples of EDD include:

- obtaining more information about the customer's or beneficial owner's business
- obtaining robust verification of the beneficial owner's identity based on information from a reliable and independent source
- gaining a better understanding of the customer's or beneficial owner's reputation and/or role in public life and assessing how this affects the level of risk associated with the business relationship
- carrying out searches on a corporate customer's directors or other individuals exercising control to understand whether their business or integrity affects the level of risk associated with the business relationship
- establishing how the customer or beneficial owner acquired their wealth to be satisfied that it is legitimate, and
- establishing the source of the customer's or beneficial owner's funds to be satisfied that they do not constitute the proceeds from crime.

5.3 Sanctions Screening Procedures

Learning Objective

9.5.4 Know how financial institutions implement sanctions screening procedures

The consequences of breaching a sanctions regime were explained in chapter 7, section 1.5. Banks and other financial institutions typically use one of the many commercially available automatic screening tools, which are kept updated by the providers. The solutions are complex and vary in detail, but both the firm's customers and all transactions and payments messages will be screened against all relevant sanctions lists. In the case of payments, the screening will take place in real time and any hit will cause the payment to be blocked, pending review. The variable quality of the data on sanctions lists can cause many false positive hits, so firms must invest not just in the software, but also in sufficient staff to screen hits.

5.4 Politically Exposed Persons (PEPs)

Learning Objective

9.5.5 Know examples of politically exposed persons (PEPs)

9.5.6 Know standards for dealing with PEPs: The Money Laundering, Terrorist Financing and Transfer of Funds (information on the Payer) Regulations (MLR 2017) and the FCA's Finalised Guidance G17/6: the treatment of PEPs for anti-money laundering purposes

FATF Recommendation 12 and the related interpretive note do not give any examples of PEPs. However, the Fifth Money Laundering Directive (5MLD) defines a 'PEP' as a person who is or has, at any time in the preceding year, been entrusted with a prominent public function in any country by:

- a state
- a community institution (eg, the European Parliament)
- an international body (eg, the UN), or
- is an immediate family member or a known close associate of such a person.

Family members of a PEP include, but are not restricted to:

- spouses or partners
- children and their spouses or partners
- parents.

Prominent public functions include:

- heads of state or government, ministers and deputy or assistant ministers
- members of parliament
- members of supreme or constitutional courts, or other high-level judicial bodies
- members of courts of auditors or the board of central banks
- ambassadors, charges d'affaires and high-ranking officers in the armed forces, and
- members of the administrative, management or supervisory bodies of state-owned enterprises.

Persons known to be close associates include any individual who:

- is known to have joint beneficial ownership of a legal entity or legal arrangement, or any other close business relations with a PEP, and
- has sole beneficial ownership of a legal entity or legal arrangement which is known to have been set up for the benefit of the PEP.

5.4.1 UK Regulations – MLR 2017

The Money Laundering, Terrorist Financing and Transfer of Funds (information on the payer) Regulations (MLR 2017) specifies the requirement for PEPs, their family members, and known close associates to be subject to enhanced CDD. For the purpose of this section, a PEP includes their family members and known close associates. MLR 2017 contains the following definitions in relation to a PEP:

1. *A politically exposed person is an individual entrusted with prominent public functions (not middle ranking or below)*
2. *A direct family member is a spouse or civil partner and children of the politically exposed person and their spouses or civil partners.*
3. *A known close associate is:*
    a. *an individual known to have joint beneficial ownership of a legal entity or a legal arrangement or any other close business relations with a politically exposed person*
    b. *an individual who has sole beneficial ownership of a legal entity or a legal arrangement which is known to have been set up for the benefit of a politically exposed person.*

It is the responsibility of the institution to assess the extent to which the risk of money laundering and terrorist financing inherent in their business is aggravated by the relationship with a PEP. All relevant information made available by the supervisor needs to be taken into consideration; this includes information on money laundering and terrorist financing practices considered relevant by the supervisory authority, indicators of transfers of criminal funds and high-risk circumstances. The supervisory authority may obtain this information from the Treasury, EC reports and recommendations, Home Office, European Supervisory Authority (ESA) and the Director General of the National Crime Agency (NCA).

Once it has been established that a customer is a PEP, the firm needs to assess the level of risk associated with them and the extent of the enhanced CDD required. Any relevant information guidance from the FCA or other approved bodies needs to be taken into consideration.

Senior management approval is required when entering into, or continuing, a business relationship with a PEP. In addition, the firm needs to take adequate measures to establish the source of wealth and funds.

When providing long-term insurance, the firm will need to assess whether the beneficial owner is a PEP prior to receipt of the first payment or before the benefit of the policy is assigned (in full or in part) to another person. Senior management needs to be informed prior to any funds being paid out under an insurance policy with a PEP as the beneficiary. Any business relationship with a PEP needs to be subject to enhanced ongoing monitoring.

Enhanced CDD needs to remain in place after the person is no longer a PEP for a period of at least 12 months after the person ceases to be a PEP or longer in case it is deemed appropriate to address any money laundering or terrorist financing risks.

5.4.2 UK Regulations – FG17/6

In order to fulfil their responsibility to provide guidance on the subject of PEPs, the FCA has issued *FG17/6 – Finalised Guidance on the Treatment of Politically Exposed Persons for Anti Money Laundering Purposes* which applies to firms that are subject to FCA oversight. The FCA expects firms to make use of information that is reasonably available to them to assess whether or not a person is a PEP, not only for direct relationships, but also when a client is introduced via an intermediary or introducer. A firm is not expected to decline or close a relationship with a PEP, but will need to deal with the client in line with the risk they pose to the firm. Only when the risk is unacceptable for the firm should they decline or close the relationship. The FCA specifically notes that senior management approval must be sought from, at a minimum, either CF11/SM17 MLRO function or higher in the event that the client poses a higher risk. Only higher risk PEPs need to be subject to continued monitoring after they have stopped being a PEP, but this does not apply to family members. The FCA guidance extends the definition of family member to also include brothers and sisters, and requires a proportionate and risk-based approach to family members beyond this definition. A person is a PEP if they are currently holding a prominent public function, or if they have held such a position in the previous 12 months. An individual who has ceased their prominent public function over 12 months ago will not typically be categorised as a PEP, unless the firm considers this individual to be posing a high risk due to some additional factors such as ongoing negative publicity emanating from the prominent public function or ongoing legal suits/investigations for reasons that are linked to the former public function.

FCA guidance identifies three risk factors: product, geography, and personal and professional.

Factor	High Risk	Low Risk
Product	• Product or relationship is capable of being misused to launder the proceeds of large-scale corruption.	• Low-risk products – simplified due diligence required.
Geography	Countries with high-risk characteristics: • high levels of corruption • political instability • weak state institutions • weak anti-money laundering defences • armed conflict • non-democratic form of government • widespread organised criminality • a political economy dominated by a small number of people/entities with close links to the state • lacking a free press and where legal or other measures constrain journalistic investigation • a criminal justice system vulnerable to political interference • lacking expertise and skills related to bookkeeping, accountancy and audit, particularly in the public sector • law and culture antagonistic to the interests of whistleblowers • weaknesses in the transparency of registries of ownership for companies, land and equities • human rights abuses.	The UK and other countries associated with low-risk characteristics: • low levels of corruption • political stability, and free and fair elections • strong state institutions • credible AML defences • a free press with a track record for probing official misconduct • an independent judiciary and a criminal justice system free from political interference • a track record for investigating political corruption and taking action against wrongdoers • strong traditions of audit within the public sector • legal protections provided for whistleblowers • well-developed registries for ownership of land, companies and equities.

Factor	High Risk	Low Risk
Personal and Professional	• personal wealth or lifestyle inconsistent with known legitimate sources of income or wealth; if a country has laws that do not generally permit the holding of a foreign bank account, a bank should satisfy itself that the customer has authority to do so before opening an account • credible allegations of financial misconduct (eg, facilitated, made, or accepted bribes) • responsibility for, or able to influence, large public procurement exercises, particularly where procurement is not subject to competitive tender, or otherwise lacks transparency • is responsible for, or able to influence, allocation of scarce government licenses such as mineral extraction concessions or permission for significant construction projects.	Subject to rigorous disclosure requirements (such as registers of interests, independent oversight of expenses). No executive decision-making responsibilities (eg, an opposition member of parliament or a member of parliament of the party in government but with no ministerial office).

The personal and professional category also applies to family and known close associates. A firm's due diligences should be appropriate to the risk assessment. For lower risk PEPs, the FCA prescribes that a firm:

- does not need to enquire of family or known close associates
- may take less intrusive and exhaustive steps to establish the source of wealth and funds
- approves the relationship at the level of the MLRO
- reduces the frequency of formal review.

For higher risk PEPs, establishing the source of wealth and funds should be more intrusive and exhaustive. In addition, the relationship should be approved at a more senior level of management and will need to be reviewed more frequently.

Firms are responsible for assessing whether a PEP is the beneficial owner of a customer, in which case, the customer should be treated as a PEP.

5.5 Financial and Investment Sanctions

Financial institutions have to take regard of a variety of sanctions regimes, including financial and investment bans. These regimes are absolute such that it will be an offence to provide the described services to a designated person. A key part of an effective CDD process will be to take sufficient information to ensure that the institution is not taking on a designated entity and to enable the institution to identify such a person subsequently.

As explained by the UK's JMLSG:

'Firms are likely to focus their screening processes on areas of their business that carry a greater likelihood of involvement with sanctions targets'.

Although the sanctions legislation applies to indirect payments, as well as direct ones, well-conducted CDD will allow firms to identify possible sanctions 'hits' in their own customer base, where their risk will be greatest.

6. Reporting Obligations

Learning Objective

9.6.1 Know how and why regulated financial institutions report suspicious transactions, trading activity and order reports

Firms arranging or executing transactions in certain financial instruments are required to submit suspicious transactions reports (STRs) to the FCA without delay. A suspicious transaction is one in which there are reasonable grounds to suspect the transaction might constitute market abuse, such as insider dealing or market manipulation.

STRs submitted to the FCA in relation to the market abuse regime are distinct from SARs which are governed by the POCA 2002 and the Terrorism Act 2000 and that are required to be made to the NCA.

The senior management of the firm should ensure that staff responsible for managing financial crime or SARs risks have access to adequate training to identify potentially suspicious transactions and submit STRs to their MLRO without delay. It is then up to the MLRO independently to evaluate the SAR and decide whether or not to pass it onto the NCA or FCA.

6.1 Indications of Possible Suspicious Transactions

The FCA has identified some examples of transactions that may indicate signals of insider dealing and/or market manipulations. These examples are intended to be a starting point for consideration of whether a transaction is suspicious. These examples are also neither conclusive nor comprehensive.

6.1.1 Possible Signals of Insider Dealing

1. A client opens an account and immediately gives an order to conduct a significant transaction or, in the case of a wholesale client, an unexpectedly large or unusual order, in a particular security – especially if the client is insistent that the order is carried out very urgently or must be conducted before a particular time specified by the client.
2. A transaction is significantly out of line with the client's previous investment behaviour (eg, type of security; amount invested; size of order; time security held).
3. A client specifically requests immediate execution of an order regardless of the price at which the order will be executed (assuming more than a mere placing of an at market order by the client).

4. There is unusual trading in the shares of a company before the announcement of price-sensitive information relating to the company.
5. An employee's own account transaction is timed just before clients' transactions and related orders in the same financial instrument.

6.1.2 Possible Signals of Market Manipulation

1. An order will, because of its size in relation to the market in that security, clearly have a significant impact on the supply of, or demand for, or the price or value of the security, especially an order of this kind to be executed near to a reference point during the trading day, eg, near the close.
2. A transaction appears to be seeking to modify the valuation of a position while not decreasing/increasing the size of that position.
3. A transaction appears to be seeking to bypass the trading safeguards of the market (eg, as regards volume limits; bid/offer spread parameters).

6.2 Obligation to Report Currency Transactions

Learning Objective

9.6.2 Know the circumstances in which financial services firms are obliged to report currency transactions and those circumstances that are exempt

In the UK, there is no requirement to report currency transactions, unless they are deemed to be suspicious. Of course, large cash payments or unusual cash transactions can trigger a SAR.

In other jurisdictions, such as the US and Australia, there are strict requirements to report cash transactions over certain thresholds ($10,000 in the US). These derive from the FATF Recommendations, where an Interpretative Note suggests that countries should consider the feasibility and utility of a system where financial institutions and other reporting sectors would report all domestic and international currency transactions above a fixed amount.

7. Consent Regimes

Learning Objective

9.7.1 Know what is meant by a 'consent regime'

9.7.2 Know the legal basis on which the consent of a Financial Intelligence Unit (FIU) must be obtained

9.7.3 Know the scope of the FIU consent regime

If they become suspicious of a transaction before it occurs, businesses in the regulated sector are required to report it to the NCA before carrying it out. They must then not complete the transaction until a specific consent is received. Although this is widely known as a consent regime, the NCA now prefers the term Defence Against Money Laundering Offence (DAMLO) disclosure. A similar regime operates to provide a defence against a terrorist financing offence under the Terrorism Act.

Where reporters obtain consent, it is important to note that it does not:

- oblige or mandate a reporter to undertake the proposed act
- imply NCA approval of the proposed act
- provide a criminal defence against other criminal offences pertaining to the proposed act
- provide derogation from professional duties of conduct or regulatory requirements, or
- override the private law rights of any person who may be entitled to the property specified in the disclosure.

Decisions on granting or refusing 'consent', in all cases, are the responsibility of the NCA and are made by the UK Financial Intelligence Unit (UKFIU) consent team who work in close cooperation with law enforcement agencies (LEAs) and other partner agencies.

Where consent is granted the reporting institution may proceed with the specified transaction. If the firm chooses to proceed, it will have a defence against the three principal money laundering offences (Sections 327–329 of POCA) relating to that activity. The NCA has produced guidance for firms, which states:

> 'The term 'consent' is frequently misinterpreted. Often it is seen as seeking permission or that where requests are granted that this is a statement that the funds are clean or that there is no criminality involved. This is not the case. Additionally, reporters sometimes seek 'consent' where they have been unable to complete customer due diligence. The process is not a substitute for taking a risk-based approach or for fulfilling your regulatory and legal responsibilities, including those under the Money Laundering Regulations 2007. Such misinterpretation and conduct risks undermining efforts to prevent money laundering and counter terrorist financing.'

Consent regimes similar to the UK's system are not common in other jurisdictions.

8. Record-Keeping Obligations

Learning Objective

9.8.1 Understand the reasons why financial institutions may have record-keeping requirements and the circumstances in which they are required to comply

8.1 Obligations

Financial institutions are under a regulatory obligation to keep all records obtained through customer due diligence measures (eg, copies or records of official identification documents like passports, identity cards, driving licences or similar documents), account files and business correspondence, including the results of any analysis undertaken (eg, inquiries to establish the background and purpose of complex, unusual large transactions), for at least five years after the business relationship is ended, or after the date of the occasional transaction. The CDD information and the transaction records should be available to domestic competent authorities upon appropriate authority.

The FATF, in its Recommendation 11 also obliges countries to ensure that their financial institutions should be required to maintain, for at least five years, all necessary records on transactions, both domestic and international, to enable them to comply swiftly with information requests from the competent authorities. Such records must be sufficient to permit reconstruction of individual transactions (including the amounts and types of currency involved, if any) so as to provide, if necessary, evidence for the prosecution of criminal activity.

In the UK, all records of transactions (whether undertaken as occasional transactions or part of an account holder/relationship) must be kept for five years beginning on the date on which the transaction is completed. All other records must be kept for five years beginning on the date on which the business relationship ends. The MLR 2017 provide financial penalties and/or potentially prosecution including imprisonment for up to two years for improper record keeping.

8.1.1 An Essential Component

Record-keeping is an essential component of the evidentiary trail that must be established to assist in any investigation with a view to any prosecution and the detection and confiscation of criminal funds by the authorities.

Firms retain records concerning customer identification and transactions as evidence of the work they have undertaken in complying with their legal and regulatory obligations, as well as for use as evidence in any investigation conducted by the relevant authorities.

In addition, the firm should retain such other records as they deem necessary to show their compliance with the regulatory provisions in relation to internal systems, compliance management and training. In the UK, the FCA requires the MLRO to provide an annual report to senior management on the firm's anti-money laundering regime. This report must be considered by the board/executive and any recommendations formally responded to and recorded. The JMLSG Guidance contains advice on preparation of the MLRO's annual report, including a template that can be used.

End of Chapter Questions

Think of an answer for each question and refer to the appropriate section for confirmation

1. What is meant by protection of customer confidentiality?
   Answer reference: Section 1.1

2. What is cash forfeiture?
   Answer reference: Section 1.3.2

3. What are some of the best practices regarding confiscation according to the Financial Action Task Force (FATF)?
   Answer reference: Section 1.4

4. Is the appointment of a money laundering reporting officer (MLRO) a legal requirement?
   Answer reference: Section 2.1

5. What are the responsibilities of senior management with regard to combating financial crime?
   Answer reference: Section 2.2

6. What is compliance risk?
   Answer reference: Section 3.1

7. Describe how technology can be used for customer due diligence (CDD).
   Answer reference: Section 4.3

8. List the possible types of data source that can be used.
   Answer reference: Section 4.5

9. What is customer due diligence?
   Answer reference: Section 5.1.1

10. What is ongoing monitoring?
    Answer reference: Section 5.1.3

11. Give four examples of politically exposed persons (PEPs).
    Answer reference: Section 5.4

12. Give examples of close associates of PEPs.
    Answer reference: Section 5.4

13. List the possible signals of market manipulation.
    Answer reference: Section 6.1.2

Glossary

Bearer Shares

Bearer shares refer to negotiable instruments that accord ownership in a legal person to the person who possesses the bearer share certificate.

Beneficial Owner

Beneficial owner refers to the natural person(s) who ultimately owns or controls a customer of the FI and/or the natural person on whose behalf a transaction is being conducted. It also includes those persons who exercise ultimate effective control over a legal person or arrangement.

Chinese Wall

An organisational barrier to the flow of information set up in large firms, to prevent the movement of confidential, sensitive information between departments and to manage any potential conflicts of interest.

Confiscation

The term confiscation, (used interchangeably with forfeiture) means the permanent deprivation of funds or other assets by order of a competent authority or court. Confiscation or forfeiture takes place through a judicial or administrative procedure that transfers the ownership of specified funds or other assets to the State. In such case, the entity that held an interest in the specified funds or other assets at the time of the confiscation or forfeiture loses all rights, in principle, to the confiscated or forfeited funds or other assets.

Confiscation or forfeiture orders are usually linked to a criminal conviction or a court decision, whereby the confiscated or forfeited property is determined to have been derived from or intended for use in a violation of the law.

Consent

Obtaining an authorisation from a law enforcement agency (in the UK it is the NCA) to proceed with a transaction once the suspicious activity report has been made.

Counter-Terrorist Financing (CTF) or Combating the Financing of Terrorism (CFT)

The measures put in place to prevent those involved in the financing and perpetration of terror and terror-related activity from accessing financial services.

Customer Due Diligence (CDD)

Client (or customer) due diligence can include, but is not limited to: establishing the identity of clients, determining expected client behaviour, and/or monitoring account activity to identify those transactions that do not conform with the normal or expected transactions for that client or type of account.

Documents

The term 'documents' in the context of combating financial crime refers to all information recorded in any form, visual or aural and by any means, whether in hand written form; photographic form (eg, microfilm, microfiche, prints, slides, videotapes, photocopies); mechanical form (eg, phonograph records, printing, typing); or electrical, electronic, or magnetic form (such as tape recordings, cassettes, compact discs, electronic or magnetic storage devices such as floppy diskettes, hard disks, memory sticks, optical disks, printer buffers, smart cards, memory calculators, electronic dialers, or electronic notebooks, as well as digital data files and printouts.

The term is also at times used interchangeably with records and materials.

Enhanced Due Diligence (EDD)

Enhanced due diligence refers to any additional information that is collected by a FI as part of the customer due diligence process or increased cautionary measures, such as ongoing monitoring of activity, applied on a risk-sensitive basis in any situation which, by its nature, can present a higher risk of financial crime.

The additional information sought, and of any additional monitoring carried out, in respect of any particular business relationship, or class/category of business relationship, depends on the financial risk that the client, or class/category of business relationship, is assessed to present to the firm.

European Commission (EC)

The European Commission is the EU's politically independent executive arm. It draws up proposals for new European legislation and implements decisions taken by the decision-making bodies of the EU, the European Parliament (the directly elected EU law-making body) and the Council of the EU (where government ministers from all EU countries meet to discuss and amend laws and policies).

European Supervisory Authorities (ESAs)

Pan-European financial services regulatory bodies, each with responsibility for a different financial sector, introduced in early 2011. The three ESAs are the European Securities and Markets Authority (ESMA), the European Banking Authority (EBA) and the European Insurance and Occupational Pensions Authority (EIOPA).

Financial Institution

In the UK, the term 'financial institution' has the meaning given to it by Regulation 55(2) of MLR 2017.

The FATF defines financial institutions (with some exceptions), to mean any natural or legal person who conducts as a business one or more of the following activities or operations for or on behalf of a customer:

1. Acceptance of deposits and other repayable funds from the public.
2. Lending.
3. Financial leasing.
4. Money or value transfer services.
5. Issuing and managing means of payment (eg, credit and debit cards, cheques, travellers' cheques, money orders and bankers' drafts, electronic money).
6. Financial guarantees and commitments.
7. Trading in:
   a. money market instruments (eg, cheques, bills, certificates of deposit, or derivatives)
   b. foreign exchange
   c. exchange, interest rate and index instruments
   d. transferable securities
   e. commodity futures trading.
8. Participation in securities issues and the provision of financial services related to such issues.
9. Individual and collective portfolio management.
10. Safekeeping and administration of cash or liquid securities on behalf of other persons.
11. Otherwise investing, administering or managing funds or money on behalf of other persons.
12. Underwriting and placement of life insurance and other investment related insurance.
13. Money and currency changing.

Financial Intelligence Unit (FIU)

A Financial Intelligence Unit in general refers to a central, national agency responsible for receiving, analysing and disseminating to the competent authorities, disclosures of financial information: (i) concerning suspected proceeds of crime and potential financing of terrorism, or (ii) required by national legislation or regulation, in order to combat money laundering and terrorism financing.

Firm

Under the Money Laundering Regulations 2017, the term 'firm' means any entity, whether or not a legal person, that is not an individual and includes a body corporate and a partnership or other unincorporated association.

Freezing

The term refers to temporarily prohibiting the transfer, conversion, disposition, or movement of property or temporarily assuming custody or control of property on the basis of an order issued by a court or other competent authority.

The term is used interchangeably with 'seizure' and 'restraining'.

Inherent Risk

Inherent risk represents the exposure of a firm to money laundering, sanctions or bribery and corruption risk faced by the firm in the absence of any control environment being applied.

Internal Controls

Policies, procedures, systems and personnel in place within an FI, designed to protect against the materialisation of a risk of a financial crime, or to ensure that risk factors are promptly identified.

Know Your Customer (KYC)

The due diligence that financial institution and other regulated entities must perform to identify their clients and ascertain relevant information pertinent to doing financial business with them. The process includes policies and procedures used to determine the true identity of a customer and the type of activity that is 'normal' for that client.

Money Service Business

According to the Money Laundering Regulations 2017, the term 'Money Service Business' means an undertaking which by way of business operates a currency exchange office, transmits money (or any representations of monetary value) by any means or cashes cheques which are made payable to customers.

Monitoring

An element of an FI's anti-money laundering programme in which client activity is reviewed for unusual or suspicious patterns, trends or outlying transactions that do not fit the normal pattern of business relationship with that customer. Transactions are often monitored using software that weighs the activity against a threshold of what is deemed 'normal and expected' for any given client.

Non-Conviction Based Confiscation

Non-conviction based confiscation means confiscation through judicial procedures related to a criminal offence for which a criminal conviction is not required.

Residual Risk

A residual risk is the risks that remains and to which an FI is exposed after controls are applied to the inherent risk. It is determined by balancing the level of inherent risk with the overall strength of the risk management activities/controls. The residual risk rating is used to assess whether the risks relating to financial crime are being adequately managed within the FI.

Risk Assessment

A risk assessment is an exercise used by a financial institution to identify key risks faced by the firm and to test the controls that a firm has in place to mitigate these risks. Risks can be both external and internal to the firm. The risk assessment aims to measure the total exposure a firm has to the risks it faces and to plan actions to reduce these risks.

Self-Regulatory Body (SRB)

A SRB is a body that represents a profession (eg, lawyers, notaries, other independent legal professionals or accountants), and which is made up of members from the profession, has a role in regulating the persons that are qualified to enter and who practise in the profession, and also performs certain supervisory or monitoring type functions.

Such bodies should enforce rules to ensure that high ethical and moral standards are maintained by those practising the profession.

Shell Bank

Shell bank means a bank that has no physical presence in the country in which it is incorporated and licensed, and which is unaffiliated with a regulated financial group that is subject to effective consolidated supervision. Physical presence means meaningful mind and management located within a country. The existence simply of a local agent or low level staff does not constitute physical presence.

Supervisors

Supervisors refers to the designated competent authorities or non-public bodies with responsibilities aimed at ensuring compliance by financial institutions and/or DNFBPs with requirements to combat money laundering and terrorist financing.

Non-public bodies (which could include certain types of SRBs) have the power to supervise and sanction financial institutions or DNFBPs in relation to the requirements of combating financial crime. These non-public bodies are empowered by law to exercise the functions they perform and these bodies are also supervised by a competent authority in relation to such functions.

Targeted Financial Sanctions

The term targeted financial sanctions means both asset freezing and prohibitions to prevent funds or other assets from being made available, directly or indirectly, for the benefit of designated persons and entities.

Terrorist

The term terrorist refers to any natural person who: (i) commits, or attempts to commit, terrorist acts by any means, directly or indirectly, unlawfully and wilfully; (ii) participates as an accomplice in terrorist acts; (iii) organises or directs others to commit terrorist acts; or (iv) contributes to the commission of terrorist acts by a group of persons acting with a common purpose where the contribution is made intentionally and with the aim of furthering the terrorist act or with the knowledge of the intention of the group to commit a terrorist act.

Terrorist Organisation

The term terrorist organisation refers to any group of terrorists that: (i) commits, or attempts to commit, terrorist acts by any means, directly or indirectly, unlawfully and wilfully; (ii) participates as an accomplice in terrorist acts; (iii) organises or directs others to commit terrorist acts; or (iv) contributes to the commission of terrorist acts by a group of persons acting with a common purpose where the contribution is made intentionally and with the aim of furthering the terrorist act or with the knowledge of the intention of the group to commit a terrorist act.

Whistleblowing

The sounding of an alarm by an employee, director or external person to express concerns about or to attempt to reveal neglect or abuses within the activities of a company.

Wolfsberg Group

An association of global banks, which aims to develop frameworks and guidance for the management of financial crime risks, particularly with respect to know your customer, anti-money laundering and counter-terrorist financing policies.

Multiple Choice Questions

Multiple Choice Questions

These multiple choice questions reflect as closely as possible the standard that you will experience in your exam. Please note, however, that they are not actual CISI exam questions.

1. Financial institutions must undertake customer due diligence when carrying out occasional transactions above what minimum amount?

    A   €5,000
    B   €10,000
    C   €15,000
    D   €20,000

2. To what does the Financial Conduct Authority's (FCA's) identified market abuse behaviour of unlawful disclosure relate?

    A   Insider information passed to a third party
    B   Exaggeration of the supply or demand for an instrument
    C   Exaggeration of the status of the issuer of an investment
    D   Disclosure of information to deliberately influence investor decisions

3. A criminal transfers money in a UK bank to multiple offshore accounts. What stage of the money laundering process does this represent?

    A   Integration
    B   Layering
    C   Phasing
    D   Placement

4. When considering the difference between the offences of bribery and corruption, only:

    A   bribery requires evidence of a gain of undue advantage
    B   bribery includes both implied and non-monetary advantage
    C   corruption requires the gain of illegitimate advantage
    D   corruption usually includes the illegitimate use of office

5. From a criminal's point of view, the PRINCIPAL purpose of money laundering is to:

    A   avoid bringing sudden windfalls of income to the attention of HM Revenue & Customs (HMRC)
    B   make the proceeds of crime appear legitimate
    C   transfer assets to a safe jurisdiction
    D   finance further criminal activity

6. A foreign subsidiary of a UK bank is discovered to be a provider of funds to a regime subject to international sanctions. What risk(s) does this discovery present?

   A   Reputational risk only
   B   Legal and reputational risks only
   C   Financial and reputational risks only
   D   Legal, financial, operational and reputational risks

7. Rob has purchased jewellery valued at £20,000, for only £4,000. If this jewellery is stolen property, what offence under the Proceeds of Crime Act (POCA) 2002 is Rob likely to have committed?

   A   Arrangement
   B   Concealment
   C   Failure to disclose
   D   Acquisition, use and possession

8. How does a firm's policy on combating financial crime, formalise the involvement required by senior management in the prevention of money laundering?

   A   It compels the firm to document how senior management intends to undertake its responsibility
   B   It requires the firm to describe the reporting line(s) of the MLRO through to senior management
   C   It requires a detailed description of the firm's anti-money laundering procedure and management oversight obligations
   D   Every firm is required to name the Head of Compliance and their role in the management of the anti-money laundering policy

9. In order to be termed as 'being bribed' under the UK Bribery Act 2010 (Section 2), the recipient of the bribe:

   A   must have received the bribe directly from the briber
   B   must have completed the performance of an improper activity
   C   needs only to have agreed to receive the bribe, without any intention to perform an improper activity
   D   need not have known or believed that the activity required was improper

10. Your bank has been asked to provide finance for the export of chemicals to a country known to use such chemicals against their own population. You advise your bank that:

    A   this is solely a moral issue for their own conscience to decide. Your personal preference is to refuse
    B   the offence of proliferation financing would only occur if the bank knew that the chemicals would be misused
    C   the offence of proliferation financing only relates to the financing of nuclear material
    D   this would be clearly an act of proliferation financing and an offence would be committed if finance is provided

11. The Market Abuse Regulation (MAR) 2014 contains:

    A   Customer due diligence requirements

    B   Enhanced audit requirements

    C   Suspicious transaction reporting regime

    D   Transparency requirements

12. If enhanced due diligence procedures are required for a beneficial owner, robust verification must be obtained from a source which is both reliable and what else?

    A   Important

    B   Finance-based

    C   Governmental

    D   Independent

13. Which of the following cannot impose a sanctions regime?

    A   UK

    B   UN

    C   The Financial Action Task Force (FATF)

    D   EU

14. Beth is accused of abuse of office, despite the absence of any evidence of bribery. Which of the following is she MOST likely to have done?

    A   Publicly supported local charitable organisations

    B   Employed a close relative

    C   Rewarded team members for exceeding targets

    D   Maximised expenses claims for late hours worked

15. Which of the following sets of descriptions best applies first to regulations and second to a code of conduct?

    A   Enforceable under law, Benchmark for behaviour

    B   Compulsory but not enforceable, Entirely mandatory

    C   Constructed through European Law, Voluntary at all times

    D   Legal but not enforceable, Best practice

16. What was the MAIN purpose of the United Nations Security Council Resolution 1267 (1999)?

    A To freeze assets belonging to states known to house terrorists from listed organisations
    B To prohibit any transfer of funds between listed states and organisations
    C To unify the laws of member states regarding the breach of sanctions against known terrorist organisations
    D To establish a sanctions regime against all individuals and entities associated with known terrorist organisations

17. Under the UK Bribery Act (2010), which of the following statements regarding the offence of 'receiving bribes' is TRUE?

    A It only covers payments in excess of a prescribed nominal amount
    B It covers payments received indirectly from third parties
    C It only covers financial offerings
    D It covers payments received as unexpected bonuses for properly carrying out relevant functions

18. To assist the combating of money laundering, which of these bodies provides technical assistance to countries to help build capacity and knowledge?

    A The World Bank
    B Wolfsberg Group
    C United Nations Security Council (UNSC)
    D Transparency International (TI)

19. What role should financial intelligence units (FIUs) play in combating financial crime?

    A Draft new legislation
    B Receive, analyse and disseminate suspicious transaction reports (STRs)
    C Establish sanction programmes
    D Train private sector personnel

20. In respect of a financial institution's enhanced due diligence procedures, the financial institution should have specific policies in place regarding the frequency of which of the following?

    A Marketing calls
    B Cash withdrawals
    C Account monitoring
    D Visits abroad

21. Which of the following is an important provision of the Sarbanes-Oxley Act 2002?

    A   Financial data must be held for a minimum of five years before destruction
    B   There is a statutory requirement to produce and audit annual reports and accounts
    C   A firm's report and accounts must be lodged with the Securities and Exchange Commission (SEC) within 90 days of production
    D   Financial reports must be comprehensive and include off-balance sheet information

22. Temporary staff in a high-risk role within a firm should be subject to the same level of vetting as:

    A   Permanent staff in similar roles
    B   Directors and executives
    C   Senior compliance officers
    D   Permanent staff in medium risk roles

23. The EU Action Plan against terrorist financing included which of these strands of action?

    A   Criminalising the use of prepaid cards
    B   Disrupting the sources of revenue used by terrorist organisations
    C   Travel bans on suspected terrorist financiers
    D   Regulatory action against banks

24. Which of the following is an FATF Recommendation?

    A   Bribery and corruption
    B   Preventative Measures
    C   National cooperation
    D   Legal framework

25. On an individual's summary conviction of an offence under the UK Bribery Act (2010), the penalty can be a:

    A   fine, of unlimited size
    B   fine, subject to a statutory minimum amount
    C   term of imprisonment, up to a maximum of 12 months
    D   term of imprisonment, up to a maximum of 24 months

26. The evolution of best practice in combating financial crime, has seen financial regulation:

    A   place less emphasis on benchmark methods and techniques
    B   endorse more localised, less international strategies
    C   give priority to terrorist financing over money laundering
    D   shift from a prescriptive-based to an outcomes-based approach

27. In respect of differences between active and passive bribery, active bribery refers to which ONE of the following?

    A   The offence committed by the person who promises or gives the bribe
    B   The offence committed by a third party associated with the criminal act
    C   The offence committed by the individual who received the bribe
    D   There is no real difference between the two

28. What is the definition of a politically exposed person under the Fourth Money Laundering Directive (4MLD)?

    A   A person who is or has at any time been in a position where they have been politically exposed
    B   A person who is or has at any time in the preceding year been entrusted with a public sector position
    C   A person who is or has at any time been entrusted with a prominent public function
    D   A person who is or has at any time in the preceding year been entrusted with a prominent public function

29. The main provisions of the Sarbanes-Oxley Act 2002 are to:

    A   prevent overseas companies from violating US law in their home countries
    B   prevent US companies from acts overseas that would be criminal in the US
    C   implement financial and corporate governance standards on companies in the US
    D   address the role of the auditor in preparing financial accounts and reports

30. Recommendation 6, published by the FATF in relation to terrorist financing, requires implementation of:

    A   vetting procedures
    B   financial sanctions
    C   cross-border intelligence sharing
    D   a national database

31. A senior officer of a UK corporation was out of the UK when an employee committed an act of bribery. The officer may be found liable for consent or connivance under the Bribery Act 2010:

    A   only where documented evidence of their consent can be found
    B   only where the officer can be shown to have rewarded the employee's action
    C   only where the act is proved to have been planned before the officer left the UK
    D   in any circumstance where a positive link to the action can be shown

32. What additional step should a firm take in respect of a politically exposed person (PEP)?

    A   Conduct enhanced ongoing monitoring of the business relationship with the PEP

    B   Put a 'block' on the PEP's account so that customer due diligence must be performed prior to every transaction

    C   Perform enhanced ongoing monitoring of the business affairs of the PEP

    D   Review the number of clients classified as 'PEPs' and 'block' further PEPs being taken on if the number is large

33. Which of the following is true regarding cash forfeiture and criminal confiscation?

    A   Cash forfeiture relates to money in a bank account

    B   Criminal confiscation normally follows conviction for an offence

    C   Police can forfeit cash without reference to a court

    D   Criminal confiscation replaces a prison sentence for an offence

34. Corruption is likely to have a negative impact on the access of the poor to which of the following public services?

    A   Education and health only

    B   Health and justice only

    C   Justice and education only

    D   Education, health and justice

35. The FATF works in collaboration with which two key bodies in order to identify national-level vulnerabilities and protect the international financial system from misuse?

    A   The Basel Committee on Banking Supervision (BCBS) and the International Monetary Fund (IMF)

    B   The IMF and the World Bank

    C   The World Bank and the Joint Money Laundering Steering Group (JMLSG)

    D   The JMLSG and the BCBS

36. The key difference between tax evasion and tax avoidance is:

    A   Tax evasion is legitimate, tax avoidance is illegal

    B   Tax avoidance is legitimate, tax evasion is illegal

    C   Tax evasion is the proper term used in the US, tax avoidance is the term used in the UK

    D   Tax evasion is carried out using legitimate forms of tax shelter

37. Which party is ultimately responsible for any errors when outsourcing screening services to third-party vendors?

    A   Hosting company

    B   Sales manager

    C   Regulator approving the vendor

    D   Financial institution

38. How can 'privilege creep' be prevented?

    A   Ensure any deviations to standard access are signed off by management

    B   Ensuring the compliance department has access to the identity and access management system

    C   Ensuring the distinction between rights and privileges is documented

    D   Preventing laptops being taken home by members of staff

39. The FATF Recommendations are:

    A   made by treaties between countries

    B   equivalent to UN Conventions

    C   soft law, to which countries sign up voluntarily

    D   derived from European Directives

40. Both Tom and Amy are classed as foreign natural and legal persons for the purposes of the US Foreign Corrupt Practices Act (FCPA) 1977.

    Both are deemed to have been involved in corrupt conduct. However, only Tom's actions are covered by the FCPA. Why is this?

    A   Only Tom was employed by a US incorporated firm

    B   Only Tom was present in the US when the corrupt conduct occurred

    C   Amy's conduct involved a foreign official and Tom's a US party candidate

    D   Amy's conduct involved a non-financial reward and Tom's a financial payment

41. Which of the following is a data protection principle? Personal information must be:

    A   disclosed to the police on request

    B   kept for no longer than absolutely necessary

    C   handled according to the company's data protection rights

    D   kept in an open source environment

42. Under UK law, it is prohibited to make any funds available to a non-designated person where the maker of the arrangement:

    A   is aware of any historic link to a designated person

    B   suspects potential onward transmission to a designated person

    C   fails to check any potential links to a designated person

    D   knows this person has previously been listed as designated

43. Which of the following is true regarding the JMLSG?

    A   Its Guidance MUST be followed

    B   It promulgates good practices in countering money laundering

    C   It is made up of financial crime supervisors

    D   Its Guidance relates to fraud and market abuse

44. A legal entity incorporated outside the EU, but operating within the UK, is legally obliged to comply with which sanctions regulations?

    A   The UK only

    B   The UK and EU

    C   The EU and its country of origin only

    D   Its country of origin only

45. The distinction between active bribery and passive bribery primarily relates to whether the bribe is:

    A   the passive subject will supply the bribe as part of the *mens rea*

    B   made face to face or made through a third party

    C   intended to influence a decision or intended to totally control a decision

    D   being given or being received

46. Which of the following is true in relation to PEPs in the UK?

    A   Rules are issued by the Prudential Regulatory Authority (PRA)

    B   Rules do not apply if a client is introduced via an intermediary

    C   Firms need to decline any close relationships with PEPs

    D   Only high risk PEPs are subject to continued monitoring once no longer a PEP

47. Jurisdiction X has been assessed in terms of technical compliance with a FATF Recommendation, resulting in the award of a rating of 'LC'. This means that the shortcomings for this Recommendation in X have been found to be:

    A major
    B moderate
    C minor
    D nil

48. A foreign corporation, operating mainly in Europe, is deemed to be in breach of the US Foreign Corrupt Practices Act (FCPA) 1977.

    The firm's corrupt action is covered by the FCPA specifically because the firm:

    A supports charities which operate worldwide
    B had previously voluntarily withdrawn from US trade
    C had an official present in the US when the action took place
    D also regularly trades securities within the US

49. When considering the battle against financial crime, it is important to remember that the dynamic nature of data means that information gathered using technology:

    A does not need to be justified on a cost/benefit basis
    B will reduce the need for other external resources
    C is not always sufficient on its own
    D will be more hardware-based than software-based

50. The FATF approach to combating financial crime, is BEST described as:

    A prescriptive
    B legally binding
    C principles-based
    D risk-based

Answers to Multiple Choice Questions

**1.	C	Chapter 9, Section 5.1**

Financial institutions should be required to undertake customer due diligence (CDD) measures when:

1. establishing business relations
2. carrying out occasional transactions:
    - above the applicable designated threshold (€15,000), or
    - that are wire transfers in the circumstances covered by the Interpretive Note to Recommendation 16
3. there is a suspicion of money laundering or terrorist financing, or
4. the financial institution has doubts about the veracity or adequacy of previously obtained customer identification data.

**2.	A	Chapter 5, Section 3.2.1**

Unlawful disclosure – where an insider improperly discloses inside information to another person.

**3.	B	Chapter 2, Section 1.2**

Layering – this is the most complex stage and often entails international movement of the funds and use of formal remittance services. The primary purpose of this stage of the process is to separate the illegal money from its source. This is done through the sophisticated layering of financial transactions that are intended to obscure the audit trail and thus cut the link of the money with the original crime. The money launderers may, during this stage, begin by moving funds from one country to another, then divide them into investments placed in advanced financial options or overseas markets; constantly moving them to elude detection. These funds may be left invested for some time in countries with weak anti-money laundering enforcement systems before moving to the third stage of the process.

**4.	D	Chapter 4, Section 1.1**

Corruption, in short, is most commonly defined *'as the misuse or the abuse of public office for private gain'*.

**5.	B	Chapter 1, Section 1.2**

Money laundering (ML) is the process utilised by criminals to disguise the origin of the proceeds of crime (such as money made from trafficking drugs) by converting them into 'clean' money, ie, funds which no longer appear to have an illegal origin.

**6.	D	Chapter 8, Section 2.4**

The categories of financial crime risks faced by regulated firms are diverse. Managing these risk factors inadequately can be catastrophic and lead to reputation risk, regulatory or legal sanctions and consequent financial costs.

Reputational damage can arise in numerous ways which affect the good reputation of a financial institution. A financial institution's reputation is negatively affected by the announcement of a serious investigation into financial crime in connection with client accounts, which has, or is likely to have, a significant financial impact through regulatory, civil or criminal monetary fines and penalties.

Legal risk can arise from different sources but is primarily rooted in uncertainty due to legal actions and in the applicability or interpretation of contracts, laws or regulations.

The Bank for International Settlements (BIS) defines operational risk as: 'The risk of loss resulting from inadequate or failed internal processes, people and systems or from external events'.

7. D Chapter 2, Section 1.3

A person commits an offence of acquisition, use and possession when they acquire, possess or use criminal property.

8. A Chapter 8, Section 3.4.1

A statement of the firm's AML/CTF policy and the procedures to implement it should necessarily clarify how the firm's senior management intends to discharge its responsibility for the prevention of money laundering and TF. This provides a framework of direction to the firm and its staff, and identifies the individuals and functions responsible for implementing particular aspects of the policy.

The firm's policy on CFC should also set out how senior management will undertake its assessment of the money laundering and terrorist financing risks the firm faces, and how these risks are to be managed.

9. D Chapter 4, Section 2.2

Being bribed (Bribery Act, Section 2) – it is an offence to request, agree to receive or accept a financial or other advantage with the intention that, as a consequence, a relevant function or activity should be performed improperly. It does not matter if the bribe is received directly or through someone else. It is immaterial whether or not the recipient or the person acting as a conduit to receive the bribe, knows or believes the performance of the function or activity is improper.

10. D Chapter 1, Section 1.5

Proliferation financing (PF) has been described by the FATF as:

> 'the act of providing funds or financial services which are used, in whole or in part, for the manufacture, acquisition, possession, development, export, trans-shipment, brokering, transport, transfer, stockpiling or use of nuclear, chemical or biological weapons and their means of delivery and related materials (including both technologies and dual use goods used for non-legitimate purposes), in contravention of national laws or, where applicable, international obligations'.

11.   C   Chapter 5, Section 3.1.1

According to the Financial Conduct Authority (FCA):

'MAR strengthens the previous UK market abuse framework by extending its scope to new markets, new platforms and new behaviours. It contains prohibitions of insider dealing, unlawful disclosure of inside information and market manipulation, and provisions to prevent and detect these.'

MAR contains disclosure obligations, which state that inside information must be made available publicly as soon as possible.

12.   D   Chapter 9, Section 5.10

Examples of enhanced due diligence include:

- obtaining more information about the customer's or beneficial owner's business
- obtaining robust verification of the beneficial owner's identity based on information from a reliable and independent source
- gaining a better understanding of the customer's or beneficial owner's reputation and/or role in public life and assessing how this affects the level of risk associated with the business relationship
- carrying out searches on a corporate customer's directors or other individuals exercising control to understand whether their business or integrity affects the level of risk associated with the business relationship
- establishing how the customer or beneficial owner acquired their wealth to be satisfied that it is legitimate, and
- establishing the source of the customer's or beneficial owner's funds to be satisfied that they do not constitute the proceeds from crime.

13.   C   Chapter 1, Section 2.1

The FATF is a 'policy-making body' that reviews money laundering/TF, develops countermeasures and promotes the adoption and implementation of the appropriate measures globally. It also monitors the progress of its members in implementing the measures to combat financial crime.

The role of the UN, EU and the UK in imposing sanctions regimes as described in chapter 7.

14.   B   Chapter 4, Section 4.1.3

Public office can also be abused for personal benefit even if no bribery occurs, through patronage and nepotism, the theft of state assets, or the diversion of state revenues.

15. A Chapter 8, Sections 3.4.2 and 3.4.3

Regulations are mandatory requirements made under enabling provisions/powers given in the law and have the same enforceability as laws. They are primarily rules and are designed to fill in the details of the broader concepts mandated by parliament in laws/statutes. Rulemaking is designed to ensure that a reasonable course of action is taken to meet a requirement given in law.

A code of conduct, in general terms, is explained as a set of rules that outline the norms and rules and responsibilities of, or proper practices for, an individual, party or organisation. Codes of conduct basically set benchmarks for behaviour in the marketplace and provide visible guidelines for behaviour. Codes in a way are an open disclosure by an organisation of the way it operates.

16. D Chapter 7, Sections 1.3.1 to 1.3.3

Under Chapter VII of the UN Charter, the UNSC can take enforcement measures to maintain or restore international peace and security. The range of sanctions can vary from comprehensive financial and trade sanctions to more targeted measures such as arms embargoes, travel bans, financial or diplomatic restrictions. Specific information on UNSCR 1267 can be found in chapter 3, section 2.2.

The EU applies sanctions in pursuit of the specific objectives of the Common Foreign and Security Policy (CFSP) as set out in the Treaty of the EU.

The UK applies financial sanctions either as part of international or European moves to bring pressure to bear on target groups or regimes (for example, because of measures adopted by the UN) or to meet domestic policy objectives.

17. B Chapter 4, Section 2.2

The advantage can be offered, promised or given by the briber directly or through someone else, eg, if a bribe is paid by a third party (such as a partner organisation) for their benefit, in this case they can be found guilty of offence.

18. A Chapter 2, Section 2.1.2

The World Bank assists countries with their AML/CFT efforts in several ways, for example via grants to help build capacity and knowledge aimed at enhancing compliance with FATF recommendations. Similar to the IMF, it provides technical assistance to develop laws, regulations and institutional frameworks; provides training to supervisors, investigators, prosecutors and judges; and disseminates good practice on new financial products, regulations and financial investigation. It has also developed a national risk assessment methodology and offers guidance and help in undertaking these assessments.

19. B Chapter 2, Section 4.4

The interpretative notes to Recommendation 29 explain the core mandate that an FIU should have and the functions that should be entrusted to an FIU. The notes provide further clarity on the obligations contained in the standard. The recommendation obliges that the FIU should serve as a national centre for the receipt and analysis of STRs.

Multiple Choice Questions

20.   C   Chapter 9, Section 5.10

An financial institution should also establish enhanced due diligence policies and procedures for customers who have been identified as higher-risk by them. In addition to established policies and procedures relating to appropriate approvals for account opening, a financial institution should also have specific policies regarding the extent and nature of enhanced due diligence, the frequency of ongoing account monitoring and updating of customer due diligence information and other records.

21.   D   Chapter 5, Section 4.1

Enhanced Financial Disclosures – Title IV describes enhanced reporting requirements for financial transactions, including off-balance-sheet transactions, proforma figures and stock transactions of corporate officers. It requires internal controls for ensuring the accuracy of financial reports and disclosures, and mandates both audits and reports on those controls.

22.   A   Chapter 8, Section 3.5

Staff in higher-risk roles should be subject to more thorough vetting and temporary staff in higher-risk roles should be subject to the same level of vetting as permanent members of staff in similar roles.

23.   B   Chapter 3, Section 3.2.1

However, following terrorist outrages in Belgium and France in recent years, in February 2016 the EU adopted an Action Plan to strengthen the fight against TF. The Action Plan focuses on two main strands of action:

- tracing terrorists through financial movements and preventing them from moving funds or other assets, and
- disrupting the sources of revenue used by terrorist organisations, by targeting their capacity to raise funds.

24.   B   Chapter 2, Section 3.2

The 40 Recommendations are broken down into categories, as follows:

a. AML/CFT Policies and Coordination (1–2).
b. Money Laundering and Confiscation (3–4).
c. Terrorist Financing and Financing of Proliferation (5–8).
d. Preventive Measures (9–23).
e. Transparency and Beneficial Ownership of Legal Persons and Arrangements (24–25).
f. Powers and Responsibilities of Competent Authorities and Other Institutional Measures (26– 35).
g. International Cooperation (36–40).

25.   C   Chapter 4, Section 2.7

Section 11 of the Act explains the penalties for individuals and companies found guilty of committing a crime under the Act. If an individual is found guilty of a bribery offence, and it is tried as a summary offence, they may be imprisoned for up to 12 months and fined up to £5,000.

26.   D   Chapter 1, Section 3.1

Regulation has evolved from a very prescriptive regime, based on extremely detailed rules, that was regarded as costly, confusing and resource-intensive, particularly for smaller firms, to a more principles- and outcomes-based regime. A large volume of detailed, prescriptive and highly complex rules also diverted attention towards adhering to the letter, rather than the purpose of regulatory standards. Regulation tends to be more outcome-focused, allowing firms to decide how best to align their business with regulatory outcomes, while holding the senior management to account for delivering. However, to assist firms in their compliance efforts, regulators produce guidance, which often includes both good and poor practice.

27.   A   Chapter 4, Section 4.1

Active bribery refers to the offence committed by the person who promises or gives the bribe with contrast with passive bribery, which is the offence committed by the official who receives the bribe. Active bribery occurs on the supply side while passive bribery is on the demand side.

28.   D   Chapter 9, Section 5.12

FATF Recommendation 12 and the related interpretive note do not give any examples of politically exposed persons. However, the 4MLD defines a PEP as a person who is or has, at any time in the preceding year, been entrusted with a prominent public function by:

- a state
- a community institution (eg, the European Parliament)
- an international body (eg, the UN)
- or is an immediate family member or a known close associate of such a person.

29.   C   Chapter 5, Section 4.1

SOX is a US federal law and is also known as the Public Company Accounting Reform and Investor Protection Act (in the Senate) and Corporate and Auditing Accountability and Responsibility Act (in the House). The SEC implements SOX.

It was enacted against a backdrop of and as a reaction to a number of major corporate and accounting scandals, notably including those affecting Enron and WorldCom which cost investors billions of dollars and shook public confidence in the US securities markets. SOX set new or expanded requirements for all US public company boards, management and public accounting firms.

30.   B   Chapter 3, Section 3.1

Some of the revised Recommendations are specific to combating terrorist financing, which are set out in Section C of the FATF Recommendations. These are:

- Recommendation 5 (the criminalisation of terrorist financing)
- Recommendation 6 (targeted financial sanctions related to terrorism and terrorist financing), and
- Recommendation 8 (measures to prevent the misuse of non-profit organisations).

31.   D   Chapter 4, Sections 2.8.1 & 2.8.2

It is straightforward under the Bribery Act to prosecute senior officers of an organisation if an offence of bribery was committed with their consent or connivance. If any organisation is guilty under Sections 1, 2 or 6 of the Act a senior officer of that organisation can also be convicted of these offences if they have given their consent or connivance.

However, if the senior officer did not give obvious consent or connive directly in bribery or corruption, an offence could still be committed by the passive acquiescence of the director or the responsible senior manager as brought out by the failure to put in place adequate procedures in the organisation.

32.   A   Chapter 9, Section 5.7

Individuals who have, or have had, a high political profile, or hold, or have held, public office, can pose a higher money laundering risk to firms as their position may make them vulnerable to corruption. This risk also extends to members of their immediate families and to their known close associates. PEP status itself does not incriminate individuals or entities. It does, however, put the customer, or the beneficial owner, into a higher risk category.

Regulation 35(1) of MLR 2017 requires firms to have appropriate risk-based procedures to:

- determine whether a customer is a PEP
- obtain appropriate senior management approval for establishing a business relationship with such a customer
- take adequate measures to establish the source of wealth and source of funds which are involved in the business relationship or occasional transaction, and
- conduct enhanced ongoing monitoring of the business relationship.

33.   B   Chapter 9, Sections 1.3.2 and 1.3.3

Cash forfeiture is a court-based procedure for recovering criminal cash seized by a law enforcement agency. Confiscation follows a conviction for an offence. If a confiscation order is not paid, an additional prison sentence may be imposed.

34.   D   Chapter 1, Section 4.1

Corruption is the major, if not the only, reason for lack of economic, political and social development in most developing countries. Corruption not only increases poverty but also impedes the access of the poor to public services such as education, health and justice.

35.   B   Chapter 1, Section 2.1

The FATF, in collaboration with other international stakeholders (eg, the IMF and the World Bank), works to identify national-level vulnerabilities with the aim of protecting the international financial system from misuse by criminals, corrupt officials and politicians.

36.   B   Chapter 6, Section 1.1

Tax avoidance is defined as the use of legally permissible methods to modify an individual's or an organisation's financial situation to lower the amount of tax owed. Tax evasion on the other hand is an illegal practice where a person, organisation or corporation intentionally avoids paying their true tax liability.

37.   D   Chapter 7, Section 1

Due to the cost involved with implementing and maintaining these systems, many firms chose to use hosting services from third-party providers. However, the firm remains ultimately responsible for any failures of the process.

38.   A   Chapter 8, Section 3.6.2

A modern IAM system should automatically match employees' job titles, locations and business unit IDs to access rights. Depending on an employee's profile, some privileges may be automatically provisioned, while others may require special authorisation. All deviations to the standard should be subject to management approval to prevent 'privilege creep'.

39.   C   Chapter 1, Section 2.1

The FATF Recommendations are 'soft law' – they are not themselves treaty obligations (although as we will see they are derived from international treaties and conventions). Countries voluntarily sign up to implement the FATF standards and submit to mutual evaluation. The findings of these evaluations are published, but the FATF cannot itself impose any sanctions for failing to comply. However, the findings can be used both by financial institutions and other governments to inform themselves about the risks posed by jurisdictions.

40.   B   Chapter 4, Section 3.1

In the case of foreign natural and legal persons, the Act covers their deeds if they are in the US at the time of the corrupt conduct.

41.   B   Chapter 9, Section 1.1

The data protection principles state that personal information must be:

- used fairly and lawfully
- used for limited, specifically stated purposes
- used in a way that is adequate, relevant and not excessive
- accurate
- kept for no longer than is absolutely necessary
- handled according to people's data protection rights
- kept safe and secure
- not transferred outside the UK without adequate protection.

42.   B   Chapter 7, Section 1.5

It is a criminal offence to knowingly (or with reasonable cause to suspect) make funds or financial services available, directly or indirectly, to a designated person. Making funds or financial services indirectly available to a designated person would involve these being routed via a third party. So, for example, it would be a criminal offence to give funds to a designated person's friend knowing or suspecting that some or all of the funds will be given to the designated person.

43.   B   Chapter 8, Section 3.4.4

The JMLSG is made up of the leading UK trade associations in the financial services sector. Its aim is to promulgate good practices in countering money laundering and to give practical assistance in interpreting the UK MLRs.

44.   B   Chapter 7, Section 1.3.2

The EU implements UN regimes by means of a directly effective EU Regulation which immediately forms part of the UK's law upon its adoption. The UK enforces those measures by means of domestic regulations which impose criminal penalties for breaches of the EU Regulation.

45.   D   Chapter 4, Section 4.1

Active bribery refers to the offence committed by the person who promises or gives the bribe with contrast with passive bribery, which is the offence committed by the official who receives the bribe.

46.   D   Chapter 9, Section 5.4.2

In order to fulfil their responsibility to provide guidance on the subject of PEPs, the FCA has issued FG17/6 – Finalised Guidance on the Treatment of Politically Exposed Persons for Anti Money Laundering Purposes which applies to firms that are subject to FCA oversight. The FCA expects firms to make use of information that is reasonably available to them to assess whether or not a person is a PEP, not only for direct relationships, but also when a client is introduced via an intermediary or introducer. A firm is not expected to decline or close a relationship with a PEP, but will need to deal with the client in line with the risk they pose to the firm. Only when the risk is unacceptable for the firm should they decline or close the relationship. The FCA specifically notes that senior management approval must be sought from, at a minimum, either CF11/SM17 MLRO function or higher in the event that the client poses a higher risk. Only higher risk PEPs need to be subject to continued monitoring after they have stopped being a PEP, but this does not apply to family members.

47.   C   Chapter 2, Section 3.3

Technical Compliance Ratings		
Rating	Symbol used in assessment	Understanding/meaning
Largely compliant	LC	There are only minor shortcomings

48.   **D**   **Chapter 4, Section 3.1**

The Act applies to any act by US businesses, foreign corporations trading securities in the US, American nationals, citizens and residents acting in furtherance of a foreign corrupt practice whether or not they are physically present in the US.

49.   **C**   **Chapter 9, Section 4.1**

Real problems arise when organisations acquire and install system-based compliance programmes that are separate and distinct from their own system of internal controls or its culture. These expensive moves invariably result in organisations burdened with fragmented programmes that are not only difficult to manage and expensive but also almost impossible to monitor. These automated programmes are ineffective in supporting comprehensive and timely decision-making by managing and supporting the development of a meaningful compliance culture within the organisation.

In short, compliance is more an issue of culture and requires a solution that goes beyond the software. However, technology can help to embed compliance into the culture of organisation.

50.   **D**   **Chapter 2, Section 3.1.1**

The FATF Recommendations create a regime for the application of an RBA by governments and regulators and provide basic guidelines to the industry for adopting it. The approach is central to the effective implementation of the Recommendations and the global fight against financial crime.

Syllabus Learning Map

Syllabus Learning Map

Syllabus Unit/ Element		Chapter/ Section
Element 1	**The Background and Nature of Financial Crime**	**Chapter 1**
1.1	**Definitions** On completion, the candidate should:	
1.1.1	Know the following terms: • financial crime • money laundering • predicate offences • terrorist financing • proliferation financing • fraud • market abuse • bribery and corruption • international financial sanctions • trade and investment sanctions • tax evasion • data protection	1
1.2	**Governmental and Quasi-Governmental Approaches to CFC** On completion, the candidate should:	
1.2.1	Know the role and objectives of FATF, its limitations and the legal context of its recommendations	2.1
1.2.2	Know the role of financial regulators, commissions and institutions in combating financial crime • Money Laundering Directives • European Supervisory Authorities • Office of Foreign Assets Control (OFAC) • Financial Conduct Authority (FCA) • US Securities and Exchange Commission (SEC) • Other domestic regulators	2.2
1.2.3	Know how regulators implement international standards and facilitate cross-border cooperation	2.3
1.2.4	Understand the role and scope of: • intelligence gathering and analysis • investigating financial crime • asset recovery and repatriation	2.4
1.3	**Best Practice** On completion, the candidate should:	
1.3.1	Know the role, evolution and practical application of best practice in CFC and establishing international standards	3
1.3.2	Understand the role of the FCA's financial crime guidance	3
1.3.3	Understand the importance of the JMLSG to UK financial services firms	3

Syllabus Unit/ Element		Chapter/ Section
1.4	**Asset Recovery** On completion, the candidate should:	
1.4.1	Know the importance of recovery for prevention, deterrence and justice	4
1.4.2	Know how the United Nations Office on Drugs and Crime (UNODC) and the World Bank Group (WBG) aim to assist developing countries and financial centres with their Stolen Asset Recovery initiative (StAR)	4
1.4.3	Know civil and criminal remedies to recovering assets and the implications of freezing orders: • criminal confiscation • civil recovery • freezing orders • search orders • disclosure of information orders • tracing • monitoring • unexplained wealth orders	4

Element 2	**Money Laundering**	**Chapter 2**
2.1	**Background** On completion, the candidate should:	
2.1.1	Understand the stages of the money laundering process: • placement, layering, integration model (PLI) • the 'enable, distance, and disguise' model	1
2.1.2	Know these associated activities as defined by the Proceeds of Crime Act (POCA) 2002: • concealment • arrangements • acquisition, use and possession • failure to disclose • tipping off • consent regime • criminal property • criminal conduct	1
2.1.3	Know the role, purpose and scope of The Money Laundering, Terrorist Financing and Transfer of Funds (information on the payer) Regulations (MLR 2017)	1
2.1.4	Understand how the stages of the money laundering process are detected by financial services firms in the regulated sectors	1

Syllabus Learning Map

Syllabus Unit/ Element		Chapter/ Section
2.2	**International Anti-Money Laundering (AML) Standards** On completion, the candidate should:	
2.2.1	Know the role of international agencies in combating money laundering: • International Monetary Fund (IMF) • World Bank	2.1
2.2.2	Know the role, purpose and scope of international instruments and conventions: • UN conventions • Directives/Regulations of the European Union – 2015/849/EC (4th Money Laundering Directive) 2018/843/EC (5th Money Laundering Directive) 2018/1673/EC (6th Money Laundering Directive) 2015/847/EC (Fund Transfer Regulations)	2.2
2.3	**The Financial Action Task Force (FATF)** On completion, the candidate should:	
2.3.1	Know the FATF's risk-based approach to AML and CFT	3.1.1
2.3.2	Know the broad categories of what the Recommendations cover	3.2
2.3.3	Know the categorisation of jurisdictions which the FATF considers to have strategic deficiencies	3.3
2.3.4	Understand the role, activities and coverage of FATF Style Regional Bodies (FSRBs)	3.3
2.4	**The Role of Other International Bodies** On completion, the candidate should:	
2.4.1	Know the role other bodies play in combating money laundering and establishing best practice: • Basel Committee on Banking Supervision • International Organization of Securities Commissions (IOSCO) • International Association of Insurance Supervisors (IAIS) • Egmont Group of Financial Intelligence Units • Wolfsberg Group • regulatory and supervisory bodies • professional bodies	4
2.4.2	Understand the importance of the guidance issued by the European Supervisory Authorities (ESAs)	4.2
2.4.3	Know the categorisation of jurisdictions which the European Union considers to have strategic deficiencies	4.3

Syllabus Unit/ Element		Chapter/ Section
Element 3	**Terrorist Financing**	**Chapter 3**
3.1	**Background** On completion, the candidate should:	
3.1.1	Understand the similarities and differences between: • money laundering and financing terrorism • proliferation finance and terrorist financing	1
3.2	**Measures to Combat the Financing of Terrorism (CFT)** On completion, the candidate should:	
3.2.1	Know the main provisions of the United Nations International Convention for the Suppression of the Financing of Terrorism	2
3.2.2	Know the work of the United Nations Security Council in relation to the financing of terrorism	2
3.3	**Standards for Combating the Financing of Terrorism (CFT)** On completion, the candidate should:	
3.3.1	Know the FATF Recommendations relative to terrorist financing	3.1
3.3.2	Know EU CFT initiatives: • money laundering directives • regulations of fund transfers • Payment Services Regulation	3.2

Syllabus Unit/ Element		Chapter/ Section
Element 4	**Bribery and Corruption**	**Chapter 4**
4.1	**Bribery and Corruption** On completion, the candidate should:	
4.1.1	Know the difference between bribery and corruption	1.1
4.2	**The UK Bribery Act 2010** On completion, the candidate should:	
4.2.1	Know the extra-territorial reach of the UK Bribery Act (2010)	2.1
4.2.2	Know the global reach of the UK Bribery Act (2010) and the offences: • Bribing another person • Receiving bribes • Bribery of a foreign public official (FPO) • Failure of commercial organisations to prevent bribery	2.2
4.2.3	Know the definition of an FPO	2.3
4.2.4	Understand the liabilities corporate entities face from 'Associated Persons'	2.4
4.2.5	Understand strict liability and the meaning of 'adequate procedures'	2.5
4.2.6	Understand the six principles for bribery prevention and their legal context	2.6
4.2.7	Know the maximum penalties applicable to individuals found guilty under the Act	2.7

Syllabus Unit/ Element		Chapter/ Section
4.2.8	Understand the circumstances under which directors and senior officers of a corporation may be found liable under the Act: • consent or connivance • passive acquiescence • failure to implement adequate procedures and potential civil liability	2.8
4.3	**The Foreign Corrupt Practices Act (FCPA) 1977** On completion, the candidate should:	
4.3.1	Understand the objectives and scope of the FCPA (1977)	3.1
4.3.2	Know the key differences between the UK Bribery Act 2010 and the FCPA 1977	3.2
4.4	**Corrupt Practice** On completion, the candidate should:	
4.4.1	Understand the main components of and differences between types of corrupt practice • active and passive bribery • embezzlement • trading in influence • abuse of office • illicit enrichment • concealment	4.1
4.5	**Combating Corruption** On completion, the candidate should	
4.5.1	Know the role that international bodies play in combating corruption	5.1
4.5.2	Understand the practical application and limitations of quantitative indicators in combating corruption	5.2
4.6	**Mutual Legal Assistance** On completion, the candidate should	
4.6.1	Know how the concept of dual criminality may be applied in cases of corruption	6

Element 5	**Fraud and Market Abuse**	Chapter 5
5.1	**Fraud** On completion, the candidate should:	
5.1.1	Know the three classes of fraud defined in the UK Fraud Act (2006) • false representation • failing to disclose information • abuse of position	1.1

Syllabus Unit/ Element		Chapter/ Section
5.2	**Types of Fraud** On completion, the candidate should:	
5.2.1	Know common examples of the types of fraudulent activity: • identity fraud and identity theft • cyber attacks • computer hacks • malware • application fraud • 419 fraud • account takeover • money mules • authorised payment fraud • smurfing	2.1
5.2.2	Know the difference between internal and external fraud	2.2
5.3	**Market Abuse** On completion, the candidate should:	
5.3.1	Know international legislation for combating market abuse: • The EU Market Abuse Regulation (2014) (MAR) • The Dodd Frank Wall Street Reform and Consumer Protection Act (Dodd Frank) and the Volcker Rule • FATF Risk-based Approach Guidance for the Securities Sector (2018) • ESMA guidance	3
5.3.2	Know the behaviours that constitute market abuse	3.2
5.3.3	Know the insider dealing provisions of the UK's Criminal Justice Act 1993 (Part 5, Section 52)	3.2
5.3.4	Know the offences relating to financial services provisions of the UK's Financial Services Act 2012 (Part 7, Sections 89, 90 and 91)	
5.3.5	Know how market abuse is detected	3.2
5.4	**Sarbanes-Oxley Act (2002)** On completion, the candidate should:	
5.4.1	Know the main provisions of the Sarbanes-Oxley Act (2002)	4

Element 6	**Tax Evasion**	**Chapter 6**
6.1	**Tax Evasion** On completion, the candidate should:	
6.1.1	Know the difference between tax evasion and tax avoidance	1.1
6.1.2	Know international EU and US approaches to improving tax compliance: • the Foreign Account Tax Compliance Act (FATCA) • Crown Dependencies and Overseas Territories (CDOT) regulation • OECD's Common Reporting Standard for Automatic Exchange of Financial Information (CRS) • EU's list of non-cooperative tax jurisdictions	1.1

Syllabus Learning Map

Syllabus Unit/ Element		Chapter/ Section
6.1.3	Understand the difference between individual and corporate liability	
6.1.4	Know how tax evasion is detected	
6.2	**Criminal Finances Act (2017)** On completion, the candidate should:	
6.2.1	Know the extra-territorial reach of the Act	2
6.2.2	Know the offences introduced by the Criminal Finances Act (2017)	2
6.2.3	Understand the liabilities corporate entities face from 'Associated Persons'	2
6.2.4	Understand strict liability and the meaning of 'reasonable procedures'	2
6.2.5	Understand the six principles for tax evasion prevention and their legal context	2
6.2.6	Know the maximum penalties under the Act	2

Element 7	Financial Sanctions	Chapter 7
7.1	**Financial Sanctions** On completion, the candidate should:	
7.1.1	Know the purpose and application of financial sanctions screening in relation to: • terrorist financing • proliferation finance	1
7.1.2	Understand the impact of the financial sanctions listing process of the: • United Nations • European Union • UK, including the role of OFSI • OFSI • OFAC • other states	1
7.1.3	Know the range of legal financial sanctions related to 'designation' • asset freezes • prohibitions • targeted sanctions	1
7.1.4	Know the potential penalties of dealing with designated persons and entities	1
Element 8	**Financial Crime Risk Management**	**Chapter 8**

Syllabus Unit/ Element		Chapter/ Section
8.1	**Considerations for the financial services sector** On completion, the candidate should:	
8.1.1	Understand how financial crime can directly impact on firms: • embezzlement • asset misappropriation • fraudulent customer activity • defrauded by organised criminals • limiting access to data • data compromise	1.1
8.1.2	Understand how firms can be exploited as a vehicle for financial crime: • criminals using the firm's services to launder the proceeds of crime • customer payments to terrorists • theft of customer data to facilitate identity fraud • trade-based money laundering	1.2
8.1.3	Understand how a firm or its representative may collude in the propagation of financial crime: • misstatement of financial circumstances • corporate malfeasance	1.3
8.1.4	Understand the relevant implications of business strategies: • corporate structure • outsourcing and oversight • use of middlemen • FinTech • green finance	1.4
8.2	**Risk** On completion, the candidate should:	
8.2.1	Know the role, significance and utilisation of national risk assessments	
8.2.2	Understand how to identify, assess and manage the risks posed on a firm's business activities by the following: • products and services • customers • sectors • countries • delivery channels	2.2

Syllabus Learning Map

Syllabus Unit/ Element		Chapter/ Section
8.2.3	Understand the risks associated with non-compliance for regulated firms: • financial • reputational • legal • operational • systemic • regulatory • criminal • prudential	2.3
8.3	**Practical Business Safeguards** On completion, the candidate should:	
8.3.1	Know the relevant risk factors firms may consider before commencing business relationships: • nature and purpose of the relationship • source of introduction • company structure • political connections • country risk • establishing beneficial ownership • the customer's or beneficial owner's reputation • source of funds/ source of wealth • expected account activity • sector risk • involvement in public contracts • charities, voluntary and not-for-profit bodies	3
8.3.2	Understand the risks from counterparties with opaque corporate and ownership structures	3.2

Syllabus Unit/ Element		Chapter/ Section
8.3.3	Understand what measures can be adopted to minimise financial crime opportunities within a firm • conflicts of interest policies • compliance monitoring • information barriers • restricting physical access • limiting access to data • effective sign off protocols • gifts and entertainment policies • remuneration policies • objective audit processes • IT security • whistleblowing • employee vetting • penetration testing and vulnerability assessment • secure disposal • staff training • segregation of duties	3.3
8.3.4	Understand how internal policies and procedures on CFC are formulated: • laws and regulations • regulators' handbooks • relevant codes of conduct • sector and regulatory guidance	3.4
8.3.5	Know effective techniques for conducting due diligence on: • directors • employees • contractors • service providers	3.5
8.3.6	Know the additional measures financial services firms can take to manage the risk of financial crime originated or enabled by an employee: • raising awareness • improving the management of IT privileges for joiners, movers and leavers • classifying and segmenting data • embedding ethical practice in relation to data security • implementing whistleblowing procedures	3.3.9 & 3.6
8.3.7	Know the role industry groups and guidance bodies play in facilitating practical solutions for business	3.8

Syllabus Learning Map

Syllabus Unit/ Element		Chapter/ Section
8.3.8	Understand how auditing contributes to corporate governance, accounting and reporting requirements • audit committees • internal audit • external auditors	3.9

Element 9	The Role of the Financial Services Sector	Chapter 9
9.1	**Relations with regulators** On completion, the candidate should:	
9.1.1	Know financial services firms' responsibilities for dealing with regulatory and other relevant authorities • protection of customer confidentiality • responses to information requests • responses to investigation orders • civil recovery, forfeiture and confiscation • global investigation, prosecution and confiscation • presentation of evidence in court • transparency with regulator	1
9.2	**Practical Business Safeguards** On completion, the candidate should:	
9.2.1	Know the role of the Money Laundering Reporting Officer (MLRO) and the Nominated Officer (NO) or equivalents	2.1
9.2.2	Understand the responsibilities of Directors and senior management in relation to CFC under the Senior Managers and Certification Regime (SM&CR) or equivalent individual accountability regimes	2.2
9.2.3	Know the regulator's expectations from firms with respect to adequate management systems and controls to combat financial crime	2.3
9.3	**Compliance** On completion, the candidate should:	
9.3.1	Know the Basel Committee on Banking Supervision's (BCBS's) definition of 'Compliance risk'	3.1
9.3.2	Understand how a compliance culture may be created and maintained, including: • tone from the top • performance management processes • appointment of Compliance/Anti-Money Laundering Reporting Officers • information gathering and analysis • application in routine operations • raising awareness • training • updates	3.1

Syllabus Unit/ Element		Chapter/ Section
9.4	**FinTech** On completion, the candidate should:	
9.4.1	Know the benefits of utilising technology to support a compliance culture and the limitations of over reliance on systems	4
9.4.2	Know how distributed ledger technology (DLT) and advanced/ objective blockchain ID can be utilised for customer due diligence (CDD)	4
9.4.3	know how the following technological solutions can be used for CDD: • digital recognition • face recognition	4
9.4.4	Know how artificial intelligence (AI) can be utilised for detecting financial crime	4
9.4.5	Know how data sources can be utilised by firms to detect financial crime: • customer complaints • trade and transaction monitoring • suspicious transaction reports (STRs) • internet and website usage patterns • customer device profiles • employee turnover statistics	4
9.4.6	Know the challenges associated with fast-paced electronic markets (FPM)	4
9.4.7	Know the role of the Global Financial Innovation Network (GFIN)	4
9.5	**Customer Due Diligence (CDD)** On completion, the candidate should:	
9.5.1	Know how regulated financial institutions implement customer due diligence (CDD) procedures • know your customer (KYC) • ongoing monitoring • non-face-to-face • correspondent banking • politically exposed persons (PEPs) • reliance on others	5.1
9.5.2	Understand how firms implement a risk-based approach	5.1
9.5.3	Know enhanced due diligence (EDD) requirements for higher risk situations	5.2
9.5.4	Know how financial institutions implement sanctions screening procedures	5.3
9.5.5	Know examples of politically exposed persons (PEPs)	5.4

Syllabus Learning Map

Syllabus Unit/ Element		Chapter/ Section
9.5.6	Know standards for dealing with PEPs • The Money Laundering, Terrorist Financing and Transfer of Funds (Information on the Payer) Regulations (MLR 2017) and the FCA's Finalised Guidance G17/6: the treatment of PEPs for anti-money laundering purposes	5.4
9.6	**Reporting obligations** On completion, the candidate should:	
9.6.1	Know how and why regulated financial institutions report suspicious transactions, trading activity and order reports	6
9.6.2	Know the circumstances in which financial services firms are obliged to report currency transactions and those circumstances that are exempt	6.2
9.7	**Consent regimes** On completion, the candidate should:	
9.7.1	Know what is meant by a 'consent regime'	7
9.7.2	Know the legal basis on which the consent of a financial intelligence unit (FIU) must be obtained	7
9.7.3	Know the scope of the FIU consent regime	7
9.8	**Record-keeping obligations** On completion, the candidate should:	
9.8.1	Understand the reasons why financial institutions may have record-keeping requirements and the circumstances in which they are required to comply	8

Examination Specification

Each examination paper is constructed from a specification that determines the weightings that will be given to each element. The specification is given below.

It is important to note that the numbers quoted may vary slightly from examination to examination as there is some flexibility to ensure that each examination has a consistent level of difficulty. However, the number of questions tested in each element should not change by more than plus or minus 2.

Element Number	Element	Questions
1	The Background and Nature of Financial Crime	5
2	Money Laundering	8
3	Terrorist Financing	4
4	Bribery and Corruption	6
5	Fraud and Market Abuse	4
6	Tax Evasion	4
7	Financial Sanctions	4
8	Financial Crime Risk Management	8
9	The Role of the Financial Services Sector	7
Total		**50**

CISI Associate (ACSI) Membership can work for you...

Studying for a CISI qualification is hard work and we're sure you're putting in plenty of hours, but don't lose sight of your goal!

This is just the first step in your career; there is much more to achieve!

The securities and investments sector attracts ambitious and driven individuals. You're probably one yourself and that's great, but on the other hand you're almost certainly surrounded by lots of other people with similar ambitions.

So how can you stay one step ahead during these uncertain times?

Entry Criteria:
Pass in either:
- Investment Operations Certificate (IOC), IFQ, ICWIM, Capital Markets in, eg, Securities, Derivatives, Advanced Certificates; or
- one CISI Diploma/Masters in Wealth Management paper

Joining Fee: £25 or free if applying via prefilled application form   **Annual Subscription (pro rata):** £125

Using your new CISI qualification* to become an Associate (ACSI) member of the Chartered Institute for Securities & Investment could well be the next important career move you make this year, and help you maintain your competence.

Join our global network of over 40,000 financial services professionals and start enjoying both the professional and personal benefits that CISI membership offers. Once you become a member you can use the prestigious ACSI designation after your name and even work towards becoming personally chartered.

* ie, Investment Operations Certificate (IOC), IFQ, ICWIM, Capital Markets

Benefits in Summary...
- Use of the CISI CPD Scheme
- Unlimited free CPD seminars, webcasts, podcasts and online training tools
- Highly recognised designatory letters
- Unlimited free attendance at CISI Professional Forums
- CISI publications including *The Review* and *Change – The Regulatory Update*
- 20% discount on all CISI conferences and training courses
- Invitation to the CISI Annual Lecture
- Select benefits – our exclusive personal benefits portfolio

The ACSI designation will provide you with access to a range of member benefits, including Professional Refresher where there are currently over 100 modules available on subjects including Anti-Money Laundering, Information Security & Data Protection, Integrity & Ethics, and the UK Bribery Act. CISI TV is also available to members, allowing you to catch up on the latest CISI events, whilst earning valuable CPD.

Plus many other networking opportunities which could be invaluable for your career.

Revision Express

You've bought the workbook... now test your knowledge before your exam.

Revision Express is an engaging online study tool to be used in conjunction with most CISI workbooks.

Key Features of Revision Express:
- Questions throughout to reaffirm understanding of the subject
- Special end-of-module practice exam to reflect as closely as possible the standard you will experience in your exam (please note, however, they are not the CISI exam questions themselves)
- Extensive glossary of terms
- Allows you to study whenever you like, and on any device

IMPORTANT: The questions contained in Revision Express products are designed as aids to revision, and should not be seen in any way as mock exams.

Price per Revision Express module: £35
Price when purchased with the corresponding CISI workbook: £108 (normal price: £119)

To purchase Revision Express:

call our Customer Support Centre on:
+44 20 7645 0777

or visit the CISI's online bookshop at:
cisi.org/bookshop

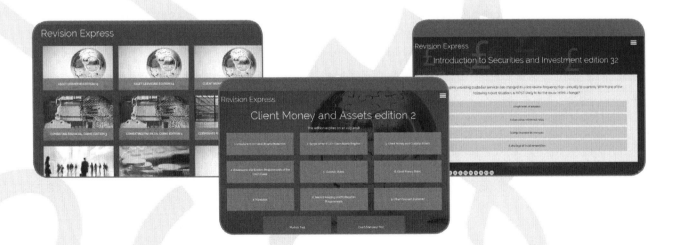

For more information on our elearning products, contact our Customer Support Centre on +44 20 7645 0777, or visit our website at cisi.org/elearning

Professional Refresher

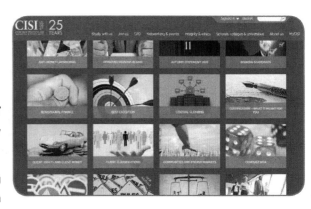

Self-testing elearning modules to refresh your knowledge, meet regulatory and firm requirements, and earn CPD.

Professional Refresher is a training solution to help you remain up-to-date with industry developments, maintain regulatory compliance and demonstrate continuing learning.

This popular online learning tool allows self-administered refresher testing on a variety of topics, including the latest regulatory changes.

There are over 120 modules available which address UK and international issues. Modules are reviewed by practitioners frequently and new ones are added to the suite on a regular basis.

Benefits to firms:
- Learning and testing can form part of business T&C programme
- Learning and testing kept up-to-date and accurate by the CISI
- Relevant and useful – devised by industry practitioners
- Access to individual results available as part of management overview facility, 'Super User'
- Records of staff training can be produced for internal use and external audits
- Cost-effective – no additional charge for CISI members
- Available for non-members to purchase

Benefits to individuals:
- Comprehensive selection of topics across sectors
- Modules are regularly refreshed and updated by industry experts
- New modules added regularly
- Free for members
- Successfully passed modules are recorded in your CPD log as active learning
- Counts as structured learning for RDR purposes
- On completion of a module, a certificate can be printed out for your own records

The full suite of Professional Refresher modules is free to CISI members, or £250 for non-members. Modules are also available individually. To view a full list of Professional Refresher modules visit:

cisi.org/refresher

If you or your firm would like to find out more, contact our Client Relationship Management team:

+ 44 20 7645 0670
crm@cisi.org

For more information on our elearning products, contact our Customer Support Centre on +44 20 7645 0777, or visit our website at cisi.org/refresher

Professional Refresher

Free to CISI members

Top 5

SCORM COMPLIANT

Integrity & Ethics
- High-Level View
- Ethical Behaviour
- An Ethical Approach
- Compliance vs Ethics

Anti-Money Laundering
- Introduction to Money Laundering
- UK Legislation and Regulation
- Money Laundering Regulations 2017
- Proceeds of Crime Act 2002
- Terrorist Financing
- Suspicious Activity Reporting
- Money Laundering Reporting Officer
- Sanctions

General Data Protection Regulation (GDPR)
- Understanding the Terminology
- The Six Data Protection Principles
- Data Subject Rights
- Technical and Organisational Measures

Information Security and Data Protection
- Cyber-Security
- The Regulators

UK Bribery Act
- Background to the Act
- The Offences
- What the Offences Cover
- When Has an Offence Been Committed?
- The Defences Against Charges of Bribery
- The Penalties

Latest

Cryptocurrencies
- Bitcoin
- Altcoins
- Central Bank Digital Currency and Cryptofiat
- Trading Cryptocurrencies
- The Impact of Cryptocurrencies

Change Management
- Types of Change
- Change Theories
- The Complexities of Change
- Leading Change
- Key Skills and Competencies

Regulatory Update
- General Regulatory Changes
- Sector Changes

Common Reporting Standard (CRS)
- What is the CRS?
- Implementation and Compliance
- Practical Issues
- The Global Perspective

Cross-Border Investment Services
- The UK System
- Overseas Regulation
- Applicability
- Face-to-Face Meetings
- Distance Communications
- Brexit Implications
- Gifts and Entertainment
- Tax Evasion, Money Laundering, and Terrorist Financing

Operations

Best Execution
- What Is Best Execution?
- Achieving Best Execution
- Order Execution Policies
- Information to Clients & Client Consent
- Monitoring, the Rules, and Instructions
- Best Execution for Specific Types of Firms

Approved Persons Regime
- The Basis of the Regime
- Fitness and Propriety
- The Controlled Functions
- Principles for Approved Persons
- The Code of Practice for Approved Persons

Corporate Actions
- Corporate Structure and Finance
- Life Cycle of an Event
- Mandatory Events
- Voluntary Events

Wealth

Client Assets and Client Money
- Protecting Client Assets and Client Money
- Segregation and Holding
- Due Diligence of Custodians and Banks
- Reconciliations
- Records and Accounts
- CASS Oversight

Investment Principles and Risk
- Diversification
- Factfind and Risk Profiling
- Investment Management
- Modern Portfolio Theory and Investing Styles
- Direct and Indirect Investments
- Socially Responsible Investment
- Collective Investments
- Investment Trusts
- Dealing in Debt Securities and Equities

Banking Standards
- Introduction and Background
- Strengthening Individual Accountability
- Reforming Corporate Governance
- Securing Better Outcomes for Consumers
- Enhancing Financial Stability

Suitability of Client Investments
- Assessing Suitability
- Risk Profiling
- Establishing Risk Appetite
- Obtaining Customer Information
- Suitable Questions and Answers
- Making Suitable Investment Selections
- Guidance, Reports and Record Keeping

International

Foreign Account Tax Compliance Act (FATCA)
- Foreign Financial Institutions
- Due Diligence Requirements
- Reporting
- Compliance

MiFID II
- The Organisations Covered by MiFID II
- The Products Subject to MiFID II
- The Origins of MiFID II
- The Impact of MiFID II
- The Products Covered by MiFID II
- Cross-Border Business Under MiFID II

UCITS
- The Original UCITS Directive
- UCITS III
- UCITS IV
- Non-UCITS Funds
- Latest Developments

cisi.org/refresher

Feedback to the CISI

Have you found this workbook to be a valuable aid to your studies? We would like your views, so please email us at learningresources@cisi.org with any thoughts, ideas or comments.

Accredited Training Partners

Support for exam students studying for the Chartered Institute for Securities & Investment (CISI) qualifications is provided by several Accredited Training Partners (ATPs), including Fitch Learning and BPP. The CISI's ATPs offer a range of face-to-face training courses, distance learning programmes, their own learning resources and study packs which have been accredited by the CISI. The CISI works in close collaboration with its ATPs to ensure they are kept informed of changes to CISI exams so they can build them into their own courses and study packs.

CISI Workbook Specialists Wanted

Workbook Authors

Experienced freelance authors with finance experience, and who have published work in their area of specialism, are sought. Responsibilities include:
- Updating workbooks in line with new syllabuses and any industry developments
- Ensuring that the syllabus is fully covered

Workbook Reviewers

Individuals with a high-level knowledge of the subject area are sought. Responsibilities include:
- Highlighting any inconsistencies against the syllabus
- Assessing the author's interpretation of the workbook

Workbook Technical Reviewers

Technical reviewers to provide a detailed review of the workbook and bring the review comments to the panel. Responsibilities include:
- Cross-checking the workbook against the syllabus
- Ensuring sufficient coverage of each learning objective

Workbook Proofreaders

Proofreaders are needed to proof workbooks both grammatically and also in terms of the format and layout. Responsibilities include:
- Checking for spelling and grammar mistakes
- Checking for formatting inconsistencies

If you are interested in becoming a CISI external specialist call:
+44 20 7645 0609

or email:
externalspecialists@cisi.org

For bookings, orders, membership and general enquiries please contact our Customer Support Centre on +44 20 7645 0777, or visit our website at cisi.org